DATE DUE

12·21·11			

The Tools for Successful Online Teaching

Lisa Dawley, Boise State University, USA

 Information Science Publishing

Hershey • London • Melbourne • Singapore

Acquisition Editor:	Kristin Klinger
Senior Managing Editor:	Jennifer Neidig
Managing Editor:	Sara Reed
Assistant Managing Editor:	Sharon Berger
Development Editor:	Kristin Roth
Copy Editor:	April Schmidt
Typesetter:	Jamie Snavely
Cover Design:	Lisa Tosheff
Printed at:	Yurchak Printing Inc.

Published in the United States of America by
    Information Science Publishing (an imprint of Idea Group Inc.)
    701 E. Chocolate Avenue
    Hershey PA 17033
    Tel: 717-533-8845
    Fax: 717-533-8661
    E-mail: cust@idea-group.com
    Web site: http://www.idea-group.com

and in the United Kingdom by
    Information Science Publishing (an imprint of Idea Group Inc.)
    3 Henrietta Street
    Covent Garden
    London WC2E 8LU
    Tel: 44 20 7240 0856
    Fax: 44 20 7379 3313
    Web site: http://www.eurospan.co.uk

Library of Congress Cataloging-in-Publication Data

Dawley, Lisa, 1960-
  The tools for successful online teaching / Lisa Dawley.
    p. cm.
  Summary: "This book is a guide for those desiring more in-depth study of how to integrate a variety of internet technology tools for successful online learning. This is an excellent resource for all online teachers, and those who design curricula for online environments"--Provided by publisher.
  Includes bibliographical references and index.
  ISBN 978-1-59140-956-4 (hardcover) -- ISBN 978-1-59140-956-4 (ebook)
  1. Computer-assisted instruction. 2. Internet in education. 3. Education--Computer network resources. I. Title.
  LB1044.87.D39 2007
  371.33'4--dc22
                            2006033664

British Cataloguing in Publication Data
A Cataloguing in Publication record for this book is available from the British Library.

All work contributed to this book is new, previously-unpublished material. The views expressed in this book are those of the authors, but not necessarily of the publisher.

The Tools for Successful Online Teaching

Table of Contents

Preface

So you want to be a successful online teacher—you are to be commended! Being a great teacher comes naturally to a select few. Others of us spend years fine tuning our craft, seeking additional learning and education, reflecting on our practice, and trying new techniques and strategies, some more successful than others. Whether you teach online at a high school or university, or design e-learning materials, this text will help you become more successful in your work.

From research and our own practice, we know there are many attributes that make a successful online teacher. Some of these attributes include self-discipline, prompt feedback to students, becoming knowledgeable with the technical aspects of the online learning environment, the ability to send students in the right direction when they are seeking technical assistance, and facilitating individual and group learning instead of lecturing.

Online teachers are more and more becoming facilitators of learning. This role is new for many teachers who are used to lecturing and testing. Others of you may already be facilitators in live classrooms, and now wonder how to transfer that form of teaching to an online environment. This text is grounded in the notion that *successful teaching involves facilitating students' achievement of learning objectives to engage and empower students as life-long learners.* Understanding the strengths and weaknesses of various online learning tools, and how these tools can be used successfully to achieve specific learning objectives, provides you the ability to become a great online teacher.

There are many texts that provide a general introduction to online teaching (e.g., Elbaum, McIntyre, & Smith, 2002; Ko & Rossen, 2004; Palloff & Pratt, 2001). This book moves beyond a general introduction to online teaching, and places an emphasis on in-depth understanding of effective use of technology tools in the online learning environment. The tools discussed in the text may or may not be part of a Learning Management System (LMS): chat, discussion forums, e-mail, whiteboards, survey and exam tools, video conferencing, blogs, wikis, instant messaging, and small group features. Our goal is to help you understand the pedagogical strengths and weaknesses of various technology tools and how to apply them in facilitating online learning—not to teach you the ins and outs of how to use an LMS such as Blackboard™, eCollege™, or Desire2Learn™. This book is particularly helpful to those teachers working at the high school or university level. Because the strategies in this book focus on creating learning relationships directly between teachers, students, and peers, this text may be less appropriate for online elementary teachers who mainly interface with parents, although the concepts could certainly be applied toward working with parents in those virtual environments. The activities and examples discussed within are easily modified to accommodate various grade levels or subject areas.

The strengths and weaknesses of each tool are discussed in detail, and educators are taught to match the strengths of the specific tool to the learning objectives they seek to achieve in their courses. Multiple examples of objectives and online learning activities are provided to help instill a deep understanding of the power of each online tool. This leaves you with a long-term ability to adapt your own curriculum over time, because you have learned options for using a variety of online tools to achieve specific learning objectives. Finally, each chapter includes a sample lesson plan that demonstrates how to integrate the tool into the learning experience. These ideas and activities provide tried and true suggestions for creating an online environment that engages and empowers learners for success. And when your students are successful in learning, you are successful in teaching.

In Chapter I, we overview societal and political trends pushing the evolution in online learning, and what it means to be a successful online teacher. Central to that goal are the concepts of student engagement and empowerment to become life-long learners. The terms "engagement," "empowerment," and "life-long learning" have become well-used jargon by many educators. What does it mean for students to be engaged and empowered? Are there cognitive, emotional, and behavioral responses that come into play when students feel engaged? Is it necessary to empower students to become life-long learners? Why? How have technological innovations in our society made necessary the ability to learn for life? In answering these questions, we will explore our basic tenant that the ability to match tasks in learning objectives to the strengths of appropriate online tools and activities is a requirement for successful teaching and learning. We are interested in your success as an educator. Chapter I sets the framework for assisting you to be successful teacher throughout your career.

Chapter II begins our discussion of online learning tools, content areas, in particular. The Content Areas inside an LMS include folders for items such as the class syllabus, lesson plans, weekly assignments, course documents and handouts, slideshows and other multimedia, teacher contact information, and subject-area content that may, or may not, be designed by the teacher. The major strength of Content Areas is the ability to organize information for the student and teacher. Organization of information is critical to creating an online class where students feel successful. A well-organized course can provide students a visual schema for thinking about the organization of course and course contents. This visual schema assists the student with long-term retention of knowledge. Time in a well-organized course is spent on learning instead of deciphering how the course works. Disorganized information, duplication of documents, unclear directions about where to locate or post assignments leads to students who are frustrated and have a difficult time focusing on learning.

Chapter III discusses the strengths and weaknesses of the most commonly used tool in online learning, e-mail. The true power of e-mail lies in its ability to promote one-on-one connection between the teacher and the student. An instructor who uses e-mail wisely, and consistently, promotes a sense of connectedness to the larger virtual community. Using e-mail to provide feedback, touch base, and respond to questions in a timely fashion often answers the question many online students have, "Is anyone out there?"

Chapter IV offers an in-depth discussion of discussion forums. Discussion forums have been the preferred whole-class asynchronous communication mechanism since the inception of online learning. Benefits of discussion forums are many. The asynchronous nature of discussion forums provides opportunity for in-depth reflection over time. They also create a sense of community through discussion of course concepts, peer interaction and feedback, making instructor feedback visible to all students, and they also exemplify one of the highly touted benefits of online learning—anywhere, anyplace, anytime.

Chapter V examines the ability to use small groups in online classes. The "Groups" feature offered in many LMSs allows the instructor to assign students to groups of varying size, and provides that group with their own independent tools such as chat, a drop box, e-mail, and a discussion board. Instructors might choose to group students in a variety of ways and for a variety of purposes. Commonly, groups are arranged around areas of common interest or expertise. For example, the instructor may establish study groups for teachers of various grade levels or by subject matter. Groups might also be established by similar time zone or work habits (those who like to turn in assignments early, for example). The most successful groups are purposeful in nature, and structured by the teacher with specific guidelines and deadlines for interaction. The strengths of online small groups are similar to those experienced by teachers who use cooperative groups in the regular classroom. Properly structured small groups can experience a tighter bonding with individual classmates, and a greater sense of connectedness to the course overall. Groups also promote the development of individual expertise by offering the student a smaller environment in which to discuss their work and developing constructs.

Chapter VI explores the merits of synchronous communication through chat and instant messaging (IM). When used well, chat can be a wonderful tool for promoting in-depth understanding on a topic and also helps to create a sense of connection for the student. Conversely, poorly structured or facilitated chats can have a disastrous effect, turning off students to the use of chat in the learning process. Teens, and many adults, are using instant messaging more and more as a daily means for communication with their peers. This benefit can translate over into the online classroom when teachers have the necessary expertise to understand effective use of the tool. Using instant messaging offers the benefits of the instructor being instantly available to the student to answer questions and discuss course assignments. This instant access to the instructor can alleviate anxiety on the part of the student who might be trying to complete an assignment within a certain time period. Conversely, we have used IM to contact students to ask a quick question or just to "touch base."

Chapter VII continues our exploration of synchronous tools by looking at video conferencing and whiteboard spaces. Video conferencing is an enhanced version of chat, offering a video and audio feed of the teacher and students, a text box for chatting and private messaging during chat, file sharing and polling capabilities, and a whiteboard area that can serve multiple purposes. In a whiteboard, an instructor or student can present interactive displays of graphic information such as drawings, brainstorming, slides, or math equations. Whiteboard areas also have the capability to share applications, and browser windows for displaying Web pages during the chat. Most video conferencing platforms also include the ability to record the session—a feature with many benefits! Strengths of video conferencing include the ability to brainstorm in groups of two or more, use of breakout rooms for small group discussion, display Web pages for simultaneous discussion, provide multimedia that enhance the discussion at hand in order to promote long-term retention of concepts, and the ability to view the instructor work out complex math equations. Cognitive psychology informs us that the ability to use visual images in relation to text is a key factor in promoting the development of our schema on a general topic (Gagne, Yekovich, & Yekovich, 1993). Weaknesses of video conferencing include the time involved in teaching students to use it effectively, the slow display time for students who might be working on dial-up, poor video or audio feeds due to old webcams, or inability to even access the video conference due to firewalls. These technical factors often hinder the potential effective use of video conferencing.

Chapter VIII examines the various assessment and survey tools currently available both in LMSs, and online. We find most LMS assessment tools to be somewhat limited at this time, many tools focusing only on multiple choice tests or essay exams. While those types of assessments are useful for some areas of instruction, they provide limited feedback for the instructor who is working to engage and empower students in the learning process. Assessment is a critical component of the learning cycle, and as such, teachers require multiple forms of assessment to facilitate learning objectives for their students. In addition to detailing potential uses of current assessment tools in LMS, we explore assessment options in online classrooms that use *other* online learning tools. For example, structured peer feedback in discussion forums is a type of formative assessment that offers students the ability to co-construct knowledge. We also examine various forms of assessment such as self-assessment, peer-assessment, assessment of the student, curriculum, and the instructor in the online class.

Chapter IX looks at the use of blogs and wikis as a part of online education. Although most LMSs do not contain blog or wiki tools at this point, these two tools have gained in popularity in the last couple of years, and we are now seeing their uses expanded to the educational environment. Blogs and wikis offer the individual student a worldwide forum for publishing their thoughts, writing, and expanding knowledge base. The blog is then open to comments from the outside world, and the wiki is open to further editing and expanding from outsiders. One of the highly touted benefits of blogs and wikis includes the empowerment of the author through the writing process. The individual student owns and directs the content of the blog. Unlike discussion forums which might constrain thinking into a hierarchical format, the student decides the direction the blog will take. In effect, the student becomes expert on his or her given topic. This results in an increase of higher-order thinking skills as the student constructs knowledge over time. An additional benefit of the blog is its lack of boundaries for student publication. Discussion forums constrain the ability to view the student's writing to a single set of classmates. Blogs open up a student's writing to the world, thus enabling the student as a global citizen.

Finally, in Chapter X, we explore the idea of learning to integrate multiple tool use when teaching online, and discuss several examples where a multiple tool set is required. Teachers are provided insight on how to stay current with emergent technologies, and some suggested tools are provided at the conclusion of the chapter.

Enjoy your adventure through this book, and begin to celebrate your own professional development as an online teacher of excellence!

Acknowledgments

This book was made possible through the contributions of knowledge I have gained from the hundreds of educators I have been fortunate enough to teach. Indeed, through their expertise, I have come to highly value the collaborative nature of online inquiry and learning. Every semester, I am honored to enter into a reciprocal learning adventure with the educators enrolled in my courses. Through our discussions, shared presentations, chats, and projects, I am continually introduced to new concepts, technology tools, and teaching methods. This is the true meaning of life-long learning as a community. As these educators and I have shared our learning with one another, I am now able to pass those understandings on to you.

I offer my deepest gratitude to Kristin Roth, development editor, at Idea Group Publishing for a level of support that empowered me to do my best work with the least stress possible—a true editor. Many additional words of thanks are also due to Melissa Slocum and Theresa Foster for their editorial assistance on the book.

Finally, I wish to thank my colleague, Dr. Carolyn Thorsen, for the opportunity to teach and refine my expertise in online teaching over the last four years. Her support encouraged me to push my own boundaries, to continue to explore and evolve as an online educator. Her professional approach to developing and modeling online education at the programmatic level has inspired my work and has helped me understand the limitless potential of distance learning. We are truly pioneers in a new form of learning that crosses boundaries of geography, race, class, and gender, and thus, we have become influential in creating a global society. And for that understanding, I offer my deepest gratitude.

Chapter I

Online Teaching
Today and Tomorrow

Online education continues to grow exponentially on a daily basis. The No Child Left Behind (NCLB) Act of 2002 signed into law by President Bush requires that all students be given access to first class learning opportunities, including online education. Policymakers and administrators are searching for ways to lower costs while increasing student achievement. Indeed, the President's proposed budget for NCLB in 2006 includes an $8 billion 46% increase for its programs (U.S. Department of Education, 2005a). The National Education Technology Plan (U.S. Department of Education, 2005b) recognizes that there has been significant growth in online instruction, making it possible for students at all levels to receive high quality supplemental or full courses of instruction personalized to their needs. At least 15 states already provide some form of virtual schooling at the state level to supplement regular classes or provide special needs. Overall, 25% of K-12 public schools across the country offer some form of online instruction (Thomas, 2005). The number of online private K-12 schools is now in the hundreds, and over 1 million high school students are now participating in online classes (O'Gorman, 2005). At the time of this writing, the governor of Michigan has just signed the first law that requires high school students to take at least one course online before they graduate (Carnevale, 2006).

These statistics are even more impressive in higher education, with over 2.3 million students taking online college courses, as of fall 2004 (Sloan-C, 2005). Almost two-thirds of all schools offering face-to-face courses also offer online courses. More than 40% of schools offering Master's degree programs also offer online programs. 80% of doctoral granting universities also offer online courses (Sloan-C, 2005).

The U.S. Department of Education has also acknowledged an "explosive growth" of online instruction that complements traditional instruction and tailors the needs of individual students (Thomas, 2005). This type of combined live and online instruction is also referred to as *hybrid* or *blended* learning. As schools recognize online learning as a chance for innovation and growth in all kinds of learning domains, the trends for incorporating online learning into curriculums continue to rise. Online learning is gaining support as schools recognize the benefits of learning which takes place anywhere and at any time. Schools see the number of rapidly growing resources along with the convenience of obtaining them. Online learning is a cost-effective approach and also provides students with an equal opportunity for learning, which can lead to greater participation by all students. It also combines many different learning strategies and activities to accommodate different learning styles. As this method of learning continues to help students around the country, the number of schools and students that take advantage of this method expands. Many students of the 21st century prefer "on-demand" virtual learning to traditional school programs. We are currently in an era where many students are more knowledgeable than their instructors when it comes to technology and the Internet. Online learning is a more fascinating option to these students, and therefore they are motivated to learn.

The unprecedented explosion of online courses has resulted in increased demands for online teachers. Who are these teachers and how are they learning to teach online? And perhaps more importantly, how does one *successfully* teach online? Unfortunately, more often than not, we find a lot of new online teachers who are struggling. Often, regular classroom teachers are asked to teach in an online environment with little or no prior experience, much less training. Professional standards for online teachers do not exist at the time of this writing, but some states, such as Georgia, are beginning to consider requirements and standards for an endorsement in online teaching for its K-12 teachers who teach online. And there are some universities that offer graduate degrees in online teaching, such as Boise State University.

Professional development and training occurs in many ways. Online teaching demands a new skill set for most teachers. In addition to being a content expert and a teaching expert, online teachers must learn to use new tools effectively to reach the learner and promote long-term learning. Beyond learning "how" to chat or post to discussion boards, online teachers are required to use those tools to achieve learning objectives of the course. To do so, one must be able to recognize the strengths and weaknesses of all the tools available to the online teacher, and then match the appropriate tool and activity to achieve the learning objective.

Defining Successful Online Teaching

Ko and Rossen (2004) offer us a simple definition of online teaching: "Teaching online means conducting a course partially or entirely through the Internet" (p. 2). I would like to build off this definition and offer that a successful online teacher is one who *promotes the achievement of learning objectives by facilitating engagement to empower students as life-long learners*. The terms "engagement," "empowerment," and "life-long learning" have become well-used jargon by many educators. What does it mean for students to be engaged and empowered in an online environment?

The value and need for an engaged and learner-centered approach to online education has been articulated by many researchers (Collison, Elbaum, Haavind, & Tinker, 2000; Conrad & Donaldson, 2004; Meyer, 2002; Salmon, 2002). Over the last 10 years, paradigm shifts in education from behaviorism to constructivist modes of pedagogy are a definite aspect of this position. Constructivists place an emphasis on learner-centered instruction. Meaning making is viewed as occurring within the individual, resulting from experience and social interaction with others. The teacher's job is seen as one of understanding how the student thinks, so the teacher can create an environment and experiences to further facilitate the student's individual meaning making.

Many online courses are self-paced and use extensive lecture notes with traditional testing. However, as Conrad and Donaldson (2004) point out, "Lecture is effective for knowledge transmission, but if it is the primary strategy used in the online environment, the course becomes a digital correspondence course with potential problems of learner isolation and high drop-out rates" (p. 6). In an online format, students are not required to attend class when they are bored. Engagement is a critical component to keep students online and learning. Granted, there are those individuals who seek out asynchronous, self-paced, lecture format courses and do quite well, but this is not the norm overall. Learning is a social event and requires interaction with multiple individuals, including peers, as the student moves through the knowledge construction process. The development of higher order thinking skills are almost always dependent on interactive teaching and learning (Walker, 2005).

As students begin to assume more responsibility for their own knowledge generation and overall learning experience, they become empowered to continually seek out new information and learning, and collaborate with peers and coworkers in problem solving and solution creations. This disposition is critical in today's technologically advanced society where information and technology change on a daily basis and we become a more global-based society.

Abdelraheem (2003) lists the characteristics of successful Web-based learning environments as follows:

- Relevant and well-designed challenging activities.

- Adequate and timely feedback from instructors.

- Adequate and timely student-to-student interaction.

- Active engagement in construction of knowledge with an easy to use and powerful navigation system.

- Deep learning encouraged through question design and links to thought-provoking sources.

- Student learning could be self-paced to suit individual student needs.

- Student autonomy encouraged since students are in charge of their own learning.

- Students can study various points of view through other online resources.

Effective online courses involve feedback, interaction, and content, and promote self-learning, as well as an understanding of learning styles. They foster an open curriculum, in which students learn from a variety of sources and are not limited to the scope and structure of the course. This is achieved through the use of various tools such as electronic presentation tools, online chat, whiteboard conferencing, e-mail, and Web-based resources. The teacher's use of the tools must promote an interactive learning experience in order for the student to experience success. When learning online, interaction can be asynchronous or synchronous. A successful teacher must determine which of these tools, and what type of timing, are going to be most effective for a particular group of students in a given course, in order to promote maximum learning.

How can the online teacher support engagement in learning? First, teachers must cultivate their own disposition towards student engagement. Palloff and Pratt (2001) agree that a successful online instructor must be willing to "let go" of traditional teaching concepts and also give up some control in the virtual classroom in order to encourage a learning community that empowers the learner; an essential characteristic of an online class environment. Although it is not impossible for an instructor to offer an online course without these attributes, the most successful courses may be presented by instructors who have or cultivate a combination of all of these important qualities.

For many students, learning to participate in an interactive learning experience, especially online, is a new way of learning. Often, they have been educated through years of skill and drill where an emphasis was placed on memorization and testing of knowledge. After many years of working with this transmission model of teaching, students become comfortable with the process. They understand what is expected of them as passive learners, and they develop skills for effectively mastering the content. Cognitive psychologists refer to this process as the automation of procedural knowledge (Gagne, Yekovich, & Yekovich, 1993)—that is, automating the process of learning how to learn.

Now imagine taking this student and placing that student in an engaged learning environment, where an emphasis is placed on knowledge generation, not knowledge mastery. They often report experiencing anxiety, uncertainty, and a need to be "told" what to do. They miss the comfort level of the teacher being the expert, and cannot comprehend the idea of the learner as an individual meaning maker. Their schema for "how to learn" has not yet developed to include concepts of the student as knowledge generator and coparticipant in construction of course goals and content.

Assisting students to engage in learning is critical in online courses, as students who are frustrated with this approach often drop out after a week or two. Common sense would tell us that a developmental approach to engagement, where students are progressively introduced to engaged learning concepts over a period of time, is best. For example, Conrad and Donaldson (2004) propose four phases of online engagement for students that occur over the duration of a course:

1. **Newcomer:** Teacher as social negotiator.

2. **Cooperator:** Teacher as structural engineer.

3. **Collaborator:** Teacher as facilitator.

4. **Initiator/partner:** Teacher as community member/challenger. (p. 11)

In Phase I, the teacher establishes the tone for the class by setting norms for engagement, encouraging connections through introductions, and inviting students to participate in goal setting for the course. For example, we have used an activity known as "Negotiating the Curriculum" (Boomer, Lester, Onore, & Cook, 1994) wherein students are asked to answer the four following questions during the first week, then post their responses on the discussion board.

1. **What do we know already?** (Or where are we now and what do we not need to learn or be taught?)

2. **What do we want and need to find out?** (Or what are our questions? What do we not know? What are our problems, curiosities, and challenges?)

3. **How will we go about finding out?** (Where will we look? What experiments and inquiries will we make? What will we need? What information and resources are available? Who will do what? What should be the order of things?)

4. **How will we know and show what we have found out?** (What are our findings about what we have learned? Who will we show? For whom are we doing the work and where next?)

The instructor then compiles the responses, and customizes the remainder of the course to meet individual learning needs. Students learn from this introductory activity that the course "belongs" to them. They experience ownership, and as a result, are more engaged from the first week.

In Phase II, the teacher can begin to ask students to work in pairs, and offer assignments that encourage peer cooperation, assessment, reflective thinking, and collaboration. As an initial step, the instructor can request students to provide peer feedback using a structured rubric or set of questions. Another activity is to have students interview a partner for a course assignment.

In Phase III, the student learns to become a collaborator, working in a small group to cooperatively complete an assignment. The most successful collaborations at this phase are provided guidelines to structure the work. For example, the teacher might assign a group leader or specific tasks to complete. In one of our courses, we often have students at this stage working in small groups to complete a Web quest where they collaboratively research and write responses to a given set of questions. Groups then compile their individual responses in a group report, edit, and publish the report as a group.

In Phase IV, students become course leaders. They initiate and direct their own learning goals and activities with the instructor serving as a community member and support person. An example activity at this stage is to have students work on a course project wherein the project goals, content, and assessment are determined by the student while utilizing the instructor's support and expertise.

Does a phased approach to promoting engagement and a potential paradigm shift in pedagogical orientation work? Copeland, Birmingham, DeMeulle, D'Emidio-Caston, and Natal (1994) report that teachers can experience a steep initial learning curve in pedagogical expertise. This occurs when teachers are offered substantial challenges to conceptions previously held about teaching, and when those challenges are offered in such a way that "prior knowledge and processing strategies were sufficiently influenced, and anomalous data and alternative theories were appropriately introduced so as to promote ... 'reflective theory change'" (p. 193). Certainly, the online learning environment can be considered a substantial challenge in and of itself. Based on our experience, a phased approach, as described previously, offers learners the support and challenges they require to experience a change in their previously held learning theories and teaching strategies.

How This Book Can Help You Be Successful

In each chapter, we look at the strengths and weaknesses of specific online teaching tools, how to use them effectively to meet tasks identified in learning objectives while promoting engagement, and empowerment, as well as some possible activities the teacher might integrate into teaching.

As in any teaching situation, objectives always drive instruction. Consider the following objective in Figure 1.1: The student will *explain* the meaning of plot and provide examples of plot.

In designing our lesson, our first task is to identify the outcome-illustrating verb. In Figure 1.1, objective, *explain,* describes the main action students must take to complete the assignment. Our next task is to then consider what online tools provide students the ability to explain. Several tools that come immediately to mind are chat, e-mail, or discussion forums. At this point, an online teacher identifies what level of learning the verb represents on Bloom's taxonomy. In this case "explain" is at the "comprehension level" on Bloom's taxonomy. The teacher will then consider the skill ability of the students and potential activities that are age appropriate. In Figure 1.1, imagine we are working with a high school class of students who have been online for several weeks. The teacher is working to promote connection with dyads of students, and so the student decides to assign students to partners who will *cooperate via chat to explain the meaning of plot to one another and then provide two examples.* Their chat transcripts can be copied and posted to the discussion forum as evidence of their *comprehension,* and thus, achievement of objective.

Figure 1.1. Designing online activities by matching outcome verbs to online tools

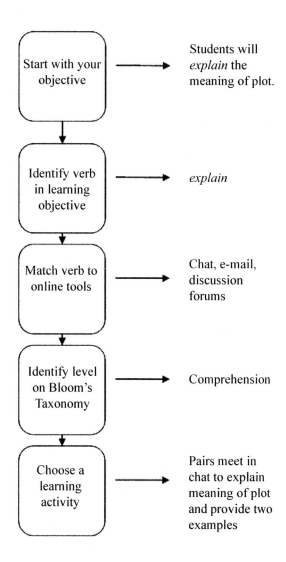

Table 1.1. Sample of learning outcome verbs matched to online tool and activities

Learning Outcome Verb	Online Tools	Activities
Explain	E-mail, discussion forums	Collaborate with partner via chat to explain the meaning of plot and provide two examples.

In subsequent chapters in the book, you will note that each activity, and suggested online tool, begins with *an outcome-illustrating verb* drawn from learning objectives (see example in Table 1.1).

Begin to consider the objectives in your teaching. What outcomes are you seeking? You will note in each chapter that the learning outcome verbs are associated with *Bloom's Taxonomy*. Bloom's Taxonomy provides key indicators in the cognitive domain involving knowledge and the development of intellectual skills. Identify the verbs in your outcomes as they determine the types of actions, and thus the types of tools we might potentially use to achieve outcomes. Consider what activities and online tools might help get you there in a way that engages and empowers your students as individual meaning makers. Use the guides at the end of each chapter as a resource to stimulate your thinking, get new ideas, and possibly try some of the activities listed within. As you gain experience with online teaching, and the strengths and weaknesses of various tools, you will learn when and how to effectively use those tools as part of your overall instructional strategy.

We often encourage beginning online teachers to compare teaching online to teaching in a "brick and mortar" setting. In a live classroom, some of your teaching tools and strategies might include overhead projection, chalk, a chalkboard, the ability to have students move their desks into small groups, have question and answer sessions, give exams, create portfolios, and more. All of these tools and strategies can exist in an online format, yet there are differences in how they are used due to the synchronous and asynchronous nature of online education, as well as the technological design of the tool itself. Therefore, our lesson design and facilitation of the lesson must accommodate these differences to help students reach their learning objectives.

Keep in mind that an underlying assumption in all of the following chapters is that students require engagement and empowerment in the online classroom in order to experience success in the educational process. All of the listed tool strengths and weaknesses, and example learning activities, are offered based on that assumption.

Comparing Learning Management Systems

The majority of, but not all, tools discussed in this book are incorporated into many learning management systems (LMS). An LMS is an e-learning platform that provides an integrated tool set (including tools such as chat, discussion board, gradebook, e-mail, and content storage such as a digital a drop box) to the online teacher and learner. Leslie (2003) defines a learning management system as:

- Software suites that enable both synchronous and asynchronous student participation with both the learning content and with other students and the instructor.

- Systems sold in a traditional vendor model that allow institutions to run the software in their own environment and hosted services provide application service provider (ASP) style relationships.

- Software packages and hosted services when they provide at least one of the following functions:

  ° Tools to facilitate multiple aspects of course design, content authoring, and content management.

  ° Tools for administering assessments and tracking the usage from both student and content perspectives.

  ° Tools that structure content delivery and course progression around conventional postsecondary course units of delivery and postsecondary schedules such as terms and semesters. (p. 8)

In all likelihood, if you use an LMS, it has been predetermined by your university or school. Some commonly used platforms include Blackboard, WebCT™, eCollege™, and Moodle™. Although, there are many other LMSs available on the market today. In Figures 1.2, 1.3, and 1.4, we see a comparison of threaded discussion in three platforms: Blackboard™, eCollege™, and WebCT™.

While LMSs may vary in appearance or in how some features are used, overall the learning and administrative tools of the LMS are fairly consistent. Most LMSs offer internal and external e-mail capabilities, chat, whiteboard, discussion boards, content storage, small grouping ability, a drop box, a grade-book, and calendar. For consistency throughout the text, many screenshots are taken in Blackboard. However, all of the strengths and weaknesses, and example activities listed in each chapter, easily apply to any LMS using that particular tool. Additionally, some online learning tools discussed in this text, such as instant messaging and blogs, are not currently incorporated into most LMSs, but are being used as supplemental tools by many online teachers. It is easy to imagine that future LMS versions will begin to incorporate these types of learning tools as they gain popularity among teachers. For example, Claroline.net, now offers a wiki tool as part of its platform.

Figure 1.2. Blackboard™ discussion forum. Used with copyright permission

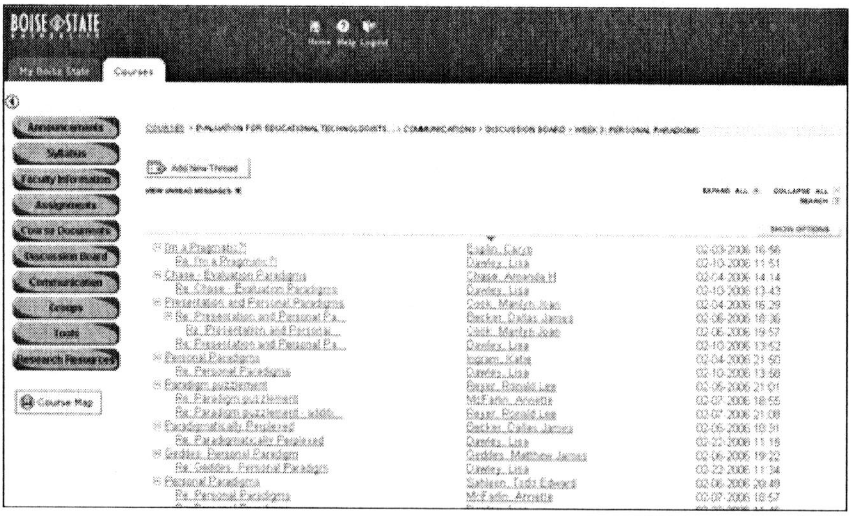

Figure 1.3. WebCT™ discussion forum. Used with copyright permission

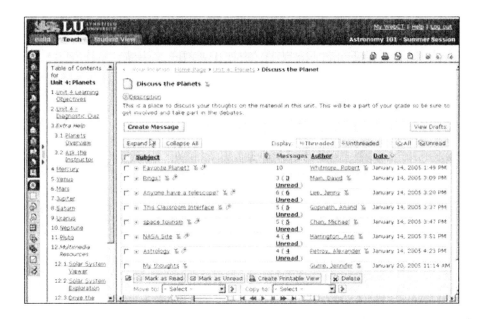

Figure 1.4. eCollege™ discussion forum. Used with copyright permission

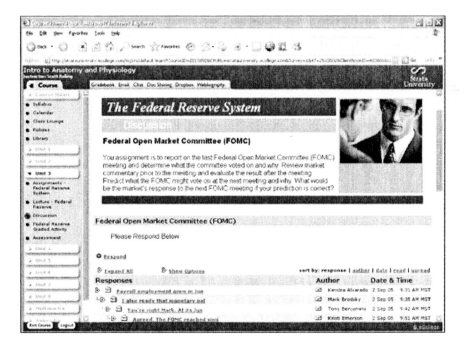

If you are interested in comparing administrative or learning tools of various learning management systems, Edu-tools.com (see *Resources* section) offers an interactive comparison tool where multiple platforms can be compared by features and technical specifications. This is extremely helpful for those educators involved in having to make decisions about LMS adoption in your district or university. For those teachers wishing to conduct a trial of an online learning environment, Blackboard offers a free 60-day trial. Moodle offers a free open-source LMS to all educators; however, it must be downloaded and hosted on your own server. Nicnet.org also provides a basic LMS free of charge to educators.

Future Trends in Online Learning

Online education continues to evolve daily. New software and e-learning platforms and tools are being introduced at a rapid pace. This growth and evolution will continue as the number of students participating in online learning continues to increase (O'Gorman, 2005), federal and state initiatives and funding increase, and as more research continues to be conducted on teaching and learning involving Internet-based technologies.

Customization of LMSs. With regard to learning management systems and online learning tools, in particular, there is a movement towards more customization of the learning environment to support the individual learner's needs. Siemens (2004), encourages us to consider what elements are required in any learning environment and what corollary tools exist online:

- Have a place for learner expression (blog/portfolio).

- Have a place for content interaction (LMSs have this).

- Have a place to connect with other learners (discussion forum LMSs have this).

- Have a place to connect the thoughts of other learners in a personal, meaningful way, that is, using RSS (aggregators that collect text based data, such as blog entries or daily news, in one location).

- Have a place to dialogue with the instructor (e-mail, VoIP, etc.; WebCT has some of this).

- Have a place to dialogue with gurus (apprentice); the heart of online communities is the mess of varying skills and expertise. Gurus are people currently in industry or established practitioners of the organizing theme of the community. LMS limits the interaction to learner and instructor.

- Have a place for learning artifacts of those who have gone before, that is, content management capabilities accessible and managed by the learner. Tools like Furl, and del.icio.us are examples of personal knowledge management (PKM) tools.

- Be modularized so additional functionality and tools can be added based on what learners want or need; a bricolage of course tools based on open standards allows for incorporation of new approaches as needed. (p. 10)

The notion of customizing online learning, and online learning tools, to the individual learner's needs and interest is grounded in constructivism, where deep learning can be nonlinear and takes place when the learner's interests and prior learning are taken into consideration, and the idea that the majority of learning, up to 75%, occurs informally, at the time the learner needs the information (Siemens, 2004). These learning opportunities can take such forms as asking the person sitting next to you, or in the next office, for information, trial and error, calling a help desk, or through observing others. Contrast this with only 25% of learning occurring formally, through trainings, seminars, and courses. Current learning management systems force the user into a suite of predefined tools, limited teaching and learning opportunities, and usually promote linear learning. The ability to choose modules of necessary tools and features to achieve the task at hand will influence future development of LMSs.

OpenSource movement. An interesting trend developing is that of the Open-Source software movement, based on the Linux operating system. With OpenSource, all software and the *software coding,* is made available free-of-charge to users (Ishii & Lutterback, 2001). This means that any user can take the coding and make modifications to create their own individualized software, if desired. MITs OpenCourseWare project is making MIT course materials available to anyone free-of-charge on the Web. Moodle, an LMS that is open source, is another example of how the educational community is supporting the constructivist notion of students creating their own knowledge and that knowledge belongs to everyone.

Evolving models of LMS usage and integration. The evolution of technology integration for learning has been fascinating to observe over the last decade. Initially, computers were used to support live learning in classrooms. They were used for simple tasks such as word processing and creating spreadsheets. As tools became more sophisticated, and as the graphic-based Internet browsers hit the market, the Internet started to become more integrated into daily classroom activities. Teachers began using computers to display notes, slideshows, show interesting Web sites, and so forth. Students had specialized software to learn about various content areas and to gather multimedia information through electronic encyclopedias. As teachers began to collect and create their own instructional materials, and as tools developed to promote online learning (such as threaded discussion and listservs), we saw the emergence of the first online classrooms. Finally, as LMSs hit the market as recently as seven or so years ago, we began to see the initial explosion of online learning.

An interesting trend now developing across all learning environments is that of blended, hybrid, or extended learning; classrooms that utilize both live and Internet-mediated instruction. Blended learning is assuming many forms and the distinctions between pure online learning and live classroom learning are becoming blurred. Some examples of this include:

- Shara teaches 8th grade biology. Her students attend live courses on campus, but are required to complete all homework and class projects online. A portion of the day is allocated to time at the computer, but it is expected students will also work online outside of the school day.

- Jim is a corporate trainer in a major biochemical corporation. A common instructional model they use is live-online-live model. Employees are introduced to new learning in a live setting. Online materials and follow-ups are made available as needed by the employees, and a final live session is then scheduled for reinforcement and follow-up.

- University of Phoenix has its new graduate students begin their program with a two-week orientation on campus. These students then work online at home for the remainder of their program.

These examples illustrate several ideas. First, online education is no longer considered a "fad" or weak form of education. It has substantiated itself as an important option in the educational realm. Second, the ways in which online learning can be combined with live learning are limitless, and a strong educator or instructional designer can design the learning environment whether online, live, or a combination of both, to fit the educational goals of the program and needs of the population it is serving. Third, traditional forms of learning (live classrooms, on campus, 16-week semesters) are changing. Educational institutions that keep up with these changes will continue to survive, while those who are less responsive to evolutionary trends will experience declining enrollments.

The Horizon Report. Issued by the New Media Consortium (2006), the Horizon Report identifies trends in distance learning over the next one to five years. Trends they predict in the next year to two include social computing and personal broadcasting. We see the emergence of this trend on a daily basis when we hear reports of teen usage on social sites such as MySpace.com. A boom has also emerged in the use of RSS feeds in blogs, as well as in the use of wikis for learning. Social networks and knowledge Web sites support learners ongoing needs to facilitate teamwork and co-construct knowledge. The emphasis is placed on communication and collaboration, not necessarily the technology itself. Examples of social networks created by users and used for educational purposes include Merlot and Wikipedia. Wikipedia is the first online encyclopedia where content is added and edited by its users.

We are also starting to see cross-use of tools and pedagogy, in the use of approaches such as blog quests, a Web quest that occurs in a blog, and wiki circles, a literature circle done via a wiki. And the increase of podcasts, for both educational and noneducational purposes, has grown significantly in the last year alone. As of today's writing, there are over 3,600 education-related podcasts available in the iTunes library alone.

In the next two to three years, it is predicted that educational gaming and the use of cell phones in education will become more commonplace. Although games are not new to the educational environment, we are now seeing the development of virtual games that promote life-like experiences where students can collaborate and problem solve toward the completion of a task in an online environment. Examples of these virtual educational games include Quest Atlantis and Virtual Learning Arcade. Simulation games such as SimsSchool provide a space for new teachers to practice their classroom management skills. With cells phones continuing development to handle multimedia, it is predicted that more mobile learning will occur via cell phone. For example, Rice University offers an entire course in learning to speak Chinese over the phone.

Power Tip: MMORPGs, The Future of Education?

Ever played a MMORPG (massive multiplayer online roleplay game)? Although most of these games, such as Everquest™, World of Warcraft™, Dark Age of Camelot™, and Star Wars Galaxies™, emphasize pvp (player vs. player) combat, not all MMORPGs do. Yesterday I had the opportunity to explore A Tale in the Desert II™; a mmorpg based in ancient Egypt. The designers have this to say about their game:

Have you ever wondered how it would be to live in Ancient Egypt? To be part of the civilization that built so many wonders? Well, now you can! In "A Tale in the Desert™", you can relive those times and unravel their secrets. Build your own pyramid, help rule the country by passing laws and advising the Pharaoh. See how far you can make the civilization advance, or just explore the land and make new friends.

A Tale in the Desert™ (ATITD) is a groundbreaking MMORPG with rich variety in game play, that lets you build kingdoms from the ground up, actively interact with your fellow-people, and live in a diverse society where you can do almost anything; be a merchant, a courier, a builder, an artist, a cook, an explorer, a strategist, a king ... or all of these—and more! In fact if you find your very own part that has not been provided for, pass a law to do it!

continued

Here's the beauty of MMORPG technology as I see it. First, it is 3-dimensional, graphic-based, has rich audio, includes the ability to interact, move within a virtual environment, and chat in either text or audio. MMORPGs are usually quest-based, where the user has to complete a quest, a series of tasks, directions, and so forth in order to gain an item or improved status in the game. Most MMORPGs include guilds or clans, wherein members join together over long periods of time to support one another in the questing process. The social component is emphasized in the design of the game and quests. So where is the potential for education?

Let's break it down piece by piece:

1. **3-Dimension, graphics, audio:** Appeals to multiple sensory modalities, encourages long-term retention due to a combination of visual with text and sound. This approach to learning also supports Gardener's theory of multiple intelligences.

2. **Ability to interact, move within virtual environment**: A user can travel to many different lands, over different terrains, using various vehicles. This form of virtual field trip allows users to experience a variety of environments, such as snowy mountains, baked deserts, and wooded forests. Quests can be designed to fit within an appropriate environment under study. For example, students in a Spanish I class could meet and talk in an environment replicating portions of Mexico. They could buy products, build a house, go to the mercado, and so forth, essentially "living" in Mexico and speaking Spanish to do so.

3. **Chat in text or audio:** MMORPGs are text-based in their chat tool, allowing users from around the world to meet and chat in the same environment. However, many MMORPG users also integrate external chat tools such as Roger Wilco or Battlecom to add live chat to their gaming experience. As discussed in #2, this live chat feature could be used by students studying a foreign language, by those who might be too young to type effectively for communication, as an adapative technology tool, or just to aid in learning by providing audio along with text.

4. **Questing:** In educational terms, team problem solving! Quests are designed to motivate users by engaging them in harder and more complex tasks over time. As one progresses through the quests, one requires the use of

continued

more complex skills and the ability to work as a team to progress through various components of a quest. There is great reward for the MMORPG player to complete the quest, both psychologically, socially, and in the final reward—either a new piece of equipment, armor, a tool needed to complete a more advanced quest, or an increase in rank in the game. In my thinking this approach to questing mirrors life and work in general. Educational game designers can take advantage of questing to design tasks that engage learners while rewarding them in the end. For example, in A Tale in the Desert II™, early quests are individual. You are required to collect grass, mud, and sand to make bricks. Once you learn to make bricks, you are then able to begin building structures with your bricks. In essence, you learn by doing, not by reading a text or seeing a slideshow about brick making.

5. **Social interaction:** The social interaction in MMORPGs is often required in order to complete the game—hey, just like real life! Players come together on a short term (groups) or long term (guilds or clans) basis. For those of us that support learning as a social process, the current design of MMORPG play is excellent for promoting social interaction.

So let us imagine you are a high school or college student who is taking a class in Ancient Egypt. Would you prefer to learn in an online class in Blackboard, or a MMORPG such as A Tale in the Desert™? How about an MMORPG for chemistry, art, band, business communications, or personal finance? The technology exists today—moving it into educational realms will take funding and an understanding of the power of MMORPG technology for educational purposes.

In the next four to five years, the New Media Consortium predicts that context-aware computer and augmented reality will begin to appear on the horizon. Context-aware computers customize their interaction with users based on context. The computer can customize the interface without user input based on such factors as lighting, time of day, or the user's location. Augmented reality refers to the ability to overlay a virtual environment on top of what the user is actually seeing in real life. An example of context aware computer and augmented reality is the Campus Tour program at Arizona State University where students can conduct self-guided tours using handheld GPS technology, and can see and hear information at various hot spots throughout the campus.

In summary, it is becoming obvious to all involved in education that the very nature of education is evolving at a rapid pace due to technological innovations and our changing global society. Online education, in all its forms, will continue to evolve at a rapid pace. A main goal of this text is to provide educators with a solid basis for analyzing and understanding the capabilities of current and emerging online learning tools, and how to match those capabilities to achieve desired learning outcomes when designing curricular activities. This understanding and ability empowers you, the educator, to continue remaining successful throughout your career regardless of innovations in technological tools.

Resources

Blackboard Trial Coursesites: http://coursesites.blackboard.com

Campus Tours at Arizona State University: http://www.asu.edu/asunews/university/gpstourlive_082704.htm

Deep in the Hearts of Learners Insights into the Nature of Online Community: http://cade.icaap.org/vol17.1/conrad.html

Edu-tools.com: http://www.edutools.info/index.jsp

Google Scholar: http://scholar.google.com/

How Interactive are YOUR Online Courses? A Rubric for Assessing Interaction in Distance Learning: http://www.westga.edu/~distance/roblyer32.html

Merlot: http://www.merlot.org/Home.po

Moodle: http://moodle.org

National Educational Technology Plan: http://nationaledtechplan.org/default.asp

National Survey of Student Engagement: http://www.iub.edu/~nsse/

Nicenet.org: http://nicenet.org

No Child Left Behind Act: http://www.ed.gov/nclb/landing.jhtml?src=pb

Ricardian Explorer: http://www.wesleyan.edu/re/

Quest for Atlantis: http://atlantis.crlt.indiana.edu/

Virtual Learning Arcade: http://www.bized.ac.uk/virtual/vla/

Wikipedia: http://www.wikipedia.org/

References

Abdelraheem, A. Y. (2003). Computerized learning environments: Problems, design challenges and future promises. *Journal of Interactive Online Learning, 2*(2). Retrieved June 22, 2006, from http://www.ncolr.org/jiol/archives/2003/fall/01/index.html

Boomer, G., Lester, N., Onore, C., & Cook, J. (1994). *Negotiating the curriculum: Educating for the 21ˢᵗ century.* London: Falmer.

Carnevale, D. (2006). Michigan considers requiring online course for high school students. Retrieved June 22, 2006, from http://chronicle.com/weekly/v52/i18/18a04501.htm

Collison, G., Elbaum, B., Haavind, S., & Tinker, R. (2000). *Facilitating online learning: Effective strategies for moderators.* Madison: Atwood.

Conrad, R., & Donaldson, J. (2004). *Engaging the online learner: Activities and resources for creative instruction.* Jossey-Bass.

Copeland, W., Birmingham, C., DeMeulle, L., D'Emidio-Caston, M. & Natal, D. (1994). Making meaning in classrooms: An investigation of cognitive processes in aspiring teachers, experienced teachers, and their peers. *American Educational Research Journal, 31,* 166-196.

Gagne, E., Yekovich, C., & Yekovich, F. (1993). *The cognitive psychology of school learning.* New York: Longman.

Ishii, K., & Lutterbeck, B. (2001, November). Unexploited resources of online education for democracy: Why the future should belong to OpenCourseWare. *First Monday, 6*(11). Retrieved June 22, 2006, from http://firstmonday.org/issues/issue6_11/ishii/index.html

Ko, S., & Rossen, S. (2004). *Teaching online: A practical guide.* Houghton Mifflin.

Leslie, S. (2003). *Important characteristics of course management systems: Findings from the Edu-tool.info project.* Paper presented at the 2003 CADE Conference. Retrieved June 22, 2006, from http://www.edtechpost.ca/gems/cms_characteristics.htm

Meyer, K. (2002). *Quality in distance education: Focus on on-line learning.* San Francisco: Jossey-Bass.

New Media Consortium. (2006). *The horizon report: 2006 edition.* Retrieved June 22, 2006, from http://www.nmc.org/pdf/2006_Horizon_Report.pdf

O'Gorman, D. (2005, April). *National trends in online education: Implications for UIS.* Retrieved June 22, 2006, from http://otel.uis.edu/techday2005/ogorman.htm

Palloff, R. M., & Pratt, K. (2001). *Lessons from the cyberspace classroom: The realities of online teaching.* San Francisco: Jossey-Bass.

Salmon, G. (2002). *E-tivities: The key to active online learning.* London: Kogan Page.

Siemens, G. (2004). *Learning management systems: The wrong place to start learning.* Retrieved June 22, 2006, from http://www.elearnspace.org/Articles/lms.htm

Sloan-C. (2005). *Growing by degrees: Online education in the United States, 2005.* Retrieved June 22, 2006, from http://www.sloan-c.org/publications/survey/pdf/growing_by_degrees.pdf

Thomas, D. (2005). U.S. Department of Education releases national education technology plan. Retrieved June 22, 2006, from http://www.ed.gov/news/pressreleases/2005/01/01072005.html

U.S. Department of Education. (2005a). *No child left behind: Expanding the promise.* Retrieved June 22, 2006, from http://www.ed.gov/about/overview/budget/budget06/nclb/index.html

U.S. Department of Education. (2005b). *National Educational technology plan.* Retrieved June 22, 2006, from http://www.ed.gov/about/offices/list/os/technology/plan/2004/index.html

Walker, G. (2005). Critical thinking in asynchronous discussions. *International Journal of Instructional Technology and Distance Learning, 2*(6), 15-22. Retrieved June 22, 2006, from http://www.itdl.org/Journal/Jun_05/article02.htm

Chapter II

Content Areas:
Syllabus, Notes, Lesson Plans, and Documents

Content areas refer to those spaces online where instructors host materials for their courses or students. In an LMS, content areas include folders for items such as the class syllabus, lesson plans, weekly assignments, course documents and handouts, teacher contact information, and subject-area content. Online content is presented in many formats, but most instructors use html or cut and paste from Word™ documents. If you are using a Web site, wiki, blog, or other mechanism for hosting content, the principles of this chapter still apply, although blogs and wikis provide students the additional ability to add to the content. The major strength of content areas is the ability to organize and share information between the students and the teacher.

Organization of information is critical to creating an online class where students are successful. A well-organized course can actually provide students a visual schema for thinking about the organization of course and content. This visual schema can assist the student with the integration and long-term retention of knowledge.

Figure 2.1. Course assignments organized by week and topic

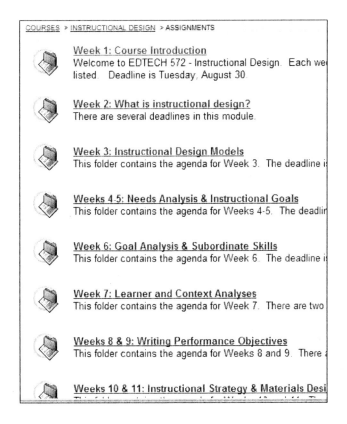

In Figure 2.1, we can see how students can quickly glance at these assignment folders to get an overview and sequence of main course topics, thus providing a schema for thinking about the topic under study. Time in a well-organized course is spent on learning instead of deciphering how the course works.

Conversely, a poorly organized course can cause confusion and anxiety for the learner. Disorganized information, duplication of documents, or unclear directions about where to locate or post assignments leads to students who are frustrated, have a difficult time learning, or who experience cognitive overload. Students in poorly organized courses often have difficulty finding the information they need, not understanding how to work through the sequence of the course, and may choose to quit the course out of frustration.

In this chapter, we examine the strengths and weaknesses of various content areas, explore the need for organization of information in online learning, and provide examples of organization strategies to assist your students in successfully achieving learning objectives. Whether you have one or multiple areas for storing content, this chapter can help.

Strengths and Weaknesses

Table 2.1 illustrates the varied strengths and weaknesses of using the content storage areas.

Strengths of content storage areas. The basic strength of content areas is organization. Because the computer is the intermediary between the teacher and student, it is also the place where information is stored. This information exists in multiple forms—text, links to references, multimedia materials

Table 2.1. Strengths and weaknesses of content storage areas

Strengths	Weaknesses
• Content areas make it easy to find necessary information with minimal clicking. • Navigation in content areas can be set up to mimic a regular syllabus, thus making it easy for the first-time online learner to comprehend the online environment. • Able to support learning by providing hierarchies of information and visual schemas. • Multiple content areas are available in some LMSs, wikis, blogs, and Web sites.	• Documents can be hosted in inconsistent places from course to course, causing confusion. • Inappropriately labeled content areas can create confusion. • Instructors who do not use folders force their students to scroll through many pages of text. • Sometimes instructors will use an area just because it is there, not really considering whether it is useful for the students. • Predefined storage areas should be "turned off" if not in use. Otherwise, students may question if something is missing or spend useless time clicking to an empty area.

(graphics, slideshows, flash presentations, movie files). The organization of those materials determines the path the student takes through an online course.

Navigation in online courses can lead users through various content areas, as needed, and some of the predefined content areas (syllabus, assignments, etc.) in many LMSs and online courses mimic a normal syllabus. This recognized chunking of information makes it easy for the first-time or novice online learner to comprehend and easily navigate the online class.

As demonstrated at the beginning of this chapter, the way an online course is organized can also support learning by providing visual schemas for understanding major topics covered in the course. Finally, LMSs, Web sites, and wikis offer multiple content storage areas and formats, making it easy for the teacher to chunk various bits of information, files, and documentation in the online course.

Weaknesses of content storage areas. An online tool's greatest strength can also be its greatest weakness. Because online teachers organize and present online content in a variety of ways, students who move from one online course to another can be confused by the inconsistent presentation of information. Students may have to memorize different locations of materials, or spend useless time clicking in one place to find information only to discover it is located in another section. Some of these organizational issues can be compounded when an instructor names a storage area inappropriately. For example, an instructor might choose to label a storage area with the term "documents." The instructor then makes the decision to insert each weekly lesson plan into the documents folder. This labeling is confusing to the student who is used to seeing supplemental course materials inside a "documents" folder. The student would be better served by accurately renaming this folder "Lesson Plans" or "Weekly Assignments," depending on how the instructor has structured the course.

Folders and subfolders are a great way to organize levels of documentation and information. For example, in the "Lesson Plans" folder, an instructor can create subfolders that hold each of the weekly lesson plans. When an instructor does not use subfolders, all those lesson plans display in the same browser frame, one long page of lesson plans that requires lengthy scrolling to get to the desired lesson plan.

Because LMSs come with predefined storage areas, many new online teachers may feel compelled to use a storage area, without considering if it is useful for their particular students or the needs of their course. For example, an instructor might have separate areas for "Syllabus" and "Course Information." Why include both areas of navigation and clutter up the simplicity of the navigation, when choosing one of these areas would do the trick? It is recommended to turn off, or deactivate, storage areas that are not useful to the class or instructor. A simple rule of thumb would be to use the least number of storage areas possible to effectively offer the course. If you have a "Discussion Boards" area activated, but do not use discussion boards, turn it off to save students time with unnecessary clicking.

Understanding Content Areas: Organized for Success!

From our early years in school, we are taught to use outline format as a tool to organize our thinking before we write. Perhaps you were also taught the use of writing webs, flowcharts, tree diagrams, maps, or jot lists as other ways of putting a random list of thoughts into a coherent whole. Children today use Kidspiration™ to create electronic flowcharts to organize their ideas.

The human brain has a need to organize information in coherent chunks. In doing so, we create schemas that help us interpret, predict, and remember many interrelated facts, information, and memories over long periods of time (Gagne, 1985). Schemata can be reflected in text, for example (Driscoll, 1997; Halliday & Hassan, 1989). Readers use their schematic representations of text, such as an outline format, to help them interpret information.

Schema theory also has implications for online course design, and corollary, how we set up our content storage areas in online courses. In order to facilitate efficient student learning, we should organize material according to conventional structures that students already know. This is particularly true for novice online learners who are already dealing with the cognitive demands of interpreting a new way of learning. This implies that those teaching introductory, first year online courses, would want to adhere tightly to conventional structures for presenting information. There is also a case to be made for simplicity in design, as Palloff and Pratt (2001) state: "Most often, a simple course site that is easy to navigate leads to the most success-ful experience" (p. 76). As students progress through online programs and gain experience with the learner environment, teachers can lead students to explore alternative approaches to online organization and structure, such as using a concept map as the class's home page.

Content and information in online courses has to be broken down into chunks in order for students to cognitively process the information (Reushle, Dorman, Evans, Kirkwood, McDonald, & Worden, 1999). Novice online learners can be particularly prone to cognitive overload in courses that do not follow "a linear structure of logically sequenced units of instruction" (Clark & Mayer, 2003, p. 241). Cognitive overload occurs when the learning experiences impose exceptional demands on the processing capacity of the cognitive system (Mayer & Moreno, 2003).

Through the use of predesignated content areas (such as syllabus, assign-ments, and documents) and folders, much of the course organization can be established. On a Web site or wiki, this type of organization is accomplished through the navigational structure. Blogs offer less options for how to host content for an entire course and are best used as a supplement to the regular online classroom.

The use of graphic organizers or course maps can also be useful to students. Course maps offer a visual representation of the hierarchy of course context and hypertext, and learners can access any screen in the hypertext from the map. Some research has shown that users access the topic map frequently but rarely use it to navigate. Instead, they tend to review the visuals levels of topics in the course and then return to the class (Clark & Mayer, 2003). This suggests that course or topic maps may be an important tool for providing an orientation to the course content and topics (Reushle et al., 1999). Course maps may also be helpful to experienced online learners by providing alternative learning paths, as some research indicates different experienced users take different pathways to learn the same information (Reushle et al., 1999).

If you are working with an LMS, blog, wiki, or other predefined content areas, much of your organization is established for you due to the layout and design of the areas themselves. Those instructors using or integrating Web pages to run online courses have more latitude in creating their structure. However, even with a highly structured LMS system, there are organizational and file management practices that can be used wisely to promote efficient and ef-fective learning. Moreover, just because a content area is provided within an LMS does not mean we have to use it if it does not serve our purposes or audience (Palloff & Pratt, 2001). For example, a teacher might not choose to use the "external links" portion of the LMS, as the teacher prefers to embed the resources in lesson plans and master documents that the students can download. The teacher is able to reuse and build on this resource from semester to semester, and views it as more efficient for the teacher and the students.

Structuring Content Areas for Success

Now that we have a basic understanding of why we need to organize content areas for success, let us explore some practical solutions and examples used in online classes. In this section, we look at some examples for structuring the following content areas: announcements, faculty information, syllabi and schedules, assignments, course documents, discussion boards, and Web pages.

Announcements. Some LMSs have a designated area for class announcements, typically as students enter the course.

This space is used by the instructor to post announcements, for example, upcoming test dates, guest lecturers, reminders about projects, or program announcements. Some LMSs, such as Claroline™, also allow the teacher to send a copy of the announcement via e-mail, thus notifying students who might not otherwise log in for several days and miss a time-sensitive announcement.

At the beginning of a new class, instructors should include a welcoming announcement that introduces the class and provides explicit directions on where to go to begin the course.

Notice the last sentence of this announcement explains to students to "review the Course Description" and "read the Week 1 Agenda in the Learning Path folder," both items located in the left navigation menu. There is no doubt about where to go next upon entering this online course. Subsequent documents in the course, such as weekly lesson plans or agendas, should provide the same type of sequencing and leading for the students.

Figure 2.2. Announcement area in LMS

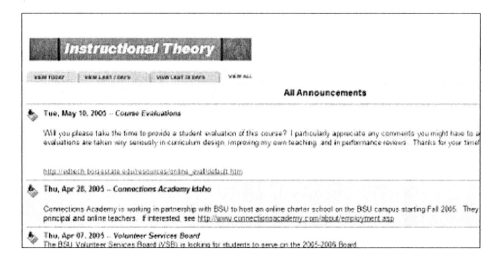

Figure 2.3. Welcoming class announcement providing directions on how to begin

Figure 2.4. Faculty information page

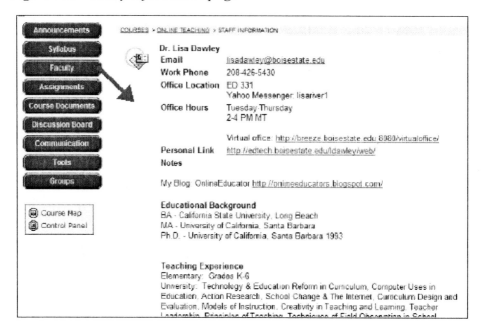

Faculty information. This area might also be labeled as "staff information," "professor," or "instructor." This area presenting the instructor's information, including e-mail, IM information, office hours, links to instructor's Web sites, or other personal or career information.

This type of page can be easily recreated on a Web site if you do not have access to a faculty information area. Here is a Web version of the above screen shot.

In your instructor information, provide students multiple options for contact, such as IM, phone, e-mail, or virtual office hours. A photo helps to personalize the information and create a visual association for the student.

Syllabus and schedule. In this area, the instructor can post syllabus and schedule. Depending on your class, you might choose to include these two documents in one master syllabus or keep them separate in the same folder.

Figure 2.5. Faculty information hosted on a Web site

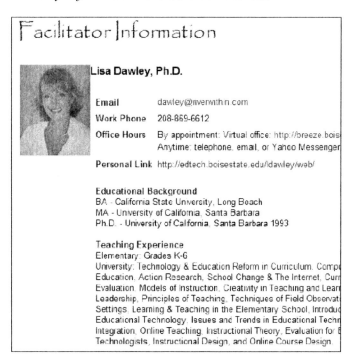

Figure 2.6. The syllabus content area

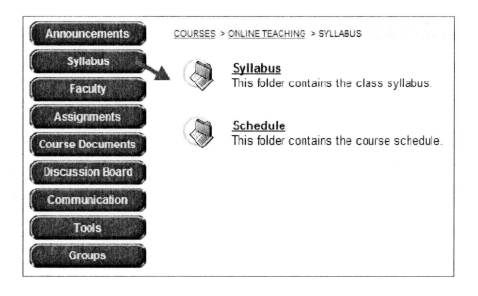

On your syllabus, address the following areas at a minimum:

- Course title and number
- Semester
- Instructor name and e-mail
- Course description
- Course text, materials, and software requirements
- Course goals and objectives
- Assignments and grading procedures
- Grading scale
- Schedule
- Course guidelines, expectations, or policies: how often to log on, how assignments are graded, and so forth

Although most instructors are familiar with the sections in a syllabus, we would like to emphasize the need to be explicit with your *course guidelines* in particular, outlining rules, roles, or norms that need to be established in the class (Palloff & Pratt, 2001).

In the course guidelines, you can provide information on when assignments are due, how often and when assignments are posted, anticipated synchronous discussions session, methods of preferred communication, and how quickly you will respond. For younger students, netiquette rules should be introduced in this section, and reinforced and discussed during the first week of class.

Also, provide a printable version of your syllabus to students, as this is their map for the course (Ko & Rossen, 2004). This .doc file can be hosted in the "Documents" section of your course, e-mailed to your students, or both.

Assignments. As we saw at the beginning of the chapter, a well organized assignment area starts with folders. Create a folder to host each week or module of the course. Give a descriptive title, such as "Week 1: Introduc-

Figure 2.7. Example of course guidelines

Course Expectations

Course work in EDTECH 707 is divided into 15 weeks of the semester. The types of assignments and the level of interactivity vary from week-to-week. This is not a self-paced course, and projects involving collaboration with peers are required. Thus, much work is not made available in advance as the purpose of the course is for students to work together at the same pace. I will always try my best to give clear directions on what, where, when, and how in the weekly assignment folder.

Communication with the instructor and/or students in the class can be readily accomplished through the e-mail, group functions, and through the virtual office in Breeze. I usually return e-mail and phone calls within 24 hours, and I am happy to schedule a time with you to discuss your questions and work. A Student Lounge Area is provided in the Discussion Board. This provides an opportunity for you to visit with other class members about any topic of interest. I encourage you to use this area to visit with other class members (much as you would in the hallway before an on-campus class).

There is also a FAQ area on the Discussion Board and I will post questions for students that I think may help the whole class. Please do not hesitate to ask questions—online environments vary greatly, as well as students' experiences with them.

Class Assignments

Instructions for where and when to submit assignments will be given in each Weekly Agenda in the Assignments folder. All assignments are due on a weekly basis by 10:00 PM MST each Tuesday at the latest unless indicated otherwise. Late assignments will result in grade reductions (10% per day until turned in).

Remember: Always save a copy of your assignment on your hard drive! I have to admit I have learned the hard way, on more than one occasion, not to type my work directly into the Blackboard window. Better to work in your word processing program and then do a copy and paste.

Finally... I am really excited about the opportunity to teach EDTECH 707. This is my seventh year of teaching in online environments. I will try everything within my power to facilitate your learning in this class. I am looking forward to working with each of you.

tion to the Course." Also provide a description of the folder contents, such as "This folder contains the agenda and survey for Week 1. The deadline for this assignment is August 14." Organize the weekly folders or unit modules in a suggested chronological sequence. Note Figures 2.8 and 2.9, showing organized and disorganized folders in the Assignments area.

In Figure 2.8, we see that folders have been titled and arranged sequentially, week by week. There is no confusion about what these folders represent, what is included inside the folder, or the due date. Now, look at Figure 2.9. Note

Figure 2.8. Organized files in Assignments folder

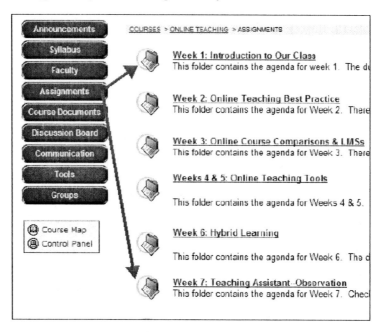

Figure 2.9. Disorganized folders in the Assignments area

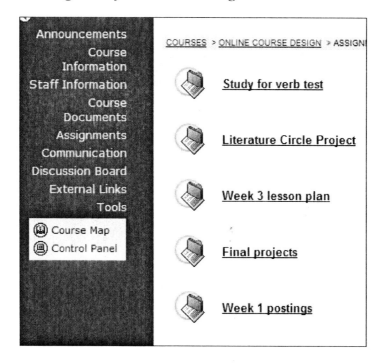

the inadequate labeling and sequencing of the folders. The teacher also forgot to include a description for each folder, so the user is not really sure what is there or when it is due. Which class would you want to take? Why?

Also, consider whether you will make all folders visible from the first day of class, or if you will selectively make them available as the course progresses week to week. With novice online learners and younger students, it is highly recommended to pace the viewing of folders for your students. For adults and self-paced courses, some instructors may prefer to make the entire course available at once. Benefits of this approach include providing the students the ability to work ahead or view planned assignments. Drawbacks to this approach may include creating anxiety in learners who feel overwhelmed by viewing 15 weeks of assignments all at once, for example.

Course documents. If you create a documents area, consider carefully what you will include in that area. It is not recommended to include items that are important enough to be in their own separate area, such as a syllabus or assignments. A good analogy is to consider the Course Documents area as the place to keep "handouts" that a teacher would give in a regular classroom (Figure 2.10).

As good practice, always include any Codes of Conduct, Acceptable Use Policies, or any other standard policies that must be provided to students. Also include a folder called "Printable Documents." Printable documents is a place to store .doc versions of syllabi, lesson plans, or handouts that you may have created in .html. Students appreciate the ability to have .doc versions to simplify printing. Many students like to print off these documents and keep them in a course binder. Finally, in Course Documents you can store any other handouts related to the course such as project guidelines, reference lists of materials, and so forth.

Some LMSs use Document storage areas as a suppository for uploading learning objects that are integrated in other sections throughout the course. Learning objects are digital objects that can be reused to support learning. In Figure 2.11, note that the teacher has created two learning object storage areas in Claroline™, called *Agendas* and *Images*.

Because the teacher is using these folders for storage of learning objects only, the teacher has turned them off, or made them invisible to students. In this class, students can only view the documents in the folders holding CEU Forms, Chat Recordings, and Printable Documents.

Figure 2.10. Course Documents area

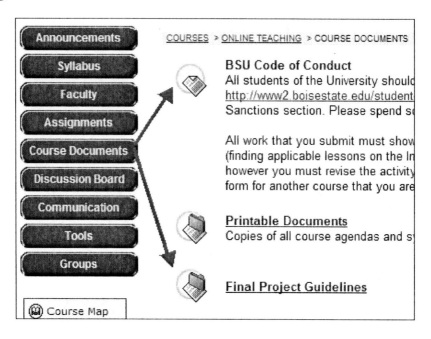

Figure 2.11. Learning object folders in a Documents storage area

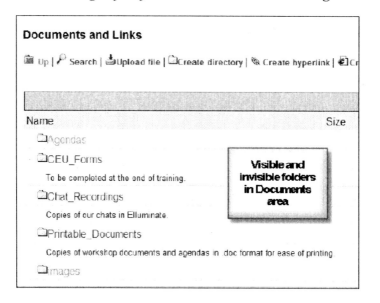

Discussion boards. All online classes should include at least one informational board and two social boards: *FAQs, The Student Lounge,* and *Week 1: Introductions.* FAQs should include commonly asked questions about where to get tech support, how to change personal settings in the LMS, or any other repetitive questions that occur from semester to semester. The Student Lounge and Week 1: Introductions boards set the stage for social interaction in the course (see Chapter IV).

Organize the remaining boards chronologically to match the outline of the assignments. Discussion boards do not have to be included for every week or module of instruction. Posting every week to discussion boards can be repetitive and create boredom in the online class. In the Figure 2.12, note how the boards are organized by week.

Because these boards were used in a workshop for teacher training, the "student lounge" was changed to "teacher's lounge" to reflect the occupation of the participants.

Figure 2.12. Example of discussion board organization

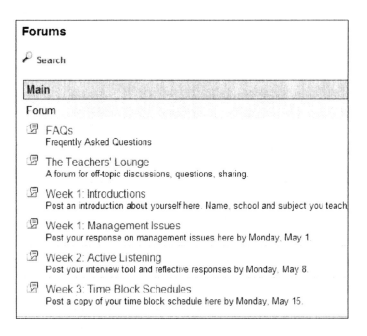

In the title for each board, list the week or module number, as well as a brief descriptor of the topic. In the description, provide a brief summary about the purpose of the board, as well as any due dates associated with the board. Even though this information may be listed in your agenda or lesson plan, the quick visual reference is helpful for keeping students on track.

External links. Some LMSs provide a location in the course for hosting a set of reference URLs that students might use throughout the course. You may or may not find this feature useful, depending on how you have been collecting URLs to integrate into your course. Many teachers keep Web sites with relevant URLs for their students. In this case, you could link to your Web site from the Content Area.

In distance learning courses, it is always helpful to provide URLs to information about netiquette, how to search for resources using the Internet (or an online library), tech support or tutorials, and subject area resources.

Web pages. Web pages can be used to host all the materials in an online course. This site may or may not be used as a supplement to an LMS. When designing Web pages or content that load inside an LMS, remember that subdivided pages load more quickly than one long document. This is especially true if you include a lot of graphics or multimedia. Readability and navigation are also greatly improved with subdivided pages. As a final consider, your subdivided Web pages are easier to edit, as you do not have to scroll through one long document.

Power Tip: Write Content in an HTML Editor, if Possible

When creating lesson plans and content for your course, it is to your benefit to write your content in an html editor such as FrontPage™ or Dreamweaver™, and then copy and paste the html code into the browser *html window* inside your LMS.

Many LMSs, such as Blackboard™ and Claroline™, allow you to write in html or WYSWYG (what you see is what you get). These tools are fine for editing small amounts of material, but *never* compose directly in the WYSWYG window.

---

continued

First, the window might close and you could lose your work (yes, this does happen). Second, by keeping your content in html, you are able to easily update and modify it from semester to semester. Third, and most importantly, if you design in html, you will retain all formatting, graphics placement, and text formatting when you paste into the LMS. Formatting can often show up askew if copying and pasting from word processing programs.

Power Tip: Keep Your Content Simple

The use of instructor-created multimedia appears to be all the rage. Students enjoy viewing video, slideshow, and flash presentations related to content. Imagery can go a long way to help students process and retain concepts presented in class; however, keep it simple. When choosing to design your lessons, and create course content, keep in mind that students often report that simple text pages, with clean lines, limited text, and a few graphics at the most, are highly valued. See Figure 2.13, for example. Remember that it is the interactive *learning experience* itself you want to promote. Online teaching is not a contest to see who can create the coolest multimedia. Multimedia is time consuming and can be expensive to create. Choose wisely for the most effective presentation.

Power Tip: Know The Law on Copyright in Distance Education

This tip might appear to be common sense for any online teacher. Not only must online teachers be sensitive to their own potential violations of copyright, but they need to be aware that they are *modeling* appropriate use of copyrighted material in distance education courses. The Technology, Education, and Copyright Harmonization (TEACH) Act was signed into law on November 2, 2002. TEACH specifies that it is not copyright infringement to use copyrighted materials for educational purposes in online courses when certain criteria are met. For detailed information on the TEACH Act, see http://www.lib.ncsu.edu/scc/legislative/teachkit/overview.html.

Example Uses for Success

Learning Objective Outcome	Content Area Activities
Interactivity and connection	• Add discussion boards that are social in nature, such as a student lounge. • Have students create blogs to reflect on their learning in the class. Create a master list of the blogs and post it as a permanent announcement, or link it on your Web site, for easy access to all blogs.
Knowledge: defines; describes; enumerates; identifies; labels; lists; matches; names; reads; records; reproduces; selects; states; views	• Post a course syllabus that includes links to other relevant sections of your course. • Create summaries of weekly discussions or activities and share these in the announcement area.
Comprehension: classifies; cites; converts; describes; discusses; estimates; explains; generalizes; gives examples; makes sense out of; paraphrases; restates (in own words); summarizes; traces; understands	• Assign readings to students on specific topics. Have them summarize that information and display it in wiki pages. • During the first week of class, have students review your faculty information. Ask them to create their own home page in the LMS sharing similar information.

continued

Application: acts; administers; articulates; assesses; charts; collects; computes; constructs; contributes; controls; determines; develops; discovers; establishes; extends; implements; includes; informs; instructs; operationalizes; participates; predicts; prepares; preserves; produces; projects; provides; relates; reports; shows; solves; teaches; transfers; uses; utilizes	• Give students access to add to your external links, if possible. Provide them criteria for determining if a link if valuable to other members of the course. • Have students review the netiquette rules in the syllabus. Create a discussion board and ask students to share examples of incidences where netiquette rules were violated and their reaction to the experience. • Consider adding a "student work" folder in the "course documents" area. This can be a place where you can upload copies of student's work that they may want to share with others.
Analysis: breaks down; correlates; diagrams; differentiates; discriminates; distinguishes; focuses; illustrates; infers; limits; outlines; points out; prioritizes; recognizes; separates; subdivides	• Have students create their own Web site offering a collection of organized resources related to course content.
Synthesis: adapts; anticipates; categorizes; collaborates; combines; communicates; compares; compiles; composes; contrasts; creates; designs; devises; expresses; facilitates; formulates; generates; incorporates; individualizes; initiates; integrates; intervenes; models; modifies; negotiates; plans; progresses; rearranges; reconstructs; reinforces; reorganizes; revises; structures; substitutes; validates	• At the conclusion of the course, ask students to revisit the assignments folder and retitle each week in their own words based on what they learned during that week. • Have a student serve as your "teaching assistant," and make them responsible for uploading and displaying course documents and information.

continued

Evaluation: appraises; compares & contrasts; concludes; criticizes; critiques; decides; defends; interprets; judges; justifies; reframes	• Assign wiki pages to your students that build on the content of the course itself. For example, if you teach a course in Learning Theories, students can work in teams to collaboratively edit wiki pages on behaviorism, constructivism, and multiple intelligences.

Example Lesson Plan

Figure 2.13. Example lesson plan with overview of content areas in the LMS

> **WEEK 1.**
> **Introduction and Overview to Online Teaching for Adult Learners**
>
> This week serves as an introduction to our course and Blackboard™. In our course, we will explore the world and practice of online teaching. Ko and Rossen (2004) offer us a simple definition of online teaching: "Teaching online means conducting a course partially or entirely through the Internet" (p. 2). I would like to build off this definition, and offer that a successful online teacher is one who promotes the achievement of learning objectives by facilitating engagement and collaboration to empower students as life-long learners. As we move through our course, you will note that we emphasize the importance of community, collaboration, and interactivity as integral aspects of online education. But just how do we as instructors promote this type of engagement? Adult learning theory, or andragogy, serves as the foundation of all our work, and in this week's assignment, you have the opportunity to begin some initial reflections on the relationship between adult learning theory and online teaching and learning.
>
> To get started, please complete the activities listed below. Good luck! Be sure to send me a note if you get stuck. Enjoy.

continued

OBJECTIVES

1.   Familiarize yourself with the Blackboard 6 learning environment.

2.   Adjust your settings and create a home page in Blackboard.

3.   Establish community by introducing yourself to others in class.

4.   Reflect on core concepts in adult learning theory.

5.   Order course texts.

6.   Complete initial class survey.

7.   Subscribe to DistanceEducator.com.

READINGS

Gibbons, H., & Wentworth, G. (2001). Andrological and pedagogical training differences for online instructors. *Online Journal of Distance Learning Administration, 4*(3). Number III. Retrieved June 23, 2006, from http://www.emich.edu/cfid/PDFs/Andrological-Pedagogical-Training.pdf

Fidishun, D. (2006). *Andragogy and technology: Integrating adult learning theory as we teach with technology.* Retrieved June 23, 2006, from http://mark-mcmanus.ca/Resources/Adult-Learners-Integrating-Adult-Learning-Theory-with-Technology.pdf

ACTIVITIES FOR WEEK 1	DUE DATE
Getting Started **1. Read the syllabus and course calendar carefully**. Make sure that you understand what will be expected of you this semester. If you have questions ask them early. **2. Get familiar with the Blackboard™ course site**. Click all of the buttons in the navigation bar and see where things are located. Things tend to stay in the same place all semester. Once you know where everything is you should have no trouble locating information. **3. Check your e-mail address in Blackboard™**. Click the **Course Tools** button in Blackboard™ and look for a link to **Personal Information**. Click the link to open your personal settings in Blackboard. Make sure that the email address shown there is the one you want to have. When I send you email it will go to this address. By default the e-mail address is your BSU student email address in the form: FirstnameLastname@mail.boisestate.edu **4. Build your student home page.** You can find this under the **Course Tools** button in Blackboard™. After clicking Course Tools you should see a link that says **Homepage**. Click that link and fill in the boxes with any information you would like to share about yourself. Go ahead and upload a picture too. This helps us get to know you better. The *assessment criteria* for the student homepage assignment is as follows: Information about you, and a digital photo of you that is correctly sized for Blackboard™. Don't go over 200x200 pixels. If your photo is too large resize it in <u>Microsoft Paint</u> or <u>Mac IPhoto</u>. The next image shows the Personal Information and Homepage links in Blackboard™.	Deadline: Tuesday evening, Jan. 24

continued

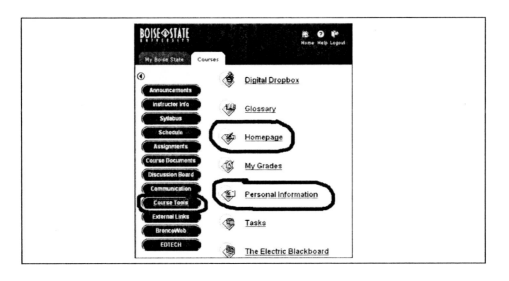

2. Class Introductions And, now, for your Introduction. Access the **Discussion Board**. You will notice a forum titled, "Class Introductions." Select Add New Thread and title it with your name. Please give us an idea of your background and experiences in education and educational technology. A little personal information is always appreciated (where you live, hobbies, career, etc).	Deadline: Tuesday evening, Jan. 24
3. Adult Learning Theory & You Read the two articles listed above. Consider the main points in each article and how those concepts (1) apply to you and your history as an adult learner, and (2) apply to you in your role as an educator. In the Week 1 discussion forum, share your reflections for each area. There are no right or wrong answers. Feel free to comment on the responses of others. What connections or similarities do you see?	Deadline: midnight MT on Tuesday, Aug 30.
4. Order Your Texts See information on Syllabus. We will use these texts next week—use next day shipping if needed. Fair warning :)	Deadline: **Do it now!**

continued

5. Survey Send me an e-mail to lisadawley@boisestate.edu that answers the following questions. Include "EDTECH 582" in the subject header. 1. Name: 2. Phone number(s): 3. E-mail: 4. My job is: 5. I have participated in other online courses (true or false) 6. I have participated on a discussion board and in chat 7. I have participated in video conferencing 8. I know how to attach text, audio or digital images to e-mail 9. I have participated in or created a blog 10. I have participated in online collaborations such as team projects or presentations. 11. Are there students listed in course roster with whom you prefer to be grouped or not grouped? 12. Is there anything you'd like me to be aware of that might affect your performance in the class? 13. Do you have any concerns or special needs? 14. Anything else you'd like to share?	Deadline: Tuesday evening, Jan. 24
6. Subscribe to DistanceEducator.com I know! Six things to do this week! It's ok, it was all pretty easy, wasn't it? ;) Take a minute to subscribe to the daily news at **Distance-educator.com**. You will begin receiving daily email on news/research/events related to distance education. It is critical for you to become aware of latest trends and news in our field. This is an easy way to make that happen. You might also find resources to complete this week's assignment! http://www. distance-educator.com/UserReg.phtml	Deadline: Tuesday evening, Jan. 24

Grading

Grading is pass/no pass this week, 40 points. You receive full credit when all assignments have been completed. If a grade isn't posted in your gradebook, it indicates I have yet to grade your assignment.

That's it for this week. Assignments will always be posted by Tuesday of each week (some modules may last two weeks or longer).

WELCOME ABOARD!

© 2006 Lisa Dawley, PhD

Resources

Creating a Course Web site: http://www.bethel.edu/its/is/teaching-technology/Dreamweaver/webtheory/webtheoryresources.htm

IHMC CMap Tools (course mapping): http://cmap.ihmc.us/

Primer for Teaching Online: Chunk Your Content: http://201.230.195.252/oldHETS/vp_teachingOnline_4.php

Match need to tool: http://www.unc.edu/cit/strategies/

References

Clark, R. C., & Mayer, R. E. (2003). *E-learning and the science of instruction.* San Francisco: Pfeiffer.

Driscoll, M. (1994). *Psychology of learning for instruction.* Boston: Allyn and Bacon.

Ko, S., & Rossen, S. (2004). *Teaching online: A practical guide.* Houghton Mifflin.

Gagne, R. M. (1985). *The conditions of learning and theory of instruction.* New York: CBS College Publishing.

Halliday, M. A., & Hassan, R. (1989). *Language, context, and text: Aspects of language in a social-semiotic perspective.* Oxford: Oxford University Press.

Mayer, R. E., & Moreno, R. (2003). Nine ways to reduce cognitive load in multimedia learning. *Educational Psychologist, 38*(1), 43–52.

Palloff, R. M., & Pratt, K. (2001). *Lessons from the cyberspace classroom: The realities of online teaching.* San Francisco: Jossey-Bass.

Reushle, S., Dorman, M., Evans, P., Kirkwood, J., McDonald, J., & Worden, J. (1999). *Critical elements: Designing for online teaching.* Paper presented at the annual meeting of the ASCILITE. Retrieved June 22, 2006, from http://www.usq.edu.au/users/evansp/not_indexed/ASCILITE99.pdf

Chapter III

E-Mail

E-mail is the most commonly used tool of the online educator. Whether the student or instructor chooses to use the internal e-mail client within an LMS or an external e-mail client, such as Outlook, it is the main tool for one-on-one communication between the online instructor and student. Herein lies the power of e-mail because all students desire a connection with their instructor.

E-mail provides the student not only a sense of connectedness, but also offers the ability for convenient and quick transfer of information (Roberson & Klotz, 2002). Whereas an instructor might check an online course discussion board a couple of times a week, e-mail is usually checked daily, thus offering students a means to receive quicker responses to their inquiries. This is especially important when the student has a technical issue that needs resolution.

E-mail also offers a sense of privacy that might not be available on a larger class discussion board. If the online discussion board is equivalent to a student asking a question in a live class, then the ability to ask a question or talk via e-mail is equivalent to a student meeting in the instructor's office to talk privately. Thus, a strong online instructor will pay heed to all e-mail received from students, and respond promptly, usually within 24 hours, even

Figure 3.1. E-mail from student requiring technical assistance

---

From: Lisa Dawley [mailto:LisaDawley@boisestate.edu]

Sent: Wednesday, November 09, 2005 8:41 AM

To: Melissa Slocum

Subject: Re: EDTECH 582: Final Project Question

Hi Melissa,

All students automatically get server space here that you can use throughout your entire program, if needed.

Here's a couple of documents to help with FTP, if you need it.

http://edtech.boisestate.edu/edtech574/Week1/ftpFlash.htm

and

http://edtech.boisestate.edu/edtech574/Week1/ftphelp.htm

Thanks, Lisa

>"Melissa Slocum" MelissaSlocum@mail.boisestate.edu>11/08/05 4:23 PM>>

Hi Lisa,

Does BSU offer any server space if I wanted publish my final web product? Or do I need to design it and provide you with a porfolio of pages in PDF format?

Thanks,

Melissa

---

if it is to say, "I don't know, but I'll need to get back to you as soon as I have more information."

All LMSs incorporate an e-mail client within their tool set. Some LMSs, such as First Class, CourseMatrix, and WebCT, incorporate internal course e-mail that does not need to go to an outside e-mail address. Other systems, such as Blackboard and eCollege, use an e-mail roster that allows the user to select who in the class will receive the e-mail, and that e-mail is then sent from within the system to an outside e-mail address previously provided by the user.

In this chapter, we examine the strengths and weaknesses of e-mail, explore the need for individual connection in online learning, and provide sample e-mail activities aligned with learning objective outcomes.

Strengths and Weaknesses

Table 3.1 illustrates the varied strengths and weaknesses of using e-mail.

Strengths of e-mail. The strengths of e-mail as an online learning tool are many. From the online student's perspective, perhaps the greatest strength of e-mail is its ability to promote a sense of connection with the instructor and the course overall (Roberson & Klotz, 2002). In an online learning environment, a sense of disconnectedness can often lead to poor quality work or to the student dropping out of the course. Any anxiety a student may be feeling prior to, or during, a course can be lessened through e-mail contact.

Table 3.1. Strengths and weaknesses of e-mail

Strengths	Weaknesses
• Enhances individual connection, as well as sense of community when used effectively • Less anxiety when students feel support from professor • Avoids scheduling conflicts • Quick response time • Easy to monitor • Can attach documents and files • Privacy • Low cost, ease of use • Can increase student involvement and motivation • Accessibility • Improves student writing overall because they are writing for an audience	• Reading and responses are time-consuming for instructor • Students can get frustrated or depressed if e-mails are not answered quickly, requiring the instructor to work 7 days a week on one class or establish boundaries for responding • Students may need to develop context sensitivity to e-mail netiquette and the norms of asynchronous communication • Loss of nonverbal communication • Text-based formatting • Potential for misunderstanding • Lack of visual contact can result in lack of inhibition, thus promoting more negativity in student's comments

Because e-mail is asynchronous, another advantage as a learning tool is that it offers a communication medium that avoids scheduling conflicts (Thorsen, 2003). This ability to communicate at the user's and instructor's own convenience is one of the highly touted benefits of online education in general. E-mail is one of the tools that allows this benefit to occur. When teaching adults or students located in various time zones, this asynchronous capability becomes an even more obvious benefit.

Another documented benefit of using e-mail is quick response time for students' inquiries (Roberson & Klotz, 2002). It is easy to monitor and does not require a separate login if using a dedicated e-mail client such as Outlook, files of any type can be attached, and it offers a private communication forum to online students. E-mail can be achieved at low or no cost, and is easily accessible via the Web. Research studies have demonstrated increased student involvement and motivation through e-mail use, as well as improved student writing, because students are writing for an audience—the instructor (Debard & Guidara, 2000; Thorsen, 2003).

Weaknesses of e-mail. The majority of online instructors would agree that along with the pleasure of connectedness through effective e-mail communication comes the pain involved with the extensive amount of time involved with e-mailing. Online courses are documented to take more instructor time per week than a live class, and e-mail is one of the major contributing factors in that time (Cavanaugh, 2005). Imagine you are an instructor with three online courses in one semester, 20 students per class. That is 60 students total who will all need to communicate via e-mail with you during the semester. This e-mail contact might be in the form of submitting assignments, but is often more in the form of (1) technical issues, (2) problems or clarifications with weekly assignments, or (3) personal problems in keeping up with online coursework. Each of these e-mails, sometime several per week from the same student, requires a separate response from you as the instructor. In addition to student e-mail, you will be doing your own fair share of e-mailing the class, making announcements, clarifying assignments, and so forth. The time involved in e-mailing can become overwhelming.

Just as e-mail has the capability to increase a sense of connection for the student, it can also do the converse if the instructor is not timely with responses. Students report becoming frustrated, depressed, or disconnected when e-mail answers are slow or nonexistent (Woods & Keeler, 2001). For instructors who are committed, this issue can be resolved by establishing boundaries at the beginning of the class for how often and when the instructor will respond to e-mail. The instructor may need to assist students in developing sensitivity to e-mail netiquette and asynchronous communication norms (Carswell, Thomas, Petre, Price, & Richards, 2000). This is especially true to overcome potential for misunderstanding—it happens all the time in e-mail. Also, it has been well-documented that the text-based nature of e-mail can lead to disinhibition, a condition where the student is more like to share negativity in their writing due to lack of visual contact (Suler, 2004). Loss of nonverbal communication can be difficult for students new to online learning, and a phone call at the beginning of an online class can help set a positive experience for the new online learner.

Understanding E-Mail: Individual Connection!

The intimate relationship between student and mentor or teacher has been recognized for ages. Famous pairings of mentors and mentees most would recognize include Socrates to Plato, Aristotle to Alexander the Great, Merlin to King Arthur, Walter Sisulu to Nelson Mandela, Ronald Regan to Christine Todd, and Anne Sullivan to Helen Keller. These types of relationships occur on a daily basis between many educators and their students. Even when taught in a course consisting of a group of students, ultimately the critical relationship of importance is between the teacher and the individual student.

Promoting this relationship is one of the arts involved in teaching. In an online environment, this ability can be heavily influenced by the tools available to the instructor for communication. As face-to-face communication is limited at best in the online environment, the instructor must learn to effectively use other tools to promote individual connections with all students. E-mail can be a source of intense interaction that can lead to deeply engaged learning. Research has shown that an average e-mail response is 106 words, while the average in-class response is only 12 words (DeBard & Guidara, 2000). However, just as the tool holds the power to promote individual connection when used effectively, it also holds the power to create feelings of isolation, loneliness, or depression in students when used ineffectively. So how does an instructor use e-mail effectively in online education?

Structuring E-Mail for Success

As the instructor, it is your job to create the norm and culture for communication patterns in your class, both asynchronous and synchronous. Students will come to the online class with prior expectations of how the course will proceed based on their former experiences—these expectations will need to be addressed by you, the teacher, in the first week of class. You can create the norms for positive course communication by following a few basic principles:

- Start out each course with an introductory e-mail. Keep it upbeat. Share required login information, books, start date, and contact information, if relevant. Set the tone for the course that personal communication from the instructor comes in the form of e-mail (see Figure 3.2).

- Respond to e-mail within 24 hours, if at all possible. What? You mean the instructor has to be available every day on e-mail? Not really. In our class syllabi, we inform students that all e-mail will be answered within 24 hours, with the exception of weekends which are reserved for family time. Now, this arrangement might not fit your teaching situation, or you might prefer another. The point is to answer e-mail as quickly as possible, and state your boundaries up front for communication you prefer. We also let our students know that a phone call is ok if they cannot wait 24 hours for a response.

- Use a phone call, instead of e-mail, if an in-depth response is required. E-mail can often be misconstrued; the longer it is, the more opportunity for misunderstandings. If a student requires a lengthy interaction, it is easier and better for the instructor to call the student and talk through the situation. Examples of this include times when students might want to discuss ideas for projects, get clarification on the direction work is taking, and so forth.

- Use e-mail to provide individual feedback, but do not do it every week. Instead, stagger e-mail feedback in entire class, peer, self, and discussion board. There is a general agreement that that feedback is an important construct for facilitating the learning process (Clariana, Wagner, & Murphy, 2000; Huett, 2004; Panasuk & LeBaron, 1999).

Figure 3.2. Introductory e-mail sent to all students before course begins

Greetings,

Welcome to EDTECH 582: Online Teaching for Adult Learners. I am your instructor, Dr. Lisa Dawley. This semester we are using Blackboard as our course management system. I know that most of you are familiar with Blackboard, but for those of you who aren't, please go to http://blackboard.boisestate.edu.

You will see a screen that requests a login—your login for this course is your student ID number. The password (unless you have changed it inside Blackboard before) is also your student ID number. You are welcome to change your passwords—I have given you directions in the Week 1 assignment that will tell you how to do so.

Once you log in, you will come to screen listing your courses. Click on "Online Teaching." Next, click on the "Assignments" button you see in the left navigation bar. Inside the folder is an agenda with directions for this week's class.

Please complete each of the tasks listed in the agenda. Do not hesitate to contact me if you experience any problems with logging on or any of the tasks you are asked to do this week. My e-mail address is: lisadawley@boisestate.edu.

I am looking forward to working with each and everyone of you this semester!

Cheers, Lisa

- Avoid late semester lag in e-mail responses. Studies have shown that frequency of e-mail responses tends to decrease and response time tends to increase as the semester goes on (Vonderwell, 2003). Work to keep e-mail responses consistent and timely throughout the semester.

- Using a student's name in the introduction and signing with your name at the end can add to a feeling of personalization and connection. With entire class e-mail, I like to begin with "Greetings all" and end with "Cheers" to keep the e-mail positive.

- Use e-mail to make an announcement each time an assignment is made available or to make other important announcements.

- Incorporate e-mail into class assignments. Students can e-mail each other, experts, conduct interviews, write for more information, and so forth. Help them understand e-mail as a tool for acquiring and synthesizing information.

- Always send a "goodbye" e-mail at the end of a class. Share highlight moments from class, dates grades will be posted, and let students know it is ok for them to contact you in the future.

- Keypals can be an interesting technique to use in online education. These e-mail relationships can be between peers or persons having knowledge about the subject under study. For example, one class of preservice teachers was paired with keypals, who were considered expert mentor teachers. As the preservice teachers went through the course, they had various questions and ideas. These were shared with the expert teachers for comment and dialogue. Another example of keypals might include pairing a student from one country with a student from another, when students are studying the country where their keypals live. They can then interview each other via e-mail about their respective country, culture, habits, norms, lifestyles, and so forth.

- If you need to make a negative comment or communicate news that might be upsetting to the student, first try to share something positive, then communicate the negative news in a way that the student can use it as constructive criticism. For example:

Hi John,

I viewed your project tonight. Overall, I like the concept a lot, and think the content and design is strong. You have two areas that need to be addressed:

1. *You need a rubric to grade your project. This was the rubric that was part of your assignment in Week 13.*

2. *At this point, the content of your project is fine. The instructional design is good. I appreciate how you integrated the*

Google group, and you demonstrate an understanding of online education—super! What needs addressing at this point is your graphic presentation of the material, as it is not conducive to easy readability online and does not address graphic design principles. So, the rubric you will make to assess your project, will include "graphic design" as one of your categories. Make sure that each of your pages addresses the four graphic design elements we discussed in Week 9.

Ok, that is it. The rubric and changes should take you just a couple more hours of work. Let me know if you have questions, ok?

Cheers, Lisa

E-mail netiquette. Most students enrolling in an online course will have experience with e-mail and usually understand basic e-mail netiquette. However, it is always helpful to include a "Netiquette" post in the class discussion forum to set the norm for the classroom, and to later refer students to if there are any problems. Tschabitscher (2005) offers 10 rules for e-mail netiquette:

1. **Use e-mail the way you want everybody to use it:** You have the future, and the present of humankind in your hands—even when you just write an e-mail.

2. **Take another look before you send a message:** Don't send anything you do not want to send.

3. **Quote original messages properly in replies:** Make your e-mail replies easy to read and understand by quoting in a smart and useful manner.

4. **Be careful with irony in e-mails:** No, really! I mean it. Honestly!

5. **Clean up e-mails before forwarding them:** Forwarding e-mails is a great way of sharing ideas, but make sure the original idea is not hidden in obfuscation.

6. **When in doubt, send plain text e-mail, not HTML:** Not everybody can receive your fancily formatted e-mails. Some may even react furi-

ously. To be safe rather than sorry, send plain text e-mails only when in doubt.

7. **Writing in all caps is like shouting:** Do not shout in your e-mails (and all caps is difficult to read).

8. **Ask before you send huge attachments:** Do not clog e-mail systems without permission.

9. **Smileys should ring an alarm:** Do not use smileys to say something you should not (and do not intend to) say in e-mails.

10. **Avoid "me too" messages:** "Me too" is not enough content, but too much annoyance. (¶2)

Power Tip: Do Student Surveys to Get Individual Information

In week one of class, survey your students to gather basic information: name, address, and contact information. An e-mail sent directly from the student to the instructor works great. These can then be filed in a subfolder in the e-mail client for future reference. That way, instructors are not required to log in to an LMS if they wish to e-mail or call a student.

You can also ask several additional questions about their needs, preferences, and experience with prior usage of online learning tools. Below is a list of potential survey questions you might consider using with your students:

Name:
Phone number(s):
Time zone:
E-mail:
My job is:

continued

I have participated in other online courses (true or false).

I have participated on a discussion board.

I have participated in chat.

I know how to attach text, audio, or digital images to e-mail.

I have participated in a blog, wiki, or podcast (describe).

I have participated in online collaborations such as team projects or presentations.

Are there students listed in the course roster with whom you prefer to be grouped or not grouped?

Is there anything you would like me to be aware of that might affect your performance in the class?

Do you have any concerns or special needs?

Anything else you would like to share?

Example Uses for Success

Learning Objective Outcome	E-Mail Activities
Interactivity and connection	• Begin each class with an introductory e-mail. Share basic information about who you are, the class, and contact information. • Pair students the first week of class. Have them e-mail each other with interview questions. Each student can post the results of their interview on the discussion board to introduce their partner to others in the class. • Survey the students the first week of class and have them email their results to you. We use this technique to gather basic information, keep this in an e-mail folder, and then have it handy for quick access throughout the semester without having to log into the course.
Knowledge: defines; describes; enumerates; identifies; labels; lists; matches; names; reads; records; reproduces; selects; states; views	• The instructor can send class e-mails at the beginning of new assignments to announce the assignment, deadlines, etc. • Students can help co-construct course goals. Solicit their input via e-mail by asking "What do you already know?" "What do you want to learn?" and "How will we show what we learned?" The results can be compiled and posted on the discussion board.

continued

Comprehension: classifies; cites; converts; describes; discusses; estimates; explains; generalizes; gives examples; makes sense out of; paraphrases; restates (in own words); summarizes; traces; understands	• Working in small groups, have students locate five Web site illustrating examples of a particular theory placed into practice. They e-mail their sites and annotations to the group leader who then compiles them and posts to the class discussion board for general class reference. • Assign a course reading. Students can e-mail the instructor, or each other, with key points from the reading. • At the end of a course, have students e-mail you reflecting on their experience in the course. They can describe key learning experiences, meaningful assignments, and offer suggestions for improvement.
Application: acts; administers; articulates; assesses; charts; collects; computes; constructs; contributes; controls; determines; develops; discovers; establishes; extends; implements; includes; informs; instructs; operationalizes; participates; predicts; prepares; preserves; produces; projects; provides; relates; reports; shows; solves; teaches; transfers; uses; utilizes	• Have students e-mail a content area expert for more information or feedback on their work. • Use the e-mail in small groups to coordinate group project work flow. • The student and teacher can use e-mail to journal with each other as a form of reflection. For example, a pre-service teacher can take notes on her daily experience, add any questions, and submit that to her mentor teacher via e-mail. The mentor teacher can then respond to any questions the pre-service teacher might have.

continued

Analysis: breaks down; correlates; diagrams; differentiates; discriminates; distinguishes; focuses; illustrates; infers; limits; outlines; points out; prioritizes; recognizes; separates; subdivides	• Use e-mail "read-arounds" to edit students' writing in-progress. A group of students is identified and then they each take turns sending their writing to the next individual in their group, who then edits their work. The edited version is sent to the next group member for more editing, and so on, until the paper eventually returns to the original author. • Students in a Web design class studying graphic elements can analyze various Web sites for graphic design principles and then e-mail the webmaster of those sites to share their findings. • Have students provide an outline for the final course projects and send to the instructor via e-mail.
Synthesis: adapts; anticipates; categorizes; collaborates; combines; communicates; compares; compiles; composes; contrasts; creates; designs; devises; expresses; facilitates; formulates; generates; incorporates; individualizes; initiates; integrates; intervenes; models; modifies; negotiates; plans; progresses; rearranges; reconstructs; reinforces; reorganizes; revises; structures; substitutes; validates	• Have ESL students correspond with keypals studying the reverse languages. Have students translate each other's e-mail. • Advanced students can create their own mailing list, solicit new members, and send out monthly e-mail newsletters on a given topic. • Younger students can create a classroom newsletter that is e-mailed home to parents on a weekly or monthly basis.

continued

Evaluation: appraises; compares & contrasts; concludes; criticizes; critiques; decides; defends; interprets; judges; justifies; reframes	• Ask students to respond to several case studies which are e-mailed randomly. These responses are then e-mailed to other students and critiqued on their strengths and weaknesses. • Have students e-mail a member of Congress with their substantiated opinion on a given topic under current debate. • Provide students with a rubric that measures quality indicators on a given product or service, for example, a children's game. Have students analyze the product and e-mail their analysis to the manufacturer. • Teachers can easily accept final projects via e-mail. Feedback can be provided via e-mail.

Example Lesson Plan

Figure 3.3. Example lesson plan using e-mail

Overview: Unit 4—Knowledge Use

At this point, we have discussed types of knowledge and how knowledge is acquired. In this unit, we look at principles of how knowledge is actually used. We will discuss concepts of problem solving, transfer, and motivation. You will also begin work on Chapter 2 of your Personal Theory Building Projects. You are assigned a partner to work with over the next three weeks (one of those weeks includes spring break). Working with your partner, you will explore firsthand the concepts of problem solving, transfer, and the role of motivation by participating in interactive online gaming. After completing your gaming activity, you will meet in chat with your partner to discuss your experience.

Readings and Resources

Required:

The Cognitive Psychology of School Learning (2nd ed.). Gagné, E. D., Yekovich, C. W., & Yekovich, F. R. (1993) Chapters 10, 11, & 16 (pp. 207-264, 425-448).

Learning and Transfer in Bransford, J. D., Brown, A. L., & Cocking, R. R. (Eds.). (1999). *How People Learn: Brain, Mind, Experience, and School*, Chapter 3 (pp. 39-66).

Online Gaming Resource

A Tale in the Desert II http://www.atitd.com/ (please review system requirements before installing)

Yahoo Games http://games.yahoo.com/

FreeGames.com http://www.free-games.com.au

ACTIVITIES FOR UNIT 4	DUE DATE
1. Personal Theory Building Project: Chapter 2 Continue work on your projects. Guidelines for Chapter 2 are located in the "Assignment" folder. I have decided to shorten the paper to two chapters instead of six, and Chapter 2 will be due toward the end of the semester. Use your study groups to support continued work, discussion, and idea sharing on your writing over the semester. First drafts will be due April 26.	
2. Partner Activity: Knowledge Use in Online Gaming You and your assigned partner(s) will meet and participate in an online game. After playing for an hour or so, you'll then meet in our class chat for a discussion of your experience. I am suggesting that you participate in **A Tale in the Desert II**, an online roleplay game of ancient Egyptian civilization. I believe this type of game allows you to most fully explore this unit's major concepts of problem-solving, transfer, and motivation. However, you might choose any other interactive online game, such as Online Scrabble. These games can be located in multiple locations on the Internet. Typically, online games do require an email login at a minimum, and sometimes a download. If you are uncomfortable providing your own email address, you can create another email account at Yahoo or MSN. Once you have completed the game, you can easily uninstall it, if you wish.	**Partner Assignments:** Peter & Cheryl Julie & Greg Paul & Laura Jared & Jason Dan & Sandy Wendy & Michelle Shane & Stephanie Kelly, Terrie & Warren

continued

ACTIVITIES FOR UNIT 4	DUE DATE
• To get started, e-mail you partner(s) to set a date and time to game and then chat together in our class. Allow 1 1/2 - 2 hours total. Decide which online game you would like to play. • Prior to meeting with your partner(s) in-game, download and install the game and make sure it runs effectively. Create a character and email your partner with your character name so they can contact you once in-game. Learn how to chat in-game, and how to send private messages so you can contact your partner. Complete the assigned readings. • Meet in-game. Be patient with your experience in the game. You won't get a lot accomplished in an hour. Remember the goal is to reflect on the concepts of problem-solving, transfer and motivation as you go through your game experience. Everyone's experience will be different. • After playing for an hour or so, meet with your partner(s) in our class Chat room. *Record your chat by clicking the "record" button in the upper right corner. Don't forget this step.* This will create a recording that I can see for grading purposes. In chat, discuss the following three questions: 1. The most important part of the problem solving process is how the problem is represented in working memory. A problem accurately represented will activate knowledge related to the problem, while an inaccurate representation will activate unrelated knowledge. What knowledge was activated for you while gaming with your partner? How did this effect your ability to problem-solve during the gaming experience? 2. A person is more able to transfer knowledge and procedures from one setting to another if the context of the problems are similar. Describe what knowledge and automated procedures you found yourself transferring to participate in the game.	Email your partner to schedule gaming and chat time: Monday, March 21. Deadline to game and conduct chat: Tuesday, April 5.

continued

ACTIVITIES FOR UNIT 4	DUE DATE
3. Uncertainty and Conceptual Conflict play a role in motivation. Discuss your motivation to play before, during and after the game, in terms of these two concepts.	

Grading

Knowledge Use Gaming activity is worth 20 points, pass/no pass, when all criteria are addressed.

Enjoy this activity! Please e-mail if you have technical issues or questions with the game. Hope you have a great spring break!

Resources

1ˢᵗ grade keypals: http://projects.edtech.sandi.net/grant/keypals/teacherpage.html

Animated Internet: How E-mail Works: http://www.learnthenet.com/english/section/e-mail.html

Classroom Ideas for E-mail: http://www.remc11.k12.mi.us/bcisd/classres/e-mail.htm
E-mail Communication and Netiquette Tips http://e-mail.about.com/cs/netiquettetips/

ePals.com: http://www.epals.com/

Global SchoolNet: http://www.globalschoolnet.org/index.html

Gmail by Google: http://gmail.google.com/gmail/help/about.html

Intercultural E-mail Activities: http://www.iecc.org/

Keypals Club: http://www.teaching.com/keypals/

Keypals Club International: http://worldkids.net/clubs/kci/

Lycos E-mail: http://mail.lycos.com/

MSN Hotmail: http://www.msn.com/

Tips on E-mail Netiquette: http://www.imagescape.com/helpweb/mail/polite.html

Yahoo Mail: http://mail.yahoo.com/

Zero Budget E-Learning: http://www.thiagi.com/ZeroBudgetE-Learning.html

References

Carswell, L., Thomas, P., Petre, M., Price, B., & Richards, M. (2000). Distance education via the Internet: The student experience. *British Journal of Educational Technology, 31*, 29-46.

Cavanaugh, J. (2005, Spring). Teaching online: A time comparison. *Online Journal of Distance Learning Administration, 3*(1). Retrieved June 23, 2006, from http://www.westga.edu/~distance/ojdla/spring81/cavanaugh81.htm

Clariana, R. B., Wagner, D., & Rohrer-Murphy, L. C. (2000). A connectionist description of feedback timing. *Educational Technology Research and Development, 48*, 5-11.

DeBard, R., & Guidera, S. (2000). Adapting asynchronous communication to meet the seven principles of effective teaching. *Journal of Educational Technology Systems, 28*(3), 219-239.

Huett, J. (2004). E-mail as an educational feedback tool: Relative advantages and implementation guidelines. *International Journal of Instructional Technology and Distance Learning, 1*(6). Retrieved June 23, 2006, from http://www.itdl.org/Journal/Jun_04/article06.htm

Panasuk, R., & LeBaron, J. (1999). Student feedback: A tool for improving instruction. *Education, 120*(2), 356-368.

Roberson, T., & Klotz, J. (2002, Winter). How can instructors and administrators fill the missing link in online instruction? [Electronic version]. *Online Journal of Distance Learning Administration, 5*(4).

Suler, J. (2004). The online disinhibition effect. *CyberPsychology and Behavior, 7*, 321-326.

Thorsen, C. (2003). *TechTactics: Instructional models for educational computing.* Boston: Allyn & Bacon.

Tschabitscher, H. (2005). *Top ten most important rules of e-mail netiquette.* Retrieved June 23, 2006, from http://e-mail.about.com/cs/netiquettetips/tp/core_netiquette.htm

Vonderwell, S. (2003). An examination of asynchronous communication experiences and perspectives of students in an online course: A case study. *Internet and Higher Education, 6*(1), 77-90.

Woods, R., & Keeler, J. (2001). The effect of instructor's use of audio e-mail messages on student participation in and perceptions of online learning: A preliminary case study. *Open Learning, 16*(3), 263-278.

Chapter IV

Discussion Forums

Discussion forums, or threaded discussion, are one of the most commonly used tools in online teaching. Discussion forums provide the ability for asynchronous (nonsimultaneous) discussion to occur over a period of time designated by the instructor. The ability to learn asynchronously is one of the highly touted benefits of online learning—anywhere, anyplace, anytime.

In a discussion forum, the author (teacher, student, or guest) can begin a new thread of discussion. In the screenshot in Figure 4.1, we see that Billie Jo has started a threaded discussion about the uses of chat. She has replied to her post from Jeanette and Jill.

In the most effective forums, the teacher gives specific guidelines of what is supposed to happen in that thread, the nature of discussion, possibly how many posts, or how long a post is supposed to be in word count. Often, threaded discussion is used for peer feedback, with students posting drafts of work in progress and other students in class commenting on their work.

Figure 4.1. Response in a threaded discussion forum

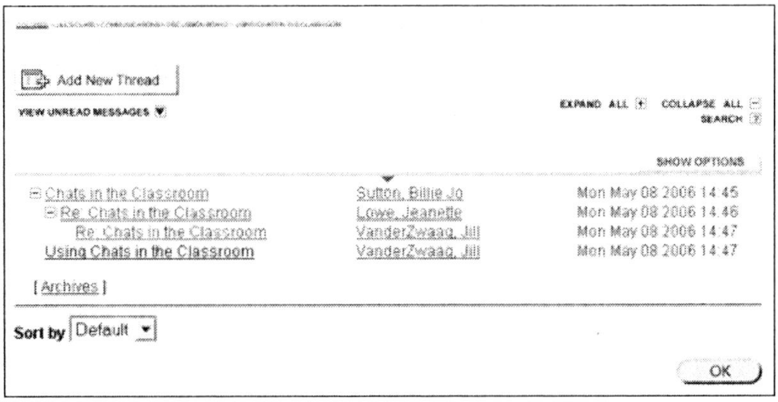

One of the mistakes new online teachers often make is overuse or misuse of the discussion forum. An emphasis is often placed on posting a response in a discussion forum and then requiring students to respond to each other every week. Because many teachers are unsure how to teach and assess in online classrooms, they will make this requirement and then grade by the number of posts a student makes. This can lead to posting wars, with students competing for the greatest number of posts. Contrary to creating engagement, this style of online learning can turn students off because it creates unnecessary competition, places the emphasis on quantity not quality, and it can be boring to read endless responses each week.

With the possible exception of providing a FAQ area, reserve the use of discussion forums for social interaction, either formal or informal. Do not post content, lesson assignments, technical requirements, or other types of documentation in the discussion forum. These documents are better located in content areas of an LMS. In our next section, we examine pedagogical strengths and weaknesses of discussion forums.

Strengths and Weaknesses

Table 4.1 illustrates the varied strengths and weaknesses of using discussion forums.

Table 4.1. Strengths and weaknesses of discussion forums

Strengths	Weaknesses

• Provides discussion capability
• Allows time for in-depth reflection
• Peer learning by viewing and responding to work of others
• Discussions can continue to build over time or over the length of the entire course
• Simultaneous discussions can occur at once, yet they are organized by topic
• Builds class community by promoting discussion on course topics
• Students can choose post times by a certain deadline
  o More time to reflect, research, and compose their thoughts
  o Easy tool for group correspondence
  o Ability to attach presentations, papers, and so forth
  o Can post group or individual work
  o All students can participate in a discussion, thus equalizing student participation
  o Develops thinking and writing skills
  o Attachments can be downloaded for further review and processing of information
  o Instructor can post intermittent feedback
  o Forums can be created by students or teachers, offering empowerment
  o Forums create a historical record of the class's progress over the semester
  o Overcomes issues of race, class, and age discrimination due to lack of visual cues
  o Guest experts can participate in course by posting information and questions
	• No ability to discuss in real-time, creating frustration for some students who want immediate feedback
	• Shy students can feel "exposed"
	• Can require multiple logins to participate in discussion during one module, thus negating self-pacing capability, if desired
	• If misused, it can promote competition instead of cooperation
	• Teacher must monitor all postings to prevent potential flaming between students
	• Students must be coached on norms for posting in discussion boards
	• Teachers may need to spend time creating rubrics to promote effective discussion
	• Responding to multiple postings can be time intensive for the instructor

Strengths of discussion forums. As we see in Table 4.1, the potential strengths of discussion boards are many. Discussion forums can be used for asynchronous whole class or small group discussions. We have even seen discussion boards set up for individual students to post progress on project development over the semester, in effect, creating an individual historical portfolio of a student's work. Attachments such as documents, slideshows, and other graphic presentations can be added to a post. Asynchronous discussion gives students time to reflect on their answers and edit their work before posting (Sherer & Shey, 2002). This often results in better quality work, not only because of the ability to reflect over time, but also because the student is aware of the work and potential feedback is being viewed by peers. Peer influence on the learning process, even for adult learners, has been documented to often have a greater impact on learning than instructor influence (Gagné, Yekovich, & Yekovich, 1997).

Because discussion forums serve as the public space for coming together, they offer a great opportunity to build community, create connection, engage and empower students in online courses. Peer learning can occur by viewing and responding to the work of others in a discussion forum. Unlike a regular classroom, discussion forums offer the ability for all students to participate in a single discussion, thus equalizing student participation (Sherer & Shey, 2002) and humanizing a large, informal class (Ko & Rossen, 2004). Discussions can also build over time, or over the length of the course, thus providing for in-depth thinking and reflection on a given topic. Corollary to this idea is the historical record created on the board – students and instructors are able to see student's development in the course over time from the written historical record. Multiple discussions can occur at the same time, yet the discussions remain organized due to the hierarchical nature of the discussion board.

Another empowering feature of discussion boards is the students' ability to create their own forums on given topics of interest. Pelz (2004) states that student led discussions allow students to ask more thought provoking questions, although some instructors might initially be uncomfortable with giving up "teacher control." Besides the teacher and students, guest experts can also be invited to begin threads with information and questions that students can engage in over the semester (Akers, 2004). Finally, many students report feelings of empowerment as writers and knowledge generators due to the lack of visual cues online. They feel they will be judged based on their thinking, not on their skin color, type of clothing, or age.

Weaknesses of discussion forums. Students unfamiliar with the operation of discussion boards often report an initial frustration with the lack of immediate feedback to their posting, sometimes logging in several times a day to see who has responded to their work (Sherer & Shey, 2002). Similar to this phenomenon is the idea of some students feeling "exposed" by presenting their work and thoughts to the entire class and resenting the lack of privacy (Tu, 2002). These feelings are usually generated by students who are more comfortable in a traditional transmission paradigm of learning, where their work was typically shared only with the instructor. These two weaknesses are best overcome with time and a sensitive instructor who establishes the norm of whole class learning and through close monitoring (Tu, 2002). Familiarity with discussion boards can be coached by the wise instructor (Akers, 2004), developing a patience with, and appreciation for, the asynchronous nature of threaded discussion.

For students who desire a more self-paced approach to online instruction, discussion forums requiring interaction can be a frustration, sometimes requiring students to log in several times in a week to accomplish an assignment. This weakness can be addressed through the instructor's sensitivity to the needs of the students, as well as through lesson design itself.

Lesson design is also critical in preventing the possibility of posting wars and flaming between students. If an emphasis is placed on quantity of posts, overzealous students can post many times, creating a sense of competition in the course. This can lead to resentment on the part of students, and possibly creating flaming. Flaming can occur in a discussion regardless of lesson design. Online teachers are wise to check their boards several times during the week to stay on top of any negative interactions that might be developing between students. Any postings that might be considered flames or attacks on another student should be immediately deleted by the instructor. That student should have their posting privileges frozen until they can be contacted regarding the severity of their offense. At times, it might be necessary to refer the student to the student code of conduct, if available, or any other policies regarding inappropriate interaction that interferes with the learning of another student. At a minimum, the two students involved in the flame attack should be told to have no further communication with one another, and a refusal to do so will result in expulsion from the course.

Understanding Discussion Forums:
Thoughtful Reflection!

If we agree that a major strength of discussion forums is the promotion of thoughtful, in-depth reflection, and knowledge construction through group interaction and idea sharing (Akers, 2004; Walker, 2005), what can the online teacher do to best promote effective interaction and reflection among the class as a whole?

Garrison, Anderson, and Archer (2000) encourage us to think about effective discussion posts as falling into one of three categories: social presence, cognitive presence, and teaching presence. In social presence, we are striving for posts that encourage students to present themselves as "real people." This can be accomplished by the instructor modeling social presence through sharing of emotion and feelings, by demonstrating evidence of reading and thinking about other's postings, and by posting responses that promote a sense of community and group commitment toward a larger purpose, the course goals and objectives.

For example, several semesters ago in an online teaching course, a student recommended starting a discussion forum to share online teaching tips. We now set up that discussion forum the first day of class every semester. This forum provides teachers a social opportunity to share their own knowledge with one another, and build on that knowledge as the class continues.

Cognitive presence posts introduce factual, conceptual, and theoretical knowledge into the discussion. The information shared must be accurate, comprehensive, and documented. This can be achieved by requiring students to provide citations and references outside of course readings, teaching students to use quotes, learning to paraphrase, and modeling how to make theoretical connections between two or more pieces of research, as well as making connections between research and practice.

Finally, teaching presence is encouraged on the discussion board by facilitation of the learning process through effective discussion. Some strategies for increasing teaching presence include (Pelz, 2004):

- Identifying areas of agreement and disagreement.

- Seeking to reach consensus and understanding.

- Encouraging, acknowledging, and reinforcing student contributions.

- Setting a climate for learning.

- Drawing in participants/prompting discussion.

- Assessing the efficacy of the process.

- Presenting content and questions.

- Focusing the discussion.

- Summarizing the discussion.

- Confirming understanding.

- Diagnosing misperceptions.

- Injecting knowledge from diverse sources.

- Responding to technical concerns. (p. 1)

Walker (2005) encourages us to consider the possibilities for critical think-ing in asynchronous discussions. When students think critically, they are engaged in problem solving and collaborative activities. However, critical thinking requires a high level of interaction. This interaction requires shaping and direction from the instructor. Some of the types of strategies proposed by Walker (2005) include:

- **Writing activities that promote critical thinking:** Analyze case stud-ies, weekly summaries, writing reports, and peer responses.

- **Using subject matter experts:** Read about an expert in a content area and conduct a real or mock interview.

- **Role playing strategies:** Dtudents can read and analyze a case related to the course content, assume roles in the case, and role play to resolu-tion.

- **Convergent questioning strategies:** Questions that require learners to analyze issues and their personal reaction to issues.

- **Divergent questioning strategies:** Questions that require students to analyze, predict, and explore alternative solutions to problems. Responses are usually open-ended, and an emphasis is put on creativity.

- **Evaluative questioning strategies:** Questions that require a comparative analysis before proposing a solution.

- **Socratic questioning strategies:** Questions that clarify, explore alternative paths, examine cause and effect, and answer the question "so what?"

We should not assume that students know how to effectively participate in, or glean value from, discussion boards (Ellis & Calvo, 2006). During the initial weeks of a class, a wise instructor will establish norms and expectations for effective communication on the boards (Suler, 2004). This can be accomplished by sharing rules for netiquette, having students read the Acceptable Use Policy if appropriate, and by providing rubrics that frame instruction. Instructors can also model and discuss appropriate ways of posting in the forums.

The amount of posts can become overwhelming or underwhelming depending on how the instructor frames the requirement for discussion. Typically, a discussion prompt and several example questions, followed by posting requirements such as "Respond to the questions in a minimum of 250 words and reply to at least two other students. In your reply, go beyond agreeing or disagreeing. What connections can you make? Offer suggestions, insights, new information gleaned from outside readings, cite your references." This gives students an understanding of how much they should post. Also, the instructor needs to be clear on grading requirements for posting. Assessment should go beyond counting the number of posts in any given course, and instead reflect quality or participation criteria that support social, cognitive, and teaching presence. Table 4.2 shows a sample rubric used to promote effective discussion board participation.

Note the rubric offers a structure and form to the posts, but still leaves room for the student to experience individual empowerment and ownership through the content of the response. Rubrics like these are particularly helpful at the beginning of a course to assist students in creating a culture of collaborative academic inquiry.

Table 4.2. Sample rubric to promote effective discussion board conversation

Rating	0	1	2	3	4	5
Quantity	BOTH response to questions AND reply to another student's response missing.	EITHER response to questions OR reply to another student's response missing.	BOTH response to questions AND reply to another student's response late.	EITHER response to questions OR reply to another student's response late.	BOTH response to questions AND reply to another student's response posted on the same day.	Response to discussion questions are posted by the deadline. Replies to another student's response are posted after most students have responded.
Response	Response is unrelated to the discussion questions. Assigned readings not mentioned.	Response briefly addresses discussion questions. Assigned readings not mentioned.	Response addresses some of the discussion questions. Assigned readings are discussed.	Response addresses most of the discussion questions. Assigned readings are discussed.	Response addresses all aspects of the discussion questions. Assigned readings quoted.	Response addresses all aspects of the discussion questions and includes additional relevant information. Assigned readings and outside sources quoted.
Reply	Reply is unrelated to the student's response. Assigned readings not mentioned.	Reply briefly addresses student's response. Assigned readings not mentioned.	Reply addresses some of the student's response. Assigned readings are discussed.	Reply addresses most of the student's response. Assigned readings are discussed.	Reply addresses all aspects of the student's response. Assigned readings quoted.	Reply addresses all aspects of the student's response and includes additional relevant information. Assigned readings and outside sources quoted.

Power Tip: Making Feedback Public

I do a lot of comparing between teaching online vs. live classes. I am fascinated with the opportunities that online technology provides that do not exist in live classes. This morning, as I was typing individual feedback in the discussion forum to my students' most recent assignment, I was reminded of both the positive and negative attributes of making feedback public.

- **Positive:** I am modeling how to provide feedback in a constructive, growth-oriented approach (or so I like to think). Since most of my students are teachers, many desiring to be online teachers, this is a necessary skill for them to observe and develop. I always frame the feedback in terms of *strengths* and *areas for improvement.*

- **Positive:** Making feedback public encourages the development of community—we are learning together, at our own pace, and based on our own needs. I never assign a grade in public feedback. I think this approach helps to transform an outdated behavioristic approach to learning where the student has to "get it right," and the teacher's job is to grade the "correctness" of each assignment.

- **Positive:** Students can learn from other's work and my perceptions about that work. Many of my students report enjoying reading my feedback to others in class. It gives them an idea of how their work compares to others (performance anxiety?). It also reinforces the classroom culture I want to promote—that you are not competing with others in the class, but rather, engaged in your own learning process and professional development.

- **Negative:** Ok, so just how to tell a student, when needed, that their work really stinks? I mean, how "nice" can an instructor be when what you really feel like saying is, "Why are you wasting my time?" This does not happen often at the graduate level, as I have a great group of students with whom I am privileged to work. But there are times when I will ask a student to reconsider, reread, and resubmit their work. Is this a form of public humiliation? Is it a turn off to student learning? Can it be a wake up call for that particular student? What impact does this type of feedback have on other students in the class? One approach I have used in the past is to publicly type, "See my e-mail for feedback" and then e-mail that student privately.

You may find that motivation to post becomes an issue in some online classes, especially those with over 20 students where students may feel hesitant to post their thinking in front of a larger group (Suler, 2004). If questioning techniques are not encouraging participation, the instructor may need to use concrete incentives, such as a grade or extra credit to build participation. Games can also be used to create positive energy in discussion forums. Suler (2004) uses a word association game where students post a word in a subject line, and the next post would do the same using a word association to the prior word.

Online disinhibition effect. Online disinhibition refers to online users who feel less inhibited in their communications due to not having to look others in the face (Suler, 2004). The computer screen serves as the medium, and more users will feel freer to express opinions, take risks, share personal information, and participate more often than they might in a live classroom. However, online disinhibition can be both a blessing and a curse. Taken to the extreme, users who are disinhibited may flame, spam, or be rude, hostile, or even threatening. This phenomenon is particularly evident in online gaming environments where such individuals are known as "haters."

The online learning environment has no room to tolerate haters or others who verge on negative forms of online disinhibition. As gaming becomes more and more popular, and tolerance for haters becomes a norm, the online teacher will be wise to redirect negative online disinhibition into more critical and questioning forms of inquiry, instead of allowing for negative destruction of the class climate and overall trust you are working to establish.

Structuring Discussion Forums for Success

So, let us get started. Prior to having your students participate in discussion forums, we suggest you establish the following three boards at the beginning of each course:

1. **Student lounge:** A designated free-talk area to discuss topics outside of class content. This board in and of itself demonstrates to students from the first day that their thinking is desired and valued.

2. **FAQs:** Information students typically need at the beginning of each class. This can be reused each semester and students can continue to post questions throughout the semester that the teacher can answer. Consider including rules for netiquette, a list of chat acronyms, instructions on how to get information during the course, and so forth. This is a perfect place to add a thread regarding class culture and student expectations for ownership and participation.

3. **Technical support:** A forum telling students where to get the answers they need to technical problems they may encounter in the class.

Helpful hint: Create the content for these forums in a Word or html document. To save time, cut and paste the information each time you start a new section of a class.

Establishing the tone and norms for discussion board communication. Norms and expectations for how students communicate on the discussion boards are available and explicitly addressed the first week of class. This is achieved in several ways:

- Provide an introduction to student netiquette (see the Resource section for a slideshow you can use with your students); share the school's acceptable use policy, if it exists.

- Ask students to introduce themselves to others in a "Class Introductions" board the first week. Be sure to post the first introduction so you can model the tone and level of information to be included. Be sure to include one personal item, such as a hobby, to establish yourself as a real person, not just an electronic lecturer.

- In your class syllabus, make students aware of your level of anticipated participation on the boards. How often do you participate each week—once, three times, five times? Also, indicate that your level of responses to posts will vary according to the assignment, and not to expect a response to every posting.

In subsequent weeks and assignments, always let your students know your anticipated level of participation on the boards. Give specific directions and criteria and explain whether formal or informal responses are required. Uses of discussion board rubrics are helpful to establish norms and when special projects are being completed, such as a role play scenario.

Finally, be a moderator of discussion, not a sage on the stage. Summarize discussions, ask questions, encourage students to ask and answer questions for one another, and provide students opportunities to lead their own discussion sessions.

Power Tip: Greet Each of Your Students Individually the First Week

Most online teachers require their students to post introductions in one form or another during the first week of the course. However, I have been surprised to hear from many students that the instructor never responds. It will go a long way in building course community, and an individual connection with your students, if you reply to every single introduction during that first week. These replies can usually be accomplished within an hour or so, depending on the class size.

Many students have reported on course evaluations that they were impressed the instructor took time to personally respond to everyone. In your response, acknowledge the information the student has shared, possibly share a personal or professional detail related to their experience and ask a question to promote communication. Finally, encourage students to contact you if they need assistance. These replies can be short—focus on creating meaningful connection instead. Here is a sample reply:

Hi Elizabeth, great to have you here! How wonderful that your school is supportive of technology integration. Have you had the opportunity to integrate any online components into your class? If not, perhaps you'll explore the idea this semester :)

Congratulations on the upcoming little one! You will have your hands full for sure once the baby comes, so let us keep in touch on your energy level and ability to get work done (I am remembering those nights of waking up every two hours!). Do you plan to return to work this semester? Best wishes for a productive and successful semester. Do not hesitate to let me know if I can assist your learning process in any way.

In the remainder of this section, we examine how to meet specific learning outcomes using a variety of activities. The activities shown are examples that you can incorporate or adapt for your online class to help achieve your learning objectives successfully through the use of discussion forums.

Example Uses for Success

Learning Objective Outcome	Discussion Forum Activities
Interactivity and connection	• At the beginning of each course, ask your students to introduce themselves in some way using the discussion forum. Be sure to respond to each individual during this week, welcoming them to the course. Encourage students to welcome one another. • Have pairs of students interview each other on a given topic and post the interview results in the discussion forum. • Have students respond to teacher posed questions as well as to peers. Require at least two postings per topic. • Teachers can create a newcomers thread that encourages students who are familiar with the online environment to give tips and answer questions for newcomers. • Students create a portrait of themselves in any medium, digitize the portrait and share it on the discussion board.

continued

Knowledge: defines; describes; enumerates; identifies; labels; lists; matches; names; reads; records; reproduces; selects; states; views	• Students conduct Web research to identify major characteristics of an assigned country, such as languages spoken, name of currency, major religions, largest exports, etc. These individual reports are posted and can be used for comparison purposes later in the unit. • Using a jigsaw technique, students work in small groups to locate and compile a list of Web resources on a given topic area. These resources are then shared on the discussion board with the remainder of the class. • Establish a discussion forum for pre-service teachers to share links to lesson plans on given content areas.
Comprehension: classifies; cites; converts; describes; discusses; estimates; explains; generalizes; gives examples; makes sense out of; paraphrases; restates (in own words); summarizes; traces; understands	• Research causes of the civil war. Discuss topics listed, reply to questions, and post a summary of the causes of the civil war. • After reading an article on Internet safety, students are asked to write a letter to the local school board outlining suggestions to improve internet safety in the school district. • The teacher poses a question asking students to estimate the number of hours most kids watch TV per week. After providing their estimations, students are then asked to locate data to verify their estimation.

continued

Application: acts; administers; articulates; assesses; charts; collects; computes; constructs; contributes; controls; determines; develops; discovers; establishes; extends; implements; includes; informs; instructs; operationalizes; participates; predicts; prepares; preserves; produces; projects; provides; relates; reports; shows; solves; teaches; transfers; uses; utilizes	• Students create a slideshow illustrating practical application of theoretical concepts discussed in course readings. They are posted as attachments and shared with the class for further discussion. • Working in pairs, students design a customized online lesson for each other on a topic of their choice related to the course content. These are posted for feedback before the student proceeds with instruction. • The instructor poses several problems to be solved. The student chooses one of the problems and offers three potential solutions that they have obtained from online resources.
Analysis: breaks down; correlates; diagrams; differentiates; discriminates; distinguishes; focuses; illustrates; infers; limits; outlines; points out; prioritizes; recognizes; separates; subdivides	• Students listen to recordings of political speeches and write a comparison of points of discussion. The comparison is posted and a discussion of political candidates ensues. • Students create a storyboard for a Web site design and post it as an attachment for peer feedback before beginning design work. • Using a flowchart software such as Inspiration, students flowchart a process for solving math equations and post it as an attachment. Peers use the flowchart to solve a sample problem, and then post their response. • Students review/evaluate software for ease of use and other properties related to the use in the classroom or online teaching environment. Results are shared, and possibly compared and discussed, in the discussion forum. • Each pre-service or in-service teacher will be asked to implement a specific lesson plan with his/her students. After completion, write an analysis of what was learned, what students learned and what you may do differently. Post your analysis as an attachment in a threaded discussion and review the other student's analyses to learn about how their experiences were similar to or different than your own.

continued

Synthesis: adapts; anticipates; categorizes; collaborates; combines; communicates; compares; compiles; composes; contrasts; creates; designs; devises; expresses; facilitates; formulates; generates; incorporates; individualizes; initiates; integrates; intervenes; models; modifies; negotiates; plans; progresses; rearranges; reconstructs; reinforces; reorganizes; revises; structures; substitutes; validates	• Create a forum solely to promote brainstorming on class project ideas. Students can share resources, topics, and build on other's ideas. • Start a webquest. The class is divided up into groups of four to five students. A leader is chosen from within group to organize group, set deadlines, and assign responsibilities from within group discussion/chat/e-mail area. Participants research topic/questions on web and submit the findings to the leader. The leader will compile the participants' reports into one group report and will post it by a specific date in class discussion board. • Students generate their own unique questions in response to a common reading. These questions are presented to the other students to answer through a threaded discussion. Every student generates one unique question and answers to at least three other questions. Students will be graded on the quality of their question as well as their posted answers. • Provide students the opportunity to create their own special interest group via the discussion forum. The student is then in charge of moderating their forum.

continued

Evaluation: appraises; compares & contrasts; concludes; criticizes; critiques; decides; defends; interprets; judges; justifies; reframes	• Debate the pros and cons of online education vs. regular education. • Students are assigned to comment on an issue using the persona of a fictional character (role play). Examples of characters: Dr. Spock, Timothy Leary, Maria Montessori, etc. Comments are posted on discussion boards. Class members respond to each other maintaining their assigned persona. • Students are assigned roles in an evaluation process. For example, establish a role-play where a school board is evaluating the potential purchase of software for the district. Roles might include concerned parent, enthusiastic teacher, school board member, school board chairperson, superintendent, and an outside evaluator. The role play can be set to play out over a designated period of time, for example, one week. During that time, students might be required to post a specific number of times, and be encouraged to log in daily (see Figure 4.2). • Each student keeps a two-column reflective journal on course readings and new learning, thoughts and questions. These journals are periodically posted and replied to by other students and the instructor.

Figure 4.2. Sample role play assignment directions

Role Play Discussion
© 2005, Chareen Snelson, Boise State University

This role play discussion is one of the participation assignment options. To count this as a participation assignment, please get involved early and stay involved in the discussion throughout the week. These types of discussions are almost always a lot of fun. One of the interesting things about a role play discussion is that it gives people an opportunity to try out a real world scenario in a safe environment. It also provides an opportunity to develop an appreciation for multiple perspectives that might be encountered in similar situations.

The scenario for this discussion centers an evaluation of educational technology in a K-12 school district. Participants will assume a role and take part in a discussion based on the scenario. Please remain civil during the discussion. Everyone is play acting a role and may write things that are meant to reflect how the characters would express themselves. It may even be contrary to their feelings and opinions.

Instructions for the Role Play Discussion:

1.   Read the scenario for the role play.

2.   Choose a character to role play during the discussion. In most cases only one person can assume a character. Some characters can be played by more than one person as noted in the character descriptions further down the page.

3.   Introduce yourself as your character on the Role Play Discussion forum in Blackboard. Do this early in the week so that your character does not get taken by someone else.

4.   Participate regularly in the discussion during the week. This will help maintain the momentum of the discussion and will also lead to a more meaningful experience.

Scenario: Instructional Software Evaluation in the Jefferson School District

*Note: The following scenario is fictitious, but includes information that is realistic. Any similarities between the scenario and an actual school district are accidental and unintentional.

The Jefferson School District is located in a small town in the western part of the United States. The school district covers only one town called Jeffersonville, which has a population of 5,257. This is an agricultural area and many of the residents work in the farming or the dairy industry. Migrant farmers arrive in Jeffersonville each spring to work and remain until late fall.

There are three schools in Jeffersonville. The elementary school covers grades 1-6, the junior high school covers grades 7-9, and the high school covers grades 10-12. During the last academic year 42% of the students were taking free or reduced priced lunch.

continued

The superintendent of Jeffersonville has grown concerned that students who graduate from Jeffersonville High School do not have adequate skills to obtain jobs or enter college without remedial coursework. Discussions held at open school board meetings have revealed that some parents fear that their children will be unprepared for the world after high school. Many parents and community members have expressed outrage that Jeffersonville Elementary School has been identified as a failing school based on criteria set by the No Child Left Behind Act. Several possible solutions have been discussed including a high stakes exam to be passed as a condition for obtaining a high school diploma. Teachers have expressed concern about the wide variety of special needs they are seeing in their classrooms. Every classroom seems to have students who are struggling for various reasons. Some have special learning needs, some do not speak English well, some have emotional problems, and the list goes on. Budget cuts have forced district officials to lay off some of the teachers, which ultimately led to an increase in class size throughout the district.

One of the school board members proposed that computer based instruction should be used to help struggling students catch up. Students who are failing academically can access the instructional software through the Internet if they have a computer and Internet access at home. They can also stay after school and go to the school computer lab to work with the software. It might also be possible to design a pull out program to get students in front of the computers to work with the software. A representative from the *Phenomenal Software* Company has provided demonstration copies of the software for everyone to examine. The software covers the content areas of math, language arts, social studies, and science for grades 1-12. It is multimedia rich software that has many tutorials and practice materials. Documentation with the software indicates that other school districts have experienced remarkable success using the product. The software will cost $10,000.00 dollars to purchase and $2000.00 per year after the first year to provide upgrades and technical support.

An open school board meeting is being held to discuss whether or not this software should be purchased and how to evaluate its effectiveness. The public has been invited to attend. Teachers, principals, parents, and students have been invited and strongly encouraged to attend.

The role play discussion in Blackboard will be an enactment of this open school board meeting. The characters have been defined as possible stakeholders in the situation just described. Choose a character from the list below and then attend the open school board meeting in Blackboard. Stay in character during the entire week. Try to have some fun with this. Feel free to embellish and add to the information provided in the scenario. Your character may know something about the situation that needs to be explained to the rest of the group during the meeting (discussion).

Choose a Character: Please pick one character for the discussion. Do not forget to introduce yourself in your first post as your character. Remain in character for the duration of the discussion.

- **School Board Chairperson:** This person is responsible for running the school board meeting. The school board chairperson is in charge of making sure that all participants are heard and receive fair treatment. If you choose this role please moderate the meeting and announce that the meeting is adjourned at the end of the week. As you moderate the meeting, keep bringing the topic back to evaluation of the software.

continued

- **School Board Member Who is Promoting the Software:** This person contacted the Phenomenal Software Company after reading about their product on the Internet. This character is gung ho in favor of using this software.

- **School Board Member Who is Not Convinced:** This person is not quite sure about the usefulness of the software especially because it is expensive.

- **Jeffersonville Elementary School Principal:** This principal is at the meeting to explain the many reasons for the failing school designation at the elementary school.

- **Jeffersonville Junior High School Principal:** This principal is simply interested in knowing the benefits and drawbacks of using the software.

- **Jeffersonville High School Principal:** This principal wants to know how the software will impact high school students who may have to pass a test to graduate. This principal is concerned about dealing with teacher and parental outrage over the proposed exam.

- **Jeffersonville School District Superintendent:** The superintendent just wants to make sure that students are learning enough to become productive members of society. The superintendent is very concerned about the elementary school as the foundation for later grades.

- **Representative from Phenomenal Software:** This is the sales representative from Phenomenal Software. The sales rep is here to answer questions about the software. (This is a fictitious software company so make up whatever you need to for this role. Try to make it realistic.)

- **Elementary Teacher1:** This teacher is working evenings and weekends to provide the best possible education but feels overwhelmed and frustrated.

- **Elementary Teacher2:** This teacher is interested in learning more about the software, but does not know if it will help with the myriad of special needs students.

- **Technology Coordinator:** This is the high school physical science teacher who also oversees tech support and technology training for the district. The technology coordinator has concerns about the software because the hardware the district owns may not be able to support it. Many of the district computers are running Windows 95 and the network is old.

- **Evaluation Consultant:** This is a university professor who was asked to help identify strategies for evaluating the software and its cost effectiveness.

- **Parent1:** This parent wants to make sure that his/her child is prepared to begin college without requiring remedial courses after high school. This parent is concerned that school has become too watered down and should be more rigorous.

- **Parent2:** This parent wants students to be taught the "old fashioned way" because that is the best way. The money should be spent on books instead of computer software.

- **Parent3:** This parent has a child with special needs. This parent is concerned that the child will not be successful in school and may fail the proposed high stakes exam.

continued

- **Business Owner:** This person is dismayed over the low basic skill level seen in people who apply for work at local businesses.

- **Dysfunctional Expert:** This person is someone who knows a lot of jargon and uses it frequently. Often, people have no idea what this person is talking about. The dysfunctional expert has an "informed opinion" about just about any topic and freely shares it. (If you pick this have fun with it.)

- **Concerned Community Member:** This character has concerns and pays taxes. We can have more than one of these characters if necessary.

- **Do it Yourself Character:** Make up a suitable character and tell us about your character in the introduction.

Example Lesson Plan

Figure 4.3. Example lesson plan using discussion boards as portfolios

Weeks 12-16: Online Teaching Final Projects

Greetings and welcome to the remaining portion of your class in Online Teaching! The final sections of our class focus on completion of your class projects as outlined in the Syllabus. We are at a place where you have the opportunity to pull together all the information you have learned in class to date, and apply that information to a particular project or product of interest to you.

This week, we will begin by writing project proposals. You will also create a rubric that you, your peers, and I will use to assess your final project. When one begins project design by first looking at outcomes, you are engaging in a design process known as "Backwards Design" or "Understanding by Design." If you are interested in learning more about backwards design, I have included a couple of links for reference. In the subsequent weeks, you will post a draft of work-in-progress, give feedback to others in class, and finally submit your project on May 9.

Note that each student in the class now has a portfolio located in the discussion board. You will use this portfolio to submit all your work for the remainder of the semester. Using your portfolio allows me and others in the course, to see the ongoing progression of your work. Enjoy!

Feel free to work ahead of deadlines.

continued

Objectives

1. Consider and prepare your final course project by submitting an initial project proposal.

2. Create a rubric to assess project outcomes .

3. Modify project design accordingly by collecting formative assessment from peers and instructor.

4. Support our online community through peer feedback.

5. Demonstrate synthesis and application of course content by completing a final project.

Resources

Understanding by Design

Overview of backward design http://www.ubdexchange.org/resources/news-articles/backward.html
Understanding by design slideshow http://www.ubdexchange.org/resources/ppts/UbD_Overview.ppt

Evaluation

Kathy Schrock's assessment and rubric information. Lots of great examples and information on creating rubrics. http://school.discovery.com/schrockguide/assess.html
Online Assessment Strategies http://www.flinders.edu.au/flexed/resources/assess.htm
My T4L Rubric Maker http://myt4l.com/index.php?v=pl&page_ac=view&type=tools&tool=rubricmaker
WWW4Teachers - check out assessment tools like RubiStar (to create rubrics), and QuizStar (to create quizzes). http://4teachers.org/
Sample Student Multimedia Evaluation Rubric from MidLink Magazine http://www.ncsu.edu/midlink/rub.mm.st.htm
Quia - Free testing site http://www.quia.com
ExamBuilder http://exambuilder.com/
Hot Potatoes, free to educators, multimedia quiz/assessment tool http://www.halfbaked-software.com/
Cheating in Online Assessment http://www.westga.edu/~distance/ojdla/summer72/rowe72.html

continued

ACTIVITIES FOR WEEKS 12-16	DUE DATE

1. Final Class Project Proposal
This assignment is worth 20 points.
Submit a proposal for your class project (see <u>Project Guidelines</u> in "Course Documents"). You may submit your proposal in either text or slideshow format. Include a flowchart or outline that illustrates the various components/pages of your project. In your proposal, please address the following categories/questions:
 	
   1. Title of Project
 	
   2. Audience (please be specific and don't generalize your audience, ex. my 9th grade Biology students)
 	
   3. Purpose of Project
 	
   4. What real-life need does this project fill for you?
 	
   5. Type of Project (slideshow, lesson plans, Web site, tutorial, lessons plans, or ??)
 	
   6. Objectives (what are the specific learning objectives driving the design of your project?)
 	
   7. Discuss how your project promotes higher-order thinking skills, critical thinking, or creativity in your audience.
 	
   8. Describe the "deliverables" or final product you will turn in to me at the end of class. Be as specific as possible.
 	
Post your proposal and flowchart into your portfolio folder on the Discussion board.
	Deadline to post

continued

2. Create Your Project Rubric **This assignment is worth 20 points.** After reviewing the resources above, create a rubric that will be used by me, yourself, and others in the class to evaluate your final project. Kathy Schrock's site gives some great examples, and RubiStar and MyT4L Rubric Maker also provides a template for designing your own. Two criteria that must be addressed in your project, and included in your rubric, are "meets a real-life need," and "includes the use, discussion, or research about online teaching tools." Other criteria are optional based on your project. I'm assuming you might include other criteria such as quality factors, alignment with content or technology standards, graphic design principles (if it is a Web site), project design meets audience needs, etc. Your point values can be set wherever you'd like...I'll be converting the final score for the grade book. After you post your rubric in your portfolio, I will let you know if it needs modifications. We might find that the rubric needs further refining after you get closer to your end product—it works that way sometimes, that's ok. Finally, please consider whether your project will include its own evaluation component, in addition. For example, if you are creating a Web site for parents, how will you assess if it's working? Will parents have a survey form they can complete? If you do choose to include an evaluation component for your site (and I recommend you do if at all possible), list "evaluation" as a category in your rubric, as well. See sample rubric at http://edtech.boisestate.edu/ldawley/582/project_rubric.doc *Post rubric containing at least six categories (two identified above), point values, and specific criteria in each cell. Post to portfolio.*	Deadline to post rubric in portfolio folder: midnight on Tuesday, April 18
3. Post Draft of Work-in-Progress **This assignment is worth 20 points.** Please post an updated rough draft of your work-in-progress. Explain what you've completed to date, and what remains to be done. If you want feedback on a specific aspect of your project, let us know that, as well. *Post draft to your portfolio.*	Deadline to post rough drafts: midnight on Tuesday, April 25

continued

4. Peer Feedback **This assignment is worth 40 points.** Provide in-depth feedback to three class members. If you also want to give feedback to others not in your group, great! In your feedback, *use their rubric* as a guideline for assessing their work. Provide suggestions, areas in which the work might be improved, solutions to problems. *Post feedback to class members using rubric located in their portfolio. Include the rubric in your post. If a student already has three replies to their work, please evaluate another student in class. We want to ensure each person gets feedback from at least three individuals.*	Deadline to post feedback in portfolios: midnight on Tuesday, May 2
5. Post Your Final Project **This assignment is worth 250 points.** In your portfolio, attach or post links to your final project.	Deadline to post final projects: midnight on Tuesday, May 9

Finally, what do you do if you need help while working on your project?

A quick e-mail to me will get you an answer of some sort usually in 24 hours. Or, give me a call and we can talk through any problems/questions you might have. Also, feel free to e-mail your class members, or post in the forum called "Final Projects." For technical issues related to Blackboard, use blackboard@boisestate.edu. Good luck and I look forward to seeing all of your completed projects!

Grading

Weeks 12-15: Pass/no pass, all criteria must be addressed. Final project is graded using student's self-created rubric.

Resources

A-Z Teacher Stuff Discussion Forums: http://forums.atozteacherstuff.com/

Blackboard: Using the Discussion Board: http://trc.edcc.edu/tutorials/_Using%20Discussion%20Boards.pdf

Bulletin Board Lesson Plan: Online Novel: http://www.geocities.com/rteirney/DiscoverLP.html

Discussion Board Tips & Pedagogy: http://www.mtsu.edu/webctsupport/faculty/manual/WebCT_DiscussionBoard_Tips-Pedagogy.pdf

ESL Café: Discussion Forums for Educators: http://www.eslcafe.com/forums/teacher/index.php

Flexible Education: Uses of Discussion Forums: http://www.flinders.edu.au/flexed/resources/discuss.htm

Facilitating Online Discussions: The Role of the Moderator: http://online.mq.edu.au/docs/facilitate.pdf

Forum Hosting Services: Without Installing Software: http://distancelearn.about.com/gi/dynamic/offsite.htm?once=true&site=http://thinkofit.com/webconf/index.htm

Teaching with Asynchronous Communication Tools: http://www.cites.uiuc.edu/edtech/teaching_methods/pedagogy/communication/communication3.html

The Virtual Professor: Using Discussion Forums: http://www.ibritt.com/resources/vp_discussion.htm

WebCT Communication Tools: http://www.webct.com/otlviewpage?name=otl_discussion_resources

Web Discussion Forums in Teaching & Learning: http://horizon.unc.edu/projects/monograph/CD/Technological_Tools/Akers.asp

References

Akers, R. (2004). *Web discussion forums in teaching and learning.* Retrieved June 24, 2006, from http://horizon.unc.edu/projects/monograph/CD/Technological_Tools/Akers.asp

Ellis, R. A. & Calvo, R. A. (2006). Discontinuities in university student experiences of learning through discussions. *British Journal of Educational Technology, 37*(1), 55-68.

Gagné, E. D., Yekovich, C. W., & Yekovich, F. R. (1997). *The cognitive psychology of school learning* (2nd ed.). New York: Longman.

Garrison, D. R., Anderson, T., & Archer, W. (2000). Critical inquiry in a text-based environment: Computer conferencing in higher education. *The Internet and Higher Education, 2*(2–3), 1–19.

Ko, S., & Rossen, S. (2004). *Teaching online: A practical guide.* Boston: Houghton Mifflin.

Pelz, B. (2004). (My) three principles of effective online pedagogy. *Journal of Asynchronous Learning Network, 8.* Retrieved June 24, 2006, from http://www.sloan-c.org/publications/jaln/v8n3/v8n3_pelz.asp

Sherer, P., & Shea, T. (2002). Designing courses outside the classroom: New opportunities with the electronic delivery toolkit. *College Teaching, 50,* 15-20.

Suler, J. (2004). The online disinhibition effect. *CyberPsychology and Behavior, 7,* 321-326.

Tu, C. (2002). The impacts of text-based CMC on online social presence. *Journal of Interactive Online Learning, 1.* Retrieved June 24, 2006, from http://www.ncolr.org/jiol/archives/2002/fall/06/index.html

Walker, G. (2005). Critical thinking in asynchronous discussions. *International Journal of Instructional Technology and Distance Learning, 2*(6), 15-22. Retrieved June 24, 2006, from http://www.itdl.org/Journal/Jun_05/article02.htm

Chapter V

Small Group Learning

We love using small group learning in our online classes. Learning to establish and facilitate small groups, especially in an online environment, is a new skill for many instructors. Hearing horror stories from other colleagues, or indeed from students themselves, causes some instructors to shy away from using the small group capabilities in an LMS, chat room, or video conferencing software. However, a well-structured and purposeful small group experience can allow the online student to work intimately with a small group of people and experience success as a team member. Successful small group work offers the student a greater sense of community, can increase enthusiasm and motivation with coursework, and can also be used as a stepping stone to larger class projects during the overall progression of a course. Collaboration also addresses multiple learning styles, reduces online isolation, provides students opportunities to test out real-world practices, and it allows students to gain competence in using teamwork, critical in the workplace.

Figure 5.1. Blackboard course groups. Used with permission

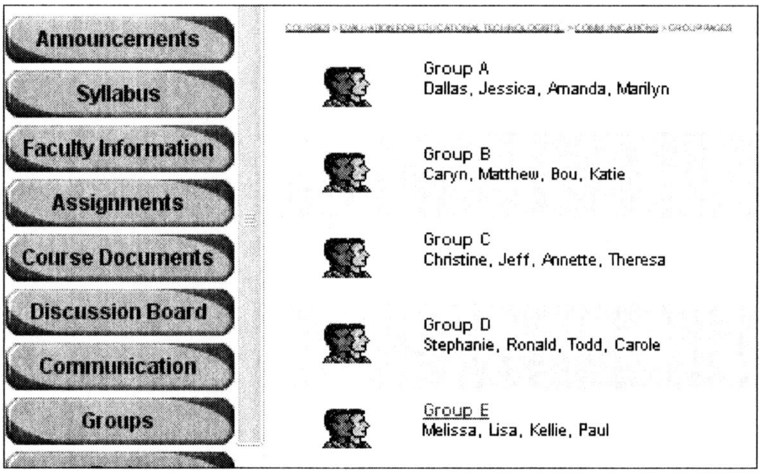

Most LMSs offer the capability to group students within an online course. In Figure 5.1, we see an example of an interface that allows students to enter their groups by clicking on "Groups" in the left navigation bar.

After clicking on "Groups," students can select the group they wish to participate in from a list.

Once in a group, students are provided with a tool set typically consisting of group e-mail (any e-mail sent from within group e-mail will only go to members in the group), a group drop box, group discussion board, and group chat. Only students added to a particular group by the instructor are able to see and participate in that group. This ability of the tool helps promote cohesion in the course by creating communication among small groups of students. One of the main goals in using groups is to promote a deepened sense of community among all class members.

In chat or video conferencing, small group discussions can be accomplished using breakout rooms, private chat rooms that allow users to leave a main discussion and breakout into smaller discussion groups.

Groups can be organized in many ways and for a variety of purposes. For example, groups might be established to work on a particular project or to create study groups on a specific topic. In courses where we enroll adult learners from a variety of fields, we sometimes establish study groups based on various industries in which the students work. For example, we can establish a study group for those who work in higher education, corporate, K-6 teachers, and so forth. This type of grouping provides students who have common work environments the ability to discuss and apply course content to their respective fields.

In this chapter, we examine the strengths and weaknesses of using small groups, explore the need for building community in online learning, and provide examples of small group activities aligned with learning objective outcomes.

Strengths and Weaknesses

Table 5.1 illustrates the varied strengths and weaknesses of using small groups.

Strengths of small groups. There is a great deal of research over the last 45 years showing that students who work together learn more than those who work alone. This research covers many subject areas and types of assignments, and is true for pairings and small groups of students (Johnson & Johnson, 1990). In addition to the amount and complexity of knowledge developed during group activity, there is also a proven effect on the length of retention of knowledge when students learn in teams. Based on the tenants of constructivism, wherein knowledge generation is viewed as being socially constructed through interactions with others, small group work offers the learner a complex environment for working with the subject matter at hand. Through the co-construction of knowledge, the exposure to multiple points of view, and the emphasis on achievement of a group task (as opposed to the memorization of content), students are led to deeper and more complex thinking on the topic at hand than if they were to work independently.

In small groups, students are typically given a problem or task to solve as a team. Proponents of small groups suggest that this teaching approach mimics today's specialized work environments where employees are often required to work as part of team toward achievement of a larger goal. In addition to learning content material, students also learn skills required of a team

Table 5.1. Strengths and weaknesses of using small groups in online classes

Strengths	Weaknesses
• Small group work can promote a deeper level of thought due to co-construction of knowledge. • Social interaction has a proven positive effect on the amount of information retained, as well as on the length of retention. • Small group learning can mimic real life tasks and problem solving, wherein students learn to work as team members to accomplish goals. • Students can learn to identify and use their strengths toward the good of the group, while relying on others to support areas in which they might be weak. • Students report feeling a connectedness to a course and program when provided opportunities for small group interaction. This connection can help reduce drop out rates in online programs. • Small group size and structure can be varied by the instructor depending on the objectives of the assignment. Thus, the student has a variety of learning experiences, from dyads, triads, and larger groups, throughout the duration of a course. This variety can help maintain interest and engagement with a course.	• Some students prefer to work individually at all times, and resent being forced to work in a group. • When assigned deadlines, small group work forces students to log in more often than they would if working individually. Students have to log in to view responses of others on discussion boards. • Adult students might find it difficult to locate a common available time for small group chat. • Nonperforming group members can be a hindrance to successful achievement of group tasks. This can create a sense of failure among other group members. • Group members may experience strong frustration when work of other members is turned in late, is weak, or not completed at all. • Younger students may lack the necessary social skills for group work and require much guidance and facilitation to work effectively together online.

member such as brainstorming, problem solving, effective communication, team leadership, and team accountability. Through their work with team members, students can begin to identify and utilize their areas of strengths, while also learning to rely on and utilize the strengths of others toward the overall achievement of the task.

Learning to work in small groups has implications that go beyond the boundaries of the small group itself. As we now begin to better understand the online learning environment, recent studies are indicating that increased social presence, that is, interactivity and a community feeling, not only contributes to achievement of *learning objectives*, but also with *learner satisfaction* in general (Palloff & Pratt, 2005). Using small groups to increase social presence is a proven strategy to increase learner satisfaction, thus having the potential to keep students engaged and enrolled in classes (Anderson & Simpson, 2004). Creating group membership, a feeling of belonging, has been demonstrated as an important variable in lowering school drop out rates overall (Wehlage & Anderson, 1989). And with drop out rates in online education edging up toward 40% in some courses (Carr & Ledwith, 2000), the effective use of small groups can be an important strategy to create long-term engagement.

Finally, course engagement and interest can be further promoted through varying the group size and type of activity. The flexible nature of small groups as a teaching strategy is a great benefit to both the student and the online teacher. The student is provided variety in their learning experience, thus being exposed to multiple ways of knowing any given subject matter. The instructors have a variety of grouping structures and approaches they can use to achieve a variety of instructional goals.

Weaknesses of small groups. Out of respect for the individual learner, it has to be noted that some people do not enjoy group assignments, and resent being assigned group work. This can be especially true for adult learners who may have had bad experiences with groups in the past, or who are working on their online course late at night after a full day's work, and do not have the extra time required to collaborate. In requiring students to work together, students are often required to log in more during the week than if they were working independently. Communication takes time, and whether this time happens synchronously or asynchronously, an extra burden of time is placed on the learner when using small groups. Additionally, requiring specified chat times for small groups can prove to be burdensome or downright impossible.

Perhaps the biggest complaint among students when working in small groups is when one group member is weak, turns in late assignments, does not communicate, or does not do his/her share of assigned work. This behavior can become particularly worrisome to peers when a group grade is being assigned by the instructor. At worst, a weak group member can ultimately leave other group members with a sense of failure if this group is unable to complete the assignment effectively. This, in turn, has the possibility of inhibiting the development of social presence in the class as the group members may perceive themselves as being ineffective when compared to other groups in the class.

Understanding Small Groups: Building Community!

Palloff and Pratt (1999, 2001, 2005) have written extensively about the concept of, and need for, building community in online education. Their work, along with many others (e.g., Conrad & Donaldson, 2004; Doran, 2001; Murphy, Drabier, & Epps, 1998; Preece, 2000; Ragoonanden & Bordeleau, 2000), has helped to establish a movement in online learning that is based on building community and connection among participants as a means to promote successful teaching and learning. Palloff and Pratt (2005) identify this movement as the *second wave* in online instruction, "which is concerned with best practices and improving both interaction and interactivity in online courses" (p. 3). This second wave moves beyond initial explorations into online learning, wherein instructors would typically require students to read material and then discuss in discussion forums. Now, as research begins to show the importance of interaction and interactivity in online courses, we are seeking to better understand how to promote community by utilizing the online tools and teaching strategies available to us, and by applying what we know about best practice.

However, as we begin to explore the use and promotion of online community, we would be wise to consider the words of White (2002): "The bottom line is that online community or online interaction is not the goal. It's one *means* for helping groups achieve their goals. It is not necessarily about 'online community' but what conditions and process are needed to enable communities to use the online environment" (¶ 3).

Palloff and Pratt (2005) define the following elements of an online community:

- **People:** The students, faculty, and staff involved in an online course.

- **Shared purpose:** Coming together to take an online course, including sharing information, interests, and resources.

- **Guidelines:** Create the structure for the online course, by providing the ground rules for interaction and participation.

- **Technology:** The vehicle for delivery of the course and a place where everyone involved can meet.

- **Collaborative learning:** Student-to-student interaction that also supports socially constructed meaning and creation of knowledge.

- **Reflective practice:** Promoting transformative learning.

- **Social presence:** Feeling of connection and community among learners. (p. 8)

So how does the successful online instructor build community and what role can the use of small groups play in this process?

Building community vs. independent learning. At the core of building community is the ability to engage students in the course. But what factors play into student engagement? The spectrum of engagement in online classes runs along a continuum (see Figure 5.2).

Figure 5.2. Engagement in online courses

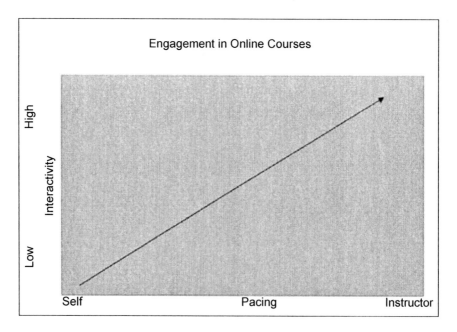

At one end of the spectrum are self-paced courses that require little, if any, interaction. Students are provided access to content and assignments that can be completed at the student's own pace. These assignments are typically submitted to the instructor and a grade is returned, with or without feedback. There is little, if any, interaction with other students in the course. These types of online courses do appeal to some types of learners; however, the majority of students require and seek more social support and interaction for an effective learning experience.

At the other end of the spectrum are online courses that are instructor-facilitated, and instructor-paced with weekly or semiweekly assignments and deadlines, and include a variety of assignments that utilize dyads, triads, and other forms of small groups to promote interactivity. There is high value placed on the benefit of peer learning, and strategies such as peer feedback and small group projects are used as an integral part of the curriculum.

Interactivity, or communication between learners (including the instructor), serves two purposes in online education. First, interactivity provides the necessary scaffolding to complete assigned class activities. Second, interactivity provides the necessary scaffolding to provide affective support between peers in class, an inherent need of human beings as they seek affiliation with various cultural groups, including the classroom or the program in which they are enrolled (Anderson & Simpson, 2004). Although interactivity may occur outside the instructor's guidelines or assignments, effective course facilitation and lesson design using peer-based and small group activities is critical to the promotion of effective interaction. In the next section, we look at strategies for the effective use of small groups to create interactivity.

Power Tip: Make that Phone Call!

A quick phone call can go a long way to creating a connection with your students. I always offer my cell phone number to all students, but few will rarely take the opportunity to call. I have used the phone in several ways: to introduce myself at the beginning of a course, to follow-up and discuss project proposals in-depth, and to throw a lifeline to students who are struggling in the course (hastily completed work, continually late assignments, poor quality work). Similar to e-mail introduction responses in the first week, students are very receptive to instructor contact and knowing that someone is really on the other end of the line.

Structuring Small Groups for Success

In this section, we offer some hands-on advice for working with small groups in the online learning environment.

Before you begin. It would be a mistake to simply assign students to groups and expect them to know how to perform effectively together. There is preparation and facilitation that is required on the instructor's part to make small group learning successful. Below are basic steps to ensure effective small group work.

First, at the beginning of each class, we survey our students for information relevant to groups we intend to create throughout the semester. The following types of information can be collected to determine potential groupings:

- **Time zone of student:** If you are teaching students in various time zones, group according to time zone. It is difficult to find a common time to chat, for example, when one student lives in Japan and the other lives in the Ukraine.

- **Experience or job background:** Group adult students with similar backgrounds or work experiences. They will have more opportunity to discuss application of the concepts being taught.

- **Comfort level with chat tools:** For purposes of small group chatting, it is important to have at least one person in the group who is familiar with chatting. That person can become the designated chat facilitator, and take ownership to lead the session.

- **Prior experience working online in groups:** When possible, it is helpful to spread out students who have experience working in small groups.

- **Grouping preferences:** If appropriate for your class, ask students if there are particular students with whom they prefer to be grouped or not grouped. When possible, students should be given the opportunity to have ownership in their group make-up. This is particularly important if a pair of students has a bad history working together in a former class.

There are also many online students who decide to sign up for an online course together. This partnership can be supported by the online teacher who is able to assign these pairs of students to the same group.

How many students should be assigned to each group? The actual number might vary depending on the given task. However, as with live small groups, the most effective number for an online class is usually between four to six participants. Having a minimum of four participants provides enough variety to keep group members active and interested, and if one student drops out or needs to change a group for whatever reason, there are still three participants left who can dialogue as opposed to just a pair. When groups start to get large, beyond five or six members, individuals can get lost in the crowd. It becomes harder to chat in larger groups, to reply to everyone's work-in-progress, and so forth. In our experience, five participants tend to be an optimum number for small grouping. Having said that, there are certain types of assignments where it might be more appropriate to assign students to dyads or triads. For example, a dyad works well when students are required to interview one another.

Getting started using small groups. Successful collaboration depends on creation of the learning community. Creating an atmosphere of safety and trust is critical to the development of a good working group online. Palloff and Pratt (2005) encourage us to:

- **Set the stage:** explain and set guidelines.

- **Create the environment:** Provide a meeting place and the parameters for how to connect.

- **Model the process:** Do it with your students before they do it on their own.

- **Guide the process:** Let them know how and when you will be involved.

- **Evaluate the process:** Always evaluate at the end of a collaborative activity.

With younger adults, or those who may be new to small group work, begin establishing the norms by which the classroom and group discussions will operate. One basic consideration is to establish rules for netiquette. Netiquette is the term used for etiquette on the Internet. This term extends to e-mail, chat, discussion boards, and live sessions. As an online teacher, it is important to educate yourself and your students about using good manners on the Internet. Just as in a classroom setting, teachers must define the rules on the first day of class and enforce them throughout the school year.

Anyone who has Internet experience or has used a chat feature on the Internet may have experienced that Internet lingo is taking on a life of its own, especially among kids in the online generation. You may have seen acronyms such as LOL (laughing out loud), BRB (be right back), or BBL (be back later). Or you may have seen emoticons such as :) or :(. Many words are being invented by kids on the Internet, too. For instance, students may invent new spellings, such as "kewl" for cool. If you have not chatted with students before, you may find yourself immersed into an entirely new language! This language is known as "leetspeak." Locate, read, and understand your school's policy dealing with netiquette, if possible. It is important that you are aware of these guidelines and incorporate them into your personal class expectations.

After establishing rules for netiquette, and collecting initial grouping preference information from your students at the beginning of a course, wait until the second or third week of class (in a typical semester-long class) before assigning students to small groups. Assigning students to groups before this time can create confusion, as there are often students who are adding or dropping the course during this time. Start small. Get your students used to the idea of peer interaction during week two. Have students begin to give peer feedback on other's work. This can be accomplished with a task as simple as, "Post a response to a minimum of two other students." In your response, list one strength of the student's assignment, one area for further consideration, and provide an additional URL regarding the topic.

In the third week, assign your students to work in pairs. This pairing might be used to complete any variety of assignments. Students can interview one another on a given topic, complete a simple Web quest together and post a single report, or meet in chat at an agreed-to time to discuss an assigned weekly reading. A chat transcript can be posted as evidence of their discussion.

Starting in the fourth week, you can begin to use a variety of grouping approaches depending on the goals and objectives of your particular course. If you plan to have students working together in groups on long-term projects, we suggest first introducing students to a small group assignment at this point that lasts a week or two. This gives students the opportunity to experience an online group activity without the pressure of working together on a long-term project. For example, students might be asked to complete the following type of activity:

Over the next week, you will work with your group members to complete a Web quest on the psychology of online gaming. Each group member, except the assigned group leader, is responsible for answering two questions from the list. Post your responses to your group discussion board by Friday. Your group leader will then compile your responses into a final report that will be posted on the class discussion board on Monday. Provide feedback to two other group's reports using the attached guidelines. Peer feedback is due by Wednesday.

There are many pedagogical approaches for using small groups in learning, and most of these transfer well to the online environment. Some of these approaches include the use of case studies, role play, brainstorming, jigsaw, simulations, debates, Web quests, and problem-based learning. If you are new to using small group pedagogy in online instruction, we recommend reading Conrad and Donaldson's (2004) *Engaging the Online Learner*. This text is filled with a variety of grouping activities used by online teachers around the country.

Making student work public. As much as possible, make student work public. Have students post assignments as attachments in discussion forums or upload to Web sites if they are keeping student portfolios. Allow your feedback, as well as peer feedback, to be made public, as well. Keep grades private, however. This ability to make learning public is one of the greatest strengths of online education in the author's opinion. This process establishes the norm that learning is collaborative, and that we all (including the instructor) have the opportunity to learn from one another. The emphasis is taken off "getting it right," and instead, is placed on the learning process itself. Students working in small groups on collaborative projects can also share their results in a larger class discussion forum. Doing so helps promote cohesion among group members, and also offers group members a benchmark by which they can compare the outcome of their efforts. As a word of caution in making work and feedback public, *never assign a grade in a public space.* Grading should be done either via the grade book or in a private e-mail to the student or group. Similarly, *never have students assign a grade to one another* as part of their peer feedback process. To do so would take the emphasis off of group learning and instead place it on competing for a grade.

Processing in small groups. Processing, or reflecting on group functioning and effort, is a critical aspect of assisting students to learn to work together effectively. Processing is done publicly, typically at the end of a chat or assignment. Processing might also be used midway through a longer term project as a means to refocus and reconnect group members. The instructor can facilitate effective processing by asking students to reflect on their group experience and share one strength of the group and one area for group improvement in the future. After each student has had an opportunity to process, the instructor can summarize and offer a final reflection on the group's effort overall.

Figure 5.3. Example of online community groups

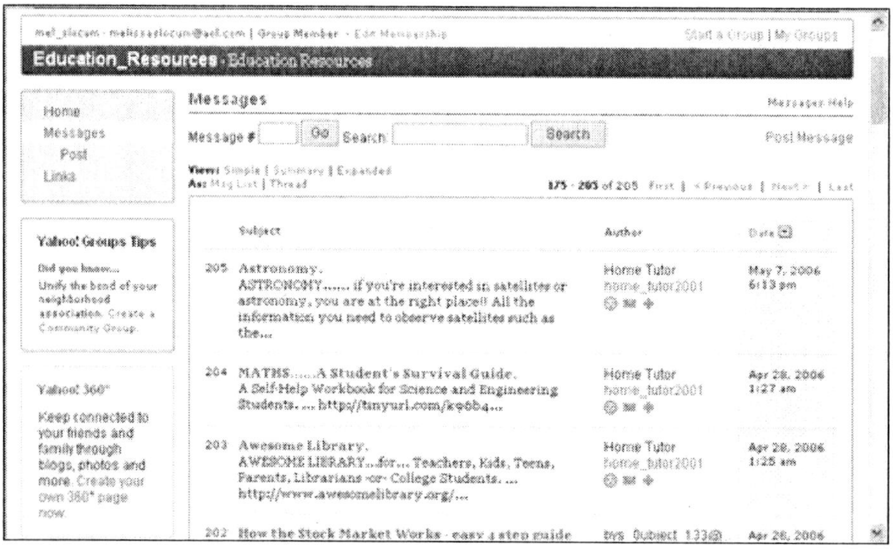

Community beyond the walls of the virtual classroom. Many online instructors are now encouraging students to develop community beyond the boundaries of the small group environment provided by the virtual classroom. Online community environments, such as those provided by Yahoo Groups, allow students to participate or establish their own groups on a given area of interest (see Figure 5.3).

These groups provide users tools such as message boards, e-mail, a calendar for scheduling events, and opinion polls. Groups of interest can be located in the Yahoo Group directory, or by using the Google Group search tool. By integrating the ability to participate in, or create, community groups as part of the class experience, instructors provide students the opportunity to extend and enrich their learning on a global level.

Example Uses for Success

Learning Objective Outcome	Small Group Learning Activities
Interactivity and connection	• Have pairs of students meet in chat to interview one another on a given topic. Ask them to discuss how the topic impacts their own lives. Require them to develop a set of interview questions prior to the chat. Post a copy of the chat transcript to the class discussion board. • Peer tutoring: Ask students to list an area of expertise related to course content. Peer experts can then list the availability for tutoring either via e-mail, discussion board, or at an assigned chat time.

continued

Knowledge: defines; describes; enumerates; identifies; labels; lists; matches; names; reads; records; reproduces; selects; states; views	• Working in groups of four, students are assigned a Web quest where they are required to locate statistics and current information on a given topic. This information is compiled in a group report and presented to the class. • Provide small groups a list of vocabulary. Groups then seek definitions to vocabulary along with supporting Web sites. These definitions can be added to a class glossary.
Comprehension: classifies; cites; converts; describes; discusses; estimates; explains; generalizes; gives examples; makes sense out of; paraphrases; summarizes; traces; understands	• Break the class into small groups. Assign each group a different reading on the same topic. Group members discuss the reading, and create a summary. The summary can be shared with other classmates and used as a basis for further discussion. • Using the topic of a given lesson (civil war, music of the 17th century, abnormal psychology, etc.), have groups of students collect Web sites containing multimedia related to the topic. These might include pictures, audio files, interviews with experts, flash presentations, and so forth. Students share these resources with the class. The teacher can then compile these resources in a master list for students to use in report writing or completing projects at a later time.

continued

Application: acts; administers; articulates; assesses; charts; collects; computes; constructs; contributes; controls; determines; develops; discovers; establishes; extends; implements; includes; informs; instructs; operationalizes; participates; predicts; prepares; preserves; produces; projects; provides; relates; reports; shows; solves; teaches; transfers; uses; utilizes	• Small groups can work together to prepare a slideshow on a given topic. For example, students might be asked to (1) illustrate the process of lesson planning, (2) provide a sample lesson, (3) provide a list of Web resources for further reading. These tasks can be divided among group members. The group leader can then be responsible for compiling the various tasks into a final product that is then presented to the class. • Create a Web-based scavenger hunt for small groups to complete. Students are asked to locate Web-based resources that provide answers to a list of questions provided by the teacher. Groups can prepare a final report listing their answers and supporting Web sites. • Have groups of students participate in an online community on a topic related to course content (appropriate for adult learners). Specific online communities can be located through Yahoo Groups or Google Groups.
Analysis: breaks down; correlates; diagrams; differentiates; discriminates; distinguishes; focuses; illustrates; infers; limits; outlines; points out; prioritizes; recognizes; separates; subdivides	• Using a Web quest structure, students are asked to locate various statistics on a given topic. In Excel, students then create charts of their statistics, conduct an analysis of the data, and write an interpretation. • Assign small groups the task of creating a wiki on a given topic (see Chapter IX for information on using wikis). Have the group outline the content of the wiki and invite others to contribute to the wiki content. Wiki's can then be shared with others in class.

continued

Synthesis: adapts; anticipates; categorizes; collaborates; combines; communicates; compares; compiles; composes; contrasts; creates; designs; devises; expresses; facilitates; formulates; generates; incorporates; individualizes; initiates; integrates; intervenes; models; modifies; negotiates; plans; progresses; rearranges; reconstructs; reinforces; reorganizes; revises; structures; substitutes; validates	• Small groups or pairs of students can work together to establish their own online community on a given topic. Because online community environments such as Yahoo Groups provide the ability to restrict membership, these types of communities can be used with younger students, as well. Parents, friends, or other interested parties can be invited to participate in the online community. This activity gives students the opportunity to share and expand their learning with a larger interested community outside the boundaries of the course. • Assign small groups the task of creating and maintaining a blog over the course of the semester (see Chapter IX). The blog can be made public or private, depending on the goals of the course. Group members alternate posting to the blog on a weekly basis. They are asked to summarize and comment on the main topics for the week. Remaining group members are then required to comment in response to the weekly posting.
Evaluation: appraises; compares and contrasts; concludes; criticizes; critiques; decides; defends; interprets; judges; justifies; reframes	• Working in small groups, students are provided a rubric for evaluating a given Web site, product, course, and so forth. Each group member posts an evaluation to the small group discussion board, and similarities and differences in results are discussed among the group members. • Provide small groups a case study on a topic under study. Group members read the case, and are then asked to assume a role of a person in the case. Over the following week, group members then role play a resolution to the case via the discussion board.

Example Lesson Plan

Figure 5.4. Example lesson plan using small group learning

WEEK 2: What is Instructional Design?

Great question! What is instructional design and what do instructional designers do? Is lesson planning the same thing as instructional design? Are curriculum designers the same as instructional designers?

There are two goals this week. **First,** begin considering what it is that instructional designers do. In order to understand the instructional design process, you need to look at it as a practice. In this module you will be introduced to the systematic design of instructional environments. The key words here are "systematic" and "design." The production of instructional and educational materials just does not happen. They are designed and produced with well defined goals or outcomes, an understanding of the learners, an analysis of the content, and resources in mind. There are many variables to consider and control for. A foundation to the "Systematic Design of Instruction" is in process and control. This is Dick, Carey, and Carey's theoretical approach to instructional design that comes out of a philosophical stance of cognitivism.

Second, I want your small group to take this time and invent ways of working together. You will have a team leader, and will identify each other's strengths. This is to be a collaborative experience. From my perspective, a major element in this class is the collaborative experience that we

---

Objectives

1.   Identify what instructional designers do.

2.   Analyze philosophical positions potentially underlying the instructional designer's work, and articulate the impact of those philosophies on the design work itself.

3.   Promote community through small group discussion.

Readings & Resources

Dick, Carey & Carey: Chapter 1

Ertmer & Quinn: pages 2-6; Case Study 6 pages 31-34

Pam Northrup: (30 minutes, slideshow)

David Merrill: http://www.id2.usu.edu/5Star/5starins.ram (15 minutes, requires RealPlayer plugin, works over 56K modem)

CramerSweeney: http://www.cramersweeney.com/instructional_design/default.cfm

---

ACTIVITIES FOR WEEK 1	DUE DATE
1. Getting Prepared • Read Dick & Carey. Then, listen to the audio-narrated slideshow by Pam Northrup (a little too much audio for me, but a great overview of basic class concepts). <u>Instructional Design Overview</u> • Watch this video with David Merrill. <u>http://www.id2.usu.edu/5Star/5starins.ram</u> (15 minutes, requires RealPlayer plugin, works over 56K modem)	
2. The Case Study • Read the Ertmer & Quinn readings above. • Review the group list to the right. Your assignments for your group are: 1st person: team leader (keep team on task, communicate with instructor if necessary, post final report on discussion board) 2nd & 3rd person: analyze case study 6 4th, 5th, 6th person: analyze CramerSweeney site Use the following guiding questions in your analysis:	**Group 1** <u>Castelin, Paul</u> <u>Collison, Gregg</u> <u>Cunningham, Julie</u> <u>Daniels, Jonathan</u> <u>Day, Shanna</u> **Group 2** <u>Evans, Bob</u> <u>Freed, Gregory</u> <u>Hong, Sung Yee</u> <u>Jensen, Maggie</u> <u>Keavy, Christine</u> **Group 3** <u>Leitner, Stacy</u> <u>Manzoor, Sajid</u> <u>Martinez, Desiree</u> <u>McKown, Shayanne</u> <u>Niezgoda, Ken</u>

continued

ACTIVITIES FOR WEEK 1	DUE DATE

2. The Case Study
 	
Question Area
Direct Questions
 	
Demographics:
1. gender of ID (Instructional Designer
2. years of working in the field
3. type of working environment:
 	
education
business
both above
 	
    4. background and training in ID
    5. who is their clientele
 	
ID Process:
 	
6. Describe the process they use in designing instruction.
 	
Theoretical Foundation:
 	
7. What ID theories steer what they do?
Does your subject work from a theoretical position to guide their work?
 	
Theory and Practice:
 	
8. What is the relationship between the theory of ID and their practice as a designer?
9. How useful is the ID Model to their work (do they use it?)?
 	
Examples:
 	
10. Describe briefly, as an example, some project they designed.
	Group 4
	Peairs, Deb
	Riley, Debbie
	Schmidt, Stephanie
	Strachan, Dwayne
	Yates, Marv Zimmerebner, Paul

continued

3. Discussion and analysis	Deadline to post individual analysis: midnight MT on Sunday, Sept. 4
Each group member should complete their individual analysis by Sunday, Sept. 4. Post these on your group discussion board (click on "Groups" in the left navigation). Over the next few days, group members should compare and contrast the two sets of analyses. The goal is for the group to 1) come to a consensus on the analysis for both the case study and CramerSweeny, 2) articulate a comparison between the two, and 3) explore the relationship between philosophical orientation and the work of ID itself.	Group discussion ends Tuesday, Sept. 6
The group leader should edit group postings, and then compile a response to post to the whole class discussion forum for Week 2. The report should cover each of the above three goals. Use a table format to show the comparison between the two cases, with a third column showing an analysis of the comparison. Add final comments to the report to cover goal #3.	Leader report posted by Thursday, Sept. 8

Grading

Grading is pass/no pass this week. This week is worth 10 points toward your class participation grade. You receive full credit when all assignments have been completed. Good luck!

Resources

Google Groups: http://groups-beta.google.com/

Learn the Net Netiquette: http://www.learnthenet.com/english/html/09netiqt.htm

Netiquette for new users: http://www.ccim.com/netiq.htm

Net Etiquette: http://www.albion.com/netiquette/index.html

Online Community Report: http://www.onlinecommunityreport.com/

Online Community Toolkit: http://www.fullcirc.com/community/communitymanual.htm

"Small Group Learning in Online Discussion: Staying in Your Own Backyard or Peering over the Garden Fence?": http://www.ascilite.org.au/conferences/auckland02/proceedings/papers/042.pdf

A Typology of Virtual Communities: http://www.ascusc.org/jcmc/vol10/issue1/porter.html

Yahoo Groups: http://groups.yahoo.com/

References

Anderson, & Simpson, W. (2004, November). *Group and class contexts for learning and support online: Learning and effective support online in small group and class contexts.* International Review of Research in Open and Distance Learning. Retrieved June 26, 2006, from http://www.irrodl.org/content/v5.3/ander-simp.html

Carr, R., & Ledwith, F. (2000). Helping disadvantaged students. *Teaching at a Distance, 18,* 77-85.

Conrad, R. M., & Donaldson, J. A. (2004). *Engaging the online learner: Activities and resources for creative instruction.* San Francisco: Jossey-Bass.

Doran, C. (2001). The effective use of learning groups in online education. *New Horizons in Adult Education, 15*(2).

Johnson, D. W., & Johnson, R. T. (1990). Cooperative learning and achievement. In S. Sharan (Ed.), *Cooperative learning: Theory and practice* (pp. 23-37). New York: Praeger.

Murphy, K., Drabier, R., & Epps, M. (1998). *Interaction and collaboration via computer conferencing.* Paper presented at the National Convention for Education Communication and Technology.

Palloff, R. M., & Pratt, K. (1999). *Building learning communities in cyberspace: Effective strategies for the online classroom.* San Francisco: Jossey-Bass.

Palloff, R. M., & Pratt, K. (2001). *Lessons from the cyberspace classroom: The realities of online teaching.* San Francisco: Jossey-Bass.

Palloff, R. M., & Pratt, K. (2005). *Collaborating online: Learning together in community.* San Francisco: Jossey-Bass.

Preece, J. (2000). *Online communities.* New York: Wiley.

Ragoonaden, K., & Bordeleau, B. (2000, July). Collaborative learning via the internet. *Educational Technology & Society, 3*(3).

Wehlage, G. G., & Anderson, E. M. (1989). *Reducing the risk: Schools and communities of support.* New York: Falmer Press.

White, N. (2002). *Networks, groups and catalysts: The sweet spot for forming online learning communities*. Retrieved June 26, 2006, from http://www.fullcirc.com/community/networkscatalystscommunity.htm

Chapter VI

Chat and
Instant Messaging

Chat and instant messaging provide teachers and students with tools that offer the opposite of a discussion forum—that is synchronous (real time) communication. Synchronous communication provides the benefits of creating a sense of community, the ability to interact more spontaneously and go in-depth on a given topic (Johntson, Anderson, & DeMeulle, 1998; Suler, 2004a), to have live group discussions with the entire class or small groups on timely matters when deadlines are short, and to involve guest speakers in the online class. Instant messaging offers the additional benefit of immediate access to the instructor or student when needed. Almost universally, students report feeling more connected to the content and other students in the class after having their first live chat. This ability to create connectedness and overcome isolation via real-time is one of the greatest strengths of chat and instant messaging (Haefner, 2000).

Figure 6.1. Blackboard™ virtual classroom

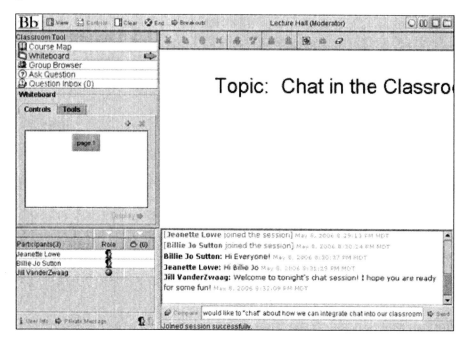

Chat involves two or more users typing into a text box, and then using the enter key, to communicate in real time (see Figure 6.1). Although there are definitely ways to chat outside of an LMS, most online instructors use the internal chat tool provided in their LMS to conduct small or entire group class chats.

As we can see in Figure 6.1, chat capability integrates into a virtual classroom or video conferencing program, another internal chat tool that incorporates a browser and slideshow area (see Chapter VII). Chat can also be conducted using instant messaging (IM), available in an external real time chat tool such as MSN Messenger™.

Although we are unaware of any LMSs that integrate an instant messaging feature at this time, many online teachers are choosing to use an external chat tool, such as MSN Messenger™, so their students can reach them online in real time. The ease of access is making instant messenger the online teacher's tool of choice for one-on-one chat.

In this chapter, we examine the strengths and weaknesses of synchronous chat tools, explore the need for student connectivity in online learning, and provide sample chat activities aligned with learning objective outcomes.

Strengths and Weaknesses

Table 6.1 illustrates the varied strengths and weaknesses of using chat and instant messaging.

Strengths of chat and IM. The main strength of chat is that it allows for dialogue in real time. For the student who is in crisis, this feature is invaluable. Beyond dealing with crises, chats are beneficial for a variety of reasons. From a learning perspective, chats increase a sense of community and connectedness with the class (see next section). Due to lack of visual cues, students can experience a sense of freedom and democracy—they can become more outspoken (Palloff & Pratt, 1999), and also experience deeper understanding on topics than they might in live classroom discussion. Driscoll (2002) notes that immediate feedback is a strength of chat, as opposed to asynchronous methods where feedback may take days or weeks. Just-in-time development can also be supported by making chat support available (Driscoll, 2002), for instance, when a teacher offers a homework period in IM. Chat or IM sessions can be held one-on-one, in small groups, and with the entire class. Outside experts can participate in live discussions with the class. Chats can be recorded and the transcripts made available for later use and recall in the course. Some chat tools offer the ability to make the student the chat facilitator, thus empowering students in their own learning (Ko & Rossen, 2004).

Weaknesses of chat and IM. Although most individuals can easily participate in chat with little instruction, one of the greatest weaknesses in the long term is students understanding that chat is a distinct form and culture of communication, often confusing to the new user (Rheingold, 2000). Although most teens are now comfortable using chat, many adult learners are still unfamiliar with its conventions and must be taught chat norms and culture as part of learning to use the tool. If students are in multiple time zones, scheduling a time for chat can be a challenge (Ko & Rossen, 2004). Also, technical

Table 6.1. Strengths and weaknesses of chat and instant messaging

Strengths	Weaknesses
Chat	**Chat**
• Allows for real time discourse and dialogue.	• Students new to chat are often overwhelmed with the style and quick pace of chats.
• Good for group work as it makes the experience more meaningful and further cements the concept of team learning	• Immediate response required (less time to think of concrete answers, etc.).
• Feedback can be given, and students' questions can be answered immediately.	• Takes a great deal of flexibility to get groups coordinated to chat at a particular time, especially when multiple time zones are involved.
• Provides a mechanism to support just-in-time development.	• One-on-one discussions require student to log into course in order to chat.
• Meaningful interaction with students helps to produce two-way conversation, which is more engaging and memorable than asynchronous or total lecture classes.	• Technical requirements or bandwidth problems make chat problematic for some students.
• There is a democracy in an online chat, where everyone is thrown together in the chat room with no physical separation of the instructor and student.	• Entire class chats need tight moderation and structuring to be successful.
• The chat environment can be less intimidating than volunteering to talk in a traditional classroom, which leads the more reserved students to be more apt to participate.	• Students can be "bumped" during chat, causing some confusion with students entering and leaving the chat room several times during a conversation.
• Chat rooms enhance the social presence of instructors and students in the course, creating a greater sense of belonging for students.	• Chat can have limitations when learning is independent and self-paced, as the tool is designed to support group interactions.
• Students like participating in online chats that are meaningful.	**Instant Messaging**
• Students who participate in chats more often for classes usually get higher grades than those students who do not participate as often.	• Requires instructor to stay logged in during the day for accessibility.
• Chat can be used for conversations, questions and answers, or even lecturing.	• Requires installation of additional software for students and teacher.
• Chats can be recorded and the transcripts can be made available to the class or instructor for future review.	• IM transcripts have to be cut and pasted into course if teacher wants to show a historical record to class.
	• Not all students will use IM unless it is a requirement.
	• Younger students can log in excessively to chat about noncourse related topics, thereby monopolizing instructional time.

continued

Table 6.1. continued

Strengths	Weaknesses
Instant Messaging • All of the above. • Best used for one-on-one instantaneous contact, that is, homework questions, office hours, supporting completion of projects, and so forth. • Using IM, the teacher can set up chats for those involved, but not enrolled, in the online class, that is, parents of K-12 online students.	

requirements for chat, such as having a java browser enabled or turning off virus software, can impede on the success of the experience. We have also experienced many users getting bumped from chat, having to log back in, and read the transcript to catch up. This can be extremely frustrating.

Some of the weaknesses of IM to be considered are that it requires separate software outside of the LMS, and users might not understand how to access, download, and install the software, the instructor is required to be logged in at specific times which imposes on the flexibility of the online instructor, and we also know online teachers of K-12 students who report students excessively logging into IM to "shoot the breeze," thus consuming an inordinate amount of the instructor's time.

Understanding Chat:
Connection and In-Depth Understanding!

What is it about chat and instant messaging that helps create "connection" for students and teachers? What is connection? In Chapter I, we explored the ideas of engagement and social interaction as being necessary in the learning process. Through interactions, students are able to construct their own knowledge, develop schemas, and participate in their own personal meaning making. They are active participants in the learning process.

Suler (2004b) gives us another insight into the idea of connection. A reported benefit of using chat is the ability to promote democratic interaction through the lack of visual cues (such as facial gestures, dress, body, etc.) that might normally inhibit expression for some people (Palloff & Pratt, 1999). Suler looks at the psychological factors involved in removing visual cues and describes this phenomenon as the "online disinhibition effect" (p. 1). Disinhibition can have positive attributes (benign disinhibition), such as encouraging those who are shy to more fully engage in a class, or negative attributes (toxic disinhibition), where the student feels an anonymity level that makes it ok to conduct such behavior as flaming or spamming. He states:

The physical body and its five senses no longer play as crucial a role as in face-to-face relationships. What others know or don't know about me is not always clear. The feeling of a linear past, present, and future becomes more obscure as we move back and forth through synchronous and asynchronous communication. As a result, this altered state of consciousness in cyberspace tends to shift or destabilize self-boundary. The distinction between inner-me and outer-other is not as clear. The person shifts to what psychoanalytic theory calls "primary process thinking" in which boundaries between self and other representations become more diffuse, and thinking becomes more subjective and emotion-centered. Within the transitional space of online communication, the psyches of self and other feel like they might be overlapping. (p. 1)

Indeed, Rheingold (2000) notes the "ephemeral nature" of chat communications can sometimes lead to users becoming addicted, forming lifelong relationships, and even falling in love with people who they have never met. He also describes chat addiction recovery groups to support those who have lost control with the medium.

Beuschel, Gaiser, and Draheim (2003) discuss the importance of providing informal communication mechanisms to learners outside of the LMS. Informal learning, as compared to formal learning, is an essential ingredient in a successful learning experience. Informal learning speaks to the social processes we engage in as we continue our work, and through these informal processes (i.e., an e-mail to a peer, or a private talk with a teacher or peer during a video conference) students are able to build relationships to continue their work (Purcell-Robertson & Purcell, 2000). For informal exchange to work, the student must feel a sense of security, and therefore maintain ownership and control over the tool. Chat via IM, in particular, provides this ownership to students, and thus an effective tool for promoting informal learning

We would argue that the use of chat and instant messaging, in the context of an online course, encourages a benign disinhibition for most students, removing boundaries to expression of ideas that might exist in a regular classroom, and creating an overlap of self and other. This capability allows the student to experience themselves in a new way, possibly for the first time. When this experience happens in a structured format with instructor support, students are cognitively, socially, and emotionally stimulated. This positive experience can thus create a deeper connection with the course, the instructor, and other students in class.

Appreciating connection at this level also helps us to comprehend how in-depth understanding can be promoted in chat. While one might assume that chat's inherent nature to type in brief tidbits would lead to shallow discussions, there is evidence that chat can provide a vehicle for in-depth discussion on one idea over time, even more so than might be experienced in a regular class (Johnston, Anderson, & DeMeulle, 1998; Suler, 2004a). The nature of chat requires users to type, post, wait, and read before responding. This "lag time" in communication imposes a communication environment that can force students to stay focused longer on one topic than they might normally. This phenomenon is usually more prevalent in groups that have chatted on several occasions. Instructors can use this phenomenon to their benefit by requiring students to chat for a given length of time on specific questions—generated either by the teacher or the students themselves.

Power Tip: Why I Like Chat

Using chat in an online course is fairly easy, and I think it gives a lot of bang for the buck—educationally speaking. Some folks complain about the lack of available options when using LMS-based chat (Blackboard's chat tool, for example), but the majority of my students report having successful and meaningful chat experiences when we follow these rules:

- **Give chat a purpose:** This is especially true for first time chats. Provide a specific task to accomplish in chat, a time period, and list of the group participants. For example, I might assign four students to chat regarding one main point of interest from the weekly readings, each student gets at least 10 minutes of the chat time to discuss their main point, and I assign a facilitator to move the group along.

- **Attend the first session:** I always attend the first chat session my students have, even if it is a small group discussion. I sit back and allow another student with chat experience to facilitate, then I jump in when needed. With younger or less experienced chatters, you might want to facilitate and model the first session yourself.

- **Create small chat groups:** No doubt about it, unless you are doing a fully moderated chat, assign students in groups of three to five students, maximum. Everyone gets a chance to participate, the opinions are varied and interesting, and the smaller group size leaves everyone feeling more socially connected to others in class.

- **Have students record their chat:** This is helpful for any member who may have missed the chat, and it also provides ownership to the students involved in the chat. I appreciate chat transcripts; they are a form of evidence, or artifact, of the learning process, and sometimes students share references or URLs during chat that can be referenced again at a later date if a transcript exists.

Structuring Chats for Success

A successful chat requires thoughtful structuring. There are a plethora of options for structuring a chat, but structuring is definitely the key! An unstructured chat can have the reverse effect—of turning off students, just as an unstructured dialogue might do in a live classroom. From our own experience, we find that the most successful interactive chats involve approximately three to five participants. Larger groups can become more confusing with multiple participants often talking over one another. However, it should also be noted that the chat facilitator has the ability to allow some, all, or none of the chat participants to speak, thus making it possible to offer large group chats where the dialogue is heavily moderated, usually with questions and answers. It is also helpful to set guidelines prior to the chat—set the topic, designate a chat "leader" whose job is to ensure each participant has an opportunity to speak on the topic at hand, set a time limit (45 to 60 minutes is usually effective), and most of all, make the chat purposeful. Why are your students meeting in chat?

Below is a copy of the chat tips we provide to students when chatting in small groups for the first time:

Chat tips and hints

1. **Be sure to test** and become familiar with our chat software before your group session. Make sure your browser is java-enabled.

2. **To keep the dialogue process flowing** smoothly, I recommend typing short lines of text and then pressing "enter" as you go. This will allow us to follow along with each other as we write, rather than sitting and waiting "in the dark" for the other person to complete a thought.

3. **Use an ellipsis** (...) at the end of a sentence to indicate you have more to say. Use a period (.) if you are finished talking. This simple technique will help minimize some of the waiting and confusion that can occur when two or more of us attempt to "talk" at the same time.

4. **When others enter the room**, it is appropriate to welcome that person with a "hi." The same applies when we all leave by saying "goodbye." If your Internet connection is inadvertently broken during the session, please reenter the room quietly.

5. **Facilitator tips:** If two people are talking at once, choose one person to lead discussion, for example: "We have two conversations here. Jim, please continue with your thoughts. When we are finished, Amy please begin your topic." To facilitate chat room discussions, it is important to know when and how to start the chat, ask questions, give encouragements, change topics, summarize, and end a chat. Good planning is a must for leading successful chat sessions. Try using a word processor to write down the topics that might be covered, the questions that might be asked, and comments that might be made. During the chat, open the word processor window and the chat room window at the same time. This makes it possible to copy and paste the prewritten text into the chat room instead of spending a lot of time typing during the chat sessions.

6. **To use Blackboard chat** effectively, print off the directions located in the student manual. That page will provide you all the information you need to use all the tools in the virtual classroom.

Good luck!

Timing of chats. Consider the timing of when your students will chat. Do the first chat early in the semester, about the third week, once all the student add or drop changes are made. Keep in mind the school calendar, as well. Are there other events going on that week that might make it hard to schedule time—sporting events, comprehensive exams, and so forth. If possible, let the small groups schedule themselves by posting times earlier in the week when they can all meet. The group leaders can then compare times, select a time, and notify the group via e-mail.

Power Tip: Safe Chat for Kids and Teens

Rick Weinberg, a technology professional developer for BOCES in Pennsylvania, introduced me to Isafe.org. Isafe.org offers planning and a curriculum for teaching Internet safety, free of charge, for kids K-12. They also provide a chat room for kids under 18 that is monitored by the i-SAFE Safety Trained Awareness Team. What a great way to introduce kids to safe chatting.

---

continued

As more K-12 schools go online or integrate online components into live class-rooms, Internet safety will continue to be a critical issue that needs ongoing consideration. Cyber dating, cyber bullying, identify theft, pornography, pla-giarism, or meetings with online friends, wanted or not, are some issues being faced by today's kids. As educators, when we are proactive in our teaching to educate kids or adults how to most effectively use today's Internet technologies, while understanding how to deal with some of the problems mentioned above, we empower learners to become responsible and safe in their own learning process. Thanks for sharing, Rick.

Provide directions and facilitate. Assign a specific chat task and outcome; in the Weekly Assignment folder provide directions for each group member to come to class with at least one interesting point from the assigned readings that they wish to further discuss. Also provide facilitation tips for the group leader (each topic should get approximately 10 minute discussion time, groups meet about an hour, everyone should get an opportunity to talk), as well as general chat tips for all group members.

Let the group leader facilitate the chat, within guidelines. Turn over owner-ship and empower your students in their own learning. The instructor should attend each chat, acting as a supporting facilitator.

Finally, process the experience; once the chat is done, give students an op-portunity for reflection on the experience. Questions to be answered: What went well? Was the outcome achieved? What steps can the group take to make their next chat more successful? This can be done in a post on a discussion board or as notes in an online journal.

Using these simple steps, many students are introduced to successful chat for the first time in their online careers, and will continue to use the tool to collaborate with others in class on future assignments. You will be astounded how many of your students will say, "I feel so much more connected to ev-eryone in this group and to the class overall!"

Power Tip: Using a Chat Script

If you are presenting a chat that involves some portion of the discussion in a lecture format, or if you are presenting to a large audience, prepare a chat script to keep you focused through your session. See this example:

Chat Script: Integrating Online Assessment Tools
By Lisa Dawley

Hi. Thanks for joining us tonight. I am assuming you are here because you are interested in learning more about no cost, online assessment tools and techniques. Is that right?

This chat has a supporting slideshow if you would like to download it for your own purposes. The link is located on main chat page on the Center for Online Educators where you clicked into the chat room.

If you have a question or comment while I am speaking, will you please indicate so by raising your hand and wait for me to acknowledge you? That will keep us from talking over one another.

Okay, I am starting on the first slide, "Overview." What is important to iterate here is that online assessment serves the same purposes as it does in a traditional classrooms. What varies are the techniques and tools you might choose to use.

The netiquette of chat. Chatting is a unique language, in and of itself. It differs from normal written and conversational text. Emotions are often communicated through symbols known as "emoticons." For example:

:-)   smiling, agreeing
:-D   laughing
:O   shocked
:-(frowning, sad

Instant messaging programs also include graphic emoticons, often called smileys, which can be clicked and put into the sentence as the user types, for example: 😊 😕 😎

Acronyms such as *lol* (laughing out loud) and *brb* (be right back) are used extensively to speed up the typing process. Other sample acronyms include:

rofl - rolling on floor laughing

afk - away from keyboard

brt - be right there

pos - parent over shoulder

Sentences in chat are often typed incomplete, with punctuation and capitalization of letters being used at the typist's discretion, "r u coming tonight?" Many teens use a form of dialogue in chat known as "leetspeek" where numbers or letters are substituted for other letters, such as "3" for "e," resulting in words like "l33t" (leet), a vernacular form of the world "elite." Other conventions of leetspeek include putting "erz" at the end of words, and typing words phonetically, such as "rockzerz" (that rocks). Leetspeek developed in online gaming where immature players engaged in the verbal game of put-downs, such as "dood, i ownerz joo!" which translates to "Dude, I own you!" meaning the player considers himself/herself better than the other. These types of players are known by the term "haters." A teacher conducting a chat with teens would be wise to monitor leetspeek and develop firm rules about its use in chat. "Hating" is a practice that is never appropriate in an online learning environment as it destroys trust and promotes negativity.

These conventions can be a turn-off to many new chat users, leaving them to wonder what happened to quality in education. In reality, chat netiquette is an emerging form of dialogue that is unfamiliar to many users. An effective online teacher learns how and when to pay heed to chat netiquette, depending on the audience and goals of the class. See the resource section in this chapter for links to emoticons, chat acronyms, netiquette, and leetspeek.

Example Uses for Success

Learning Objective Outcome	Chat and IM Activities
Interactivity and connection	• Introduce your students to chat and the tools inside your chat room by having a special "Welcome to Our Class!" session where the course is overviewed and some initial questions and answers take place. • At the end of each chat, ask the students to share a final reflection on the chat. This can be any new learning, related to the topic or not, a new question they now have, or thoughts about the content in general. • Send out a welcome e-mail to your class with your instant messaging address, along with a link to directions on how to download the tool.
Knowledge: defines; describes; enumerates; identifies; labels; lists; matches; names; reads; records; reproduces; selects; states; views	• Play Jeopardy in chat. The instructor develops a set of questions related to the readings prior to the chat. As the instructor reads the question in chat, the first one to answer correctly wins. Each student must answer a minimum number of questions before the chat is over, and all students remain logged in until everyone has a chance to finish. • Assign students a question related to the topic that can be answered in multiple ways, such as, "What are the benefits of exercise?" Each student comes prepared to chat to share one benefit they discovered, along with a supporting URL.

continued

Comprehension: classifies; cites; converts; describes; discusses; estimates; explains; generalizes; gives examples; makes sense out of; paraphrases; restates (in own words); summarizes; traces; understands	• Invite a guest speaker to participate in a class chat. Allow the speaker to begin with a short lecture or overview of their topic. Have students prepare questions ahead of time that the guest speaker can then answer. Have a moderated discussion at the end. • In small groups, ask students to discuss the three main points of a reading. After each group member discusses a main point, a second group member is then required to restate or paraphrase the point using their own words. The first student then confirms if this paraphrasing captures their original intent.
Application: acts; administers; articulates; assesses; charts; collects; computes; constructs; contributes; controls; determines; develops; discovers; establishes; extends; implements; includes; informs; instructs; operationalizes; participates; predicts; prepares; preserves; produces; projects; provides; relates; reports; shows; solves; teaches; transfers; uses; utilizes	• Assign students roles in groups, or let them assign themselves. These roles can include coordinating the chat time, facilitating the chat, finding a guest speaker to participate, summarizing the chat and posting a response to the discussion forum. • Each member of a small group designs a Web page on the current topic. Group members meet in chat to discuss the various strengths and weaknesses of each page, and group members then make corrections accordingly. • Let students assume the role of guest speaker in chat. Invite students to become knowledgeable on an assigned topic, and invite them to be the current week guest speaker while you facilitate the chat. • If you teach adults, encourage your students to participate in topic related chats outside of class. For example, if you teach science teachers, have them attend a chat given by NASA experts. Invite them to share their experience with the class.

continued

Analysis: breaks down; correlates; diagrams; differentiates; discriminates; distinguishes; focuses; illustrates; infers; limits; outlines; points out; prioritizes; recognizes; separates; subdivides	• Provide students with readings or Web sites offering contradictory opinions on a topic. Students then meet in chat to first discuss the pros, then the cons, of each opinion. The group can then present their findings to the class in a slideshow or written report. • Teams of students meet in chat to outline the major topics of a group written report. After outlining the major topics, and page length, students then assign themselves a section to complete independently.
Synthesis: adapts; anticipates; categorizes; collaborates; combines; communicates; compares; compiles; composes; contrasts; creates; designs; devises; expresses; facilitates; formulates; generates; incorporates; individualizes; initiates; integrates; intervenes; models; modifies; negotiates; plans; progresses; rearranges; reconstructs; reinforces; reorganizes; revises; structures; substitutes; validates	• Assign pairs or groups of students to locate additional materials on the current week's topic. Each person shares their site in the browser while peers discuss value of the content. • Have students meet one-on-one in IM or chat with you to discuss their proposals for class projects. Proposals should be written and provided to the instructor prior to chat. Instructor feedback on the project design can be given step by step for the project. • Practice foreign language translation in chat. The instructor offers a sentence in the native language, and requires a student to translate the sentence into the foreign language.

continued

	• Have pairs of students meet in chat to provide peer feedback on one another's work. This is particularly helpful for work-in-progress. The chat should be structured so each student has time to share: (1) strengths of the work, (2) suggestions for improvement, (3) additional resources the student should consider.
	• In groups of four or five, ask students to evaluate the course. They discuss the strengths of the course, areas for improvement, and offer concrete suggestions for improvement. Appoint someone from the group to post a summary response to the discussion board.
Evaluation: appraises; compares and contrasts; concludes; criticizes; critiques; decides; defends; interprets; judges; justifies; reframes	• Discuss recent world events. Ask students to make connections between those world events and how they impact our daily lives. Have students make analogies between world events and the history of their own county. Ask students to both defend and critique world events.
	• Use chat to support action research. Assign students to work in pairs or small groups and meet on a weekly basis to make connections between theory and practice. How are theoretical concepts playing out in their daily work? What lessons have they learned? Have students analyze their chat transcripts for themes and write a summary paper.

Example Lesson Plan

Figure 6.3. Example lesson plan using chat

Weeks 4 & 5 Agenda: Effective use of Online Teaching Tools

Greetings and welcome to Weeks 4 & 5 of class. Last week you began to identify criteria for what counts as quality in an online course—quality instruction, design, assessment, and interaction. This module we move our focus from the big picture of comparing online courses and learning management systems to specifically examine the effective use of online learning tools such as chat, e-mail, discussion forums, and blogs, for example, and videoconferencing, in particular. *Just exactly what technology tools are online teachers using, and what are those tools' strengths and weaknesses?*

You will participate in a class chat inside Breeze to discuss features of specific online teaching tools. Additionally, you will begin work with your assigned partner to begin design on a tutorial or chat inside Breeze that will be made available to assist other educators to further their knowledge about online teaching. This activity provides you the ability to provide professional development to your peers, one of the ISTE Standards for Technology Leaders.

Objectives

1.   Identify learning objectives best achieved using various online teaching tools.

2.   Analyze strengths and weaknesses of online teaching tools.

3.   Continue community building by participating in a facilitated, small group chat.

4.   Plan for a Breeze professional development project with your assigned partner.

Readings

1.   **Chapter 5 & 12:** Ko & Rossen

2.   **Chapter 1:** Palloff & Pratt

3.   **One additional peer-reviewed research article of your choice** (see Activity #1)

---

continued

Resources

OTTER: Online Teaching Tools and Tips http://www.otter-project.com/ – great list of online teaching tools reviewed with comparison charts, links, and referenced readings

Educational Technology Journals
>   National Education Technology Plan
>   Technological Horizons in Education Journal
>   Journal of Education Online
>   American Journal of Distance Education
>   Learning & Leading with Technology
>   Contemporary Issues in Technology & Teacher Education
>   European Journal of Open & Distance Learning
>   Journal of Asynchronous Learning Networks
>   Journal of Distance Learning Administration
>   Journal of Online Teaching and Learning
>   Distance-Educator.com

Chat

How to Use Blackboard Communication Tools http://www.cwru.edu/net/csg/CI/virchat.html
Using Chat in the Classroom http://safety.ngfl.gov.uk/schools/document.php3?D=d38
Educational Chat Rooms http://www.siec.k12.in.us/~west/edu/chat.htm
Teachers.net: Special Education chat board http://teachers.net/mentors/special_education/
NASA chat http://education.jpl.nasa.gov/students/chat.html
ePals.com Classroom Exchange http://www.epals.com/chat/

Breeze

1.   Guidelines for Participating in Breeze http://edtech.boisestate.edu/ldawley/582/breeze_sessions.htm

2.   How to use the Breeze admin panel http://breeze.boisestate.edu:8080/p46235047/

3.   Breeze Resource Center, including tutorials on Breeze http://www.macromedia.com/resources/breeze/

continued

ACTIVITIES FOR WEEKS 4 & 5	DUE DATE

1. Build Community in a Facilitated Chat
This week's chat is worth 40 points.
We will meet in Breeze to participate in a live video chat. You should have your webcams set up and available for use at this session. Review our guidelines for participating in Breeze. Login at http://breeze.boisestate.edu:8080/virtualoffice
 	
  1. Choose *one* session for participation:
 	
    • Thursday, Feb. 9, 5:30 PM MT
 	
    • Saturday, Feb. 11, 11:00 AM MT
 	
    • Monday, Feb. 13, 6:00 PM MT
 	
  1. Expect a minimum of 60 minutes for chat. Groups may choose to go longer, if they desire.
 	
  2. Prepare for a small group chat. **Each group member** is responsible to bring **at least one** pertinent question/issue/point from the week's assigned reading to the chat discussion. **Each group member** has equal time for discussion on their question. During this session, we will also explore the Breeze environment to prepare you for your experience teaching in Breeze with your partner.
	Participate by Monday, Feb. 13; see available dates

3. Plan for a Breeze Professional Development Training with Your Partner **This activity is worth 100 points.** This activity is a first for our program at BSU. Congratulations for having the tenacity to work on the cutting-edge of online teaching. In this assignment, you will work with a partner over the period of the next six weeks to plan, coordinate, and host a video chat in Breeze as a way to provide professional development to other online teachers. ISTE Standards for Technology Leaders (the standards on which our program is accredited) require our students to not only learn about topics relevant for educational technologists, but to also provide professional development to other educators on those topics. This activity is one means to achieve that standard. These training sessions will be made publicly available here at the Center for Online Educators, and announcements will be sent out through our mailing list. Please see the guidelines for this activity. Enjoy!	Deadline: host partner Breeze chat by Tuesday, March 26 at the latest.

continued

Grading
Participation in chat this week is credit/noncredit. See guidelines for rubric on Partner Professional Development activity.

Wow! This is really powerful learning we are entering into over the next 6 week period. You will definitely emerge from this period more highly informed and experienced as an online educator. The work will take some coordination of times and activities, but I anticipate the outcome of the learning experience to be more than worth it. Enjoy this time getting to know another colleague in your own pursuit of professional development.

Resources

Acceptable Use Policies: http://techcorps.org/resources/internetsafety/primer.html#AUP

Chat Acronyms: http://www.sharpened.net/glossary/acronyms.php

Core Rules of Netiquette: http://www.albion.com/netiquette/corerules.html

Educational Chat Rooms: http://www.siec.k12.in.us/~west/edu/chat.htm

Emoticons for Communication: http://www.windweaver.com/emoticon.htm

ePals.com Classroom Exchange: http://www.epals.com/chat/

Facilitating Great Discussions: Online and Face-to-Face: http://my.simmons.edu/services/technology/ptrc/pdf/discussion_jobaid.pdf

Flexible Education: http://www.flinders.edu.au/flexed/resources/chathome.htm

How to Use Blackboard Communication Tools: http://www.cwru.edu/net/csg/CI/virchat.html

Leetspeek: A Parent's Primer to Computer Slang: http://www.microsoft.com/athome/security/children/kidtalk.mspx

MSN Messenger: http://messenger.msn.com/

NASA Quest: chat http://quest.arc.nasa.gov/about/index.html

Online Community Report: http://www.onlinecommunityreport.com

Online Community Toolkit: http://www.fullcirc.com/community/communitymanual.htm

Sample Chat Lesson Plan: http://www.riverwithin.com/week4assignment.htm

Teachers.net: Special Education chat board: http://teachers.net/mentors/special_education/

Typology of Virtual Communities: http://www.ascusc.org/jcmc/vol10/issue1/porter.html

Using Chat in Teaching: http://online.mq.edu.au/docs/chat.pdf

Using Chat in the Classroom: http://safety.ngfl.gov.uk/schools/document.php3?D=d38

Yahoo Chat: http://chat.yahoo.com/

References

Beuschel, W., Gaiser, B., & Draheim, S. (2003). Communication needs of online students. In A. Aggarwal (Ed.), *Web-based education: Learning from experience* (pp. 203-222). Hershey, PA: Idea Group Publishing.

Driscoll, M. (2002). *Web-based training: Creating e-learning experiences.* San Francisco: Jossey-Bass/Pfeiffer

Haefner, J. (2000). Opinion: The importance of being synchronous. *Academic Writing.* Retrieved June 29, 2006, from http://wac.colostate.edu/aw/teaching/haefner2000.htm

Johnston, J., Anderson, R. S., & DeMeulle, L. (1998). Prospects for collaborative self-study on the Internet. In. M. L. Hamilton (Ed.), *Reconceptualizing teaching practice: Self-study in teacher education* (pp. 208-223). London: Falmer Press.

Ko, S., & Rossen, S. (2004). *Teaching online: A practical guide.* Boston: Houghton Mifflin.

Palloff, R., & Pratt, K. (1999). *Building learning communities in cyberspace: Effective strategies for the online classroom.* Jossey-Bass.

Purcell-Robertson, R. M., & Purcell, D. F. (2000). Interactive distance learning. In L. Lau (Ed.), *Distance learning technologies: Issues, trends and opportunities* (pp. 16-21). Hershey, PA: Idea Group Publishing.

Rheingold, H. (2000). *The virtual community: Homesteading on the electronic frontier.* Retrieved June 29, 2006, from http://www.rheingold.com/vc/book/6.html

Suler, J. (2004a). *Psychological dynamics of online synchronous conversations in text-driven chat environments.* Retrieved June 29, 2006, from http://www.rider.edu/~suler/psycyber/texttalk.html

Suler, J. (2004b). *The psychology of cyberspace*. Retrieved June 29, 2006, from http://www.
rider.edu/~suler/psycyber/disinhibit.html

Chapter VII

Audio/Video Conferencing and Whiteboard

Video conferencing is a synchronous and interactive form of communication that occurs when two or more people engage in face-to-face audio and visual exchanges using cameras, microphones, monitors, and document software (Digital Bridges, 2006). The use of video through the Internet is becoming part of our daily lives. Rainey (2005) reports that over 16%, or 20 million, Americans have viewed a person or place using a webcam. The growth in the use of video has occurred for three reasons: a moderate webcam costs approximately $30-50, they are plugged in and played with the use a USB port, and the increasing access to broadband (46% of American homes now have broadband access [Rainey, 2006]) makes it easy to display and access images from webcams.

Moore and Kearsley (2005) note three main types of video conferencing:

1.   Small room conferences that were designed primarily for groups of no more than about 12 participants at any site.

2.   Classroom conferences use compressed video to enable large groups to see and be seen on classroom monitors.

3.   Desktop conferences use personal computers linked by computer video-conferencing software. (p. 85)

The first two types of conferencing have a history in distance learning and a documented effectiveness in both adult and K-12 education (Cavanaugh, 2001). For example, preservice teachers are observed while working in classrooms by university supervisors who view their work (Johnson, Maring, Doty, & Fickle, 2006). As broadband access and emerging forms of online education continues to increase, we are beginning to see more and more teachers utilizing desktop video conferencing, which becomes the focus of this chapter. However, many of the principles we discuss also apply to small room and classroom conferencing.

Video conferencing can occur using a variety of software and Internet-based tools, and depending on the particular tool, might integrate other features such as a whiteboard area, application sharing (showing your computer screen to another user), polling, file sharing, a graphing calculator, and text messaging. Typically, a host can record a video conference session, also making the software popular for recording tutorials that students can later access through a URL. Whiteboard areas are a common feature associated with video conferencing. Typically they contain interactive space where participants can simultaneously type text, solve math equations, pull up Web browsers, share applications, or load multimedia, such as a Powerpoint slideshow. Popular video conferencing software includes such products as Breeze, Elluminate, Netmeeting, and Polycom.

Note the speaker on camera is pictured in the upper left corner. A list of participants is below her, along with a text chat window for those who do not have microphones. Also included in this video conference is a file share "pod" in the lower right corner. This is where the speaker has uploaded documents that participants can click on and download to their computer. The whiteboard space in this particular conference has a slideshow loaded onto it.

Figure 7.1. An example of a Breeze video conference

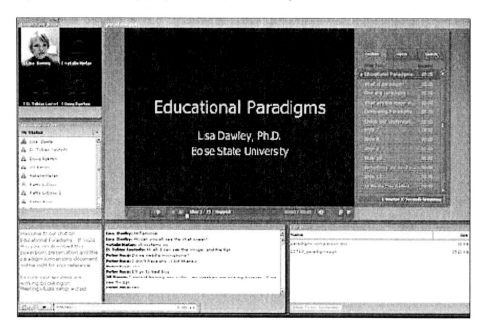

However, these types of video conferencing software are costly for the typical consumer. Individual users without access to video conferencing software are finding they can meet some of their needs through the expanded features now offered by many instant messaging programs, such as Yahoo Instant Messaging (IM), and MSN IM. These free IM tools allow the user to incorporate the use of webcams, conduct "phone calls," type in text, and share documents. However, they do not incorporate a whiteboard space. For the online teacher, these types of hybrid video conferencing options can be a great addition to add to the teacher's tool set.

In this chapter, we examine the strengths and weaknesses of video conferencing tools and whiteboards, explore the need for visual interactivity in online learning, and provide sample video conferencing and whiteboard activities aligned with learning objectives.

Table 7.1. Strengths and weaknesses of video conferencing and whiteboard areas

Strengths	Weaknesses
Video Conferencing	**Video Conferencing**
• Ability to see facial expressions of participants during conversation, allows for better interpretation of understanding through visual cues.	• Participants need initial training in how to effectively use and participate in video conferencing.
• Provides a sense of "connectedness" to instructor and other students in class through webcam images. The student becomes a real person, as opposed to just a voice or text posted on a discussion board.	• Requires purchase of a webcam, although many computers now come with a built-in cameras or one can be purchased for around $30.
• Users gain a more global view of the world by interacting with participants from various locations	• First-time use requires set-up of speakers and microphone, typically done using a wizard inside the program.
• Emerging new forms of pedagogy, such as cybermentoring, are possible due to video conferencing	• Users on low bandwidth may have issues with video or audio streaming, thus resulting in delayed audio feeds, jumpy video display, or being disconnected.
• Software is Web-based and easy to access.	• Host server requires ongoing maintenance of software and user accounts.
• Ability to poll students and collect polling data	• Mainstream software is still expensive to the average consumer.
• Ability to share copies of documents and multimedia	• Firewalls can prevent access to video conferences, an issue with some employers and schools.
• Ability to have conversations occur using video, voice, or text, all three happening in the same environment.	• Required meeting times can impose on adult distance learners' schedules, especially when accommodating various time zones.
• Main speaker can be talking while others can continue side comments or questions in the text chat, thus allowing for simultaneous conversations.	• Some software does not allow for simultaneous audio discussion. Users are required to "trade" the microphone.
• Breakout rooms can be added to a main session, allowing for pairs or small groups of users to have side conversations.	• May not allow time for reflection due to fast pacing of discussion
• Host can record a session, thus making the session available for playback to others via a URL.	• Students with hearing or visual disabilities may not be able to participate in video conferencing.
• Capabilities of the tool allow it to be used for a variety of purposes, including discussion sessions, guest lectures, virtual office hours, portfolio demonstration sessions, assessments by polling and questioning, demonstration of software, creating recorded tutorials, and more.	• Because research is newer in K-12 video conferencing, fewer pedagogical materials area available to teachers.
	• Students feel neglected and will disengage if a raised hand or comment in the chat box goes unnoticed or unacknowledged for a long period.

Strengths and Weaknesses

Table 7.1 illustrates the varied strengths and weaknesses of using video conferencing and whiteboards.

Strengths of video conferencing and whiteboard areas. Because virtual conferencing software provides several different tool sets and levels of functionality within one platform, its strengths are many. The most obvious strength is the use of video. Faces on videos communicate nonverbal facial cues that lead to effective interpretation of conversation—a raised eyebrow, a smile on a face, a shrug of the shoulder all communicates messages to the viewer. The speaker becomes a real person, not just a voice or text. This level of connection also assists in preventing online disinhibition, where the user might feel free to act in inappropriate ways due to the anonymity experienced in asynchronous learning environments (Suler, 2004). Regular participants in video conferences are able to gain a more global view of the world by interacting with others in various locations, sometimes around the world. The technology is also promoting emergent forms of pedagogy, such as cybermentoring, where preservice teachers are able to provide tutoring to students from remote locations (Johnson, Maring, Doty, & Fickle, 2006).

Most video conferencing software is Web-based, and easy to begin to use with a minimal amount of training. Software features often include the ability to have conversation occur in multiple forms (text, audio, and video), file sharing between users, ability to poll users during interaction, use of breakout rooms for small group discussion, ability to record the session and make it available in a URL, and include private or shared graphing calculators. The graphing calculator can be used to perform and illustrate such mathematical functions as add, subtract, multiply, divide, logarithm, sine, cosine, and so forth.

Webcams used in video conferencing can also come with options—avatars such as a shark, George Washington, or an alien, can be substituted for the viewer's face.

Because the avatars move according to the user's expressions, they often appear life-like. They promote humor and add visual interest in the class. For example, students studying the solar system might enjoy adopting alien avatars to fit the mood of the session. As generations continue to grow up in a world of video games, the overlap of features common to gaming environments, such as the choice of an avatar, are familiar and thus engaging to many users.

A unique feature of video conferencing is the ability to combine audio, video, and text simultaneously. If a speaker is on audio, others can watch and respond visually. They can also type comments in the text chat that add dimension to the current audio discussion. The main speaker can choose to include those comments in the discussion, or keep the conversation going in a particular direction.

With the use of breakout rooms, teachers can use collaborative and small group learning strategies. Video conferencing platforms are also used for pedagogical purposes such as discussion sessions, guest lectures, virtual office hours, portfolio demonstrations, assessments, and questioning sessions.

When sessions are a required as part of the curriculum or learning experience, such as for high school students progressing through a predefined curriculum, promoting live engagement in the course supports effective progress. Informal communication mechanisms made available in video conferencing also promote motivation for group work.

Figure 7.2. Example of a webcam avatar

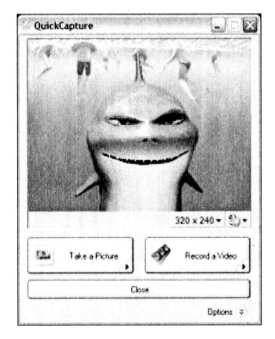

Depending on the specific software in use, the functionality of the whiteboard varies. Typically, users can brainstorm and write simultaneously in the whiteboard space, better promoting collaboration. On the whiteboard, users have tools that include text, shapes, a color palette, erase, and the ability to create multiple whiteboard screens.

Application sharing gives control to one user to share his/her desktop and anything opened on the desktop, such as software or a Web browser. This allows the teacher or student to share documents, view graphics, discuss Web sites, illustrate use of particular software, work on math problems, teach file management, or write collaboratively.

Users can typically load multimedia files, such as slideshows or flash presentations, to run during the discussion session. However, some platforms require the use of a small plug-in to convert the multimedia file prior to uploading.

Weaknesses of video conferencing and whiteboard areas. Although it is easy to begin using most video conferencing software, participants still require initial training and a couple of sessions to begin to operate effectively. Users must also gain experience working with technical contingencies (McFerrin & Furr, 2006). This learning curve for students may not be worth the effort in a class where an instructor may only offer a few video conferencing sessions. For the most effective participation, users must purchase a webcam if they do not have one built into their computer. First time use requires the user to go through a wizard to set up the speakers, microphone, and camera.

A real weakness of video conferencing at the time of this writing, is the limited access to broadband connection by a majority of Americans, over 60% (Rainey, 2006). Users on dial-up will find themselves frustrated with delayed audio feeds, jerky video, or getting disconnected multiple times in one session. However, one might assume that a majority of online learners would be more inclined to invest in broadband access to support their educational experience. Firewalls an also prevent efficient access to video conferencing rooms, an issue with some employers and schools districts that needs to be addressed.

Because mainstream software is expensive to the individual consumer, employers bring many new users onto video conferencing. The host is then responsible for ongoing maintenance of the server, software, and user accounts.

As far as meeting learner's needs, required meeting times impose problems on adults who are overcommitted with multiple responsibilities, especially when they come from a variety of time zones. Trying to find a common time to meet with a student who lives in Saudi Arabia and works full-time is quite a challenge! Being required to participate in an extended video conference session can be physically tiring or boring, and has then potential to create disengagement and frustration. Keep sessions to less than an hour and frequently change activities (McFerrin & Furr, 2006). Special needs students with hearing or visual disabilities may not be able to participate in a video conference unless special accommodations are made. In addition, for students who need time for reflection before giving an answer, the fast pace of synchronous discussion may not allow for reflective thinking and practice. If these are your goals, you might be best suited to use an asynchronous communication tool, such as a blog or discussion board (Conrad & Donaldson, 2004).

Users might not be comfortable with the inability to speak without raising their hand, or using the microphone, as some video conferencing platforms require due to inability to speak simultaneously. Finally, for K-12 teachers interested in using video conferencing, few pedagogical materials are yet to exist for assistance to those educators, as the use of video conferencing with that age range is researched and developed less (Cavanaugh, 2001).

Regarding the whiteboard, the text sharing area does not hold large amounts of text on a single page. Multiple pages might be needed, with users having to flip back and forth between pages to read their notes. The text tools are somewhat primitive compared to what is normally used in a word processing program, and users are unable to edit text easily. Participants are also unable to write or mark on documents pulled up in the whiteboard area by another user.

Although the multimedia capabilities of the whiteboard intrigue many users, they are not without their problems. Often, multimedia has to go through a conversion process using a plug-in before uploading to the whiteboard area. Moreover, after conversion, some transitions and special effects will not display correctly in the whiteboard area.

Only one user at a time can "share" applications or multimedia in the whiteboard, thus not allowing for comparison between users. For the user who does have the share permission, it is difficult to share more than one window because users have to close one window before opening another.

Understanding Audio/Video Conferencing: Interactive Auditory and Visual Learning!

Our university semester has just ended, and I received this e-mail from one of my students, an instructor at an out-of-state university. To me, this communication sums up the power of video conferencing.

I loved participating in the Breeze sessions. It helped me feel that I knew you and it gave a more personal touch. I felt more connected with you in these courses than I have with any other instructor in an online course. It must be the Breeze sessions where we can see each other, hear each other and interact on a more personal manner. The phone calls, office visits, and e-mails also helped. Your presence was strong and real. I still wish I could have taken an on-ground course from you, yet I am left satisfied for the first time with an online course. I hope to take some of what I have learned from you and incorporate in my own teaching.

One complaint shared by many students participating in online courses is a lack of feeling connected to other students or the instructor, due to the inability to see the faces or hear the voices of other individuals. Missing visual cues can lead to misunderstandings or misinterpretations of text-based comments in an online class. Using webcams and video conferencing, learners and teachers have immediate visual feedback, which, in turn, creates productive dialogue (Yermish, 2000).

Increased access to video, and its potential to support both formal and informal communication through video conferencing, deserves our highest attention. Beuschel, Gaiser, and Draheim (2003) distinguishes formal communication from informal communication as being planned and intentional, and the latter as being opportunistic and spontaneous. Both of these forms of communication can occur simultaneously through a planned video conference. For example, a teacher can schedule a video conference session with the students to discuss a particular agenda (formal communication). The instructor can structure the session to allow informal communication to occur simultaneously through text chat, private chat, breakout rooms, or through open-ended questions that the teacher may pose.

Informal communication in the learning process has been shown to be pivotal in not only meeting social needs, but it also creates collective motivation for group and team project assignments (Beuschel, Gaiser, & Draheim, 2003), thus supporting learning as a social process. An online course that solely uses asynchronous communication methods is severely lacking in the types of informal communication it offers its students. When conversation lingers over many days or weeks, it becomes difficult to create a team. It is no wonder then, that many students in these types of courses often dread group assignments.

Let us look at these principles in practice by comparing a course that uses only asynchronous methods vs. one that also incorporates video conferencing. Can you identify the opportunities for formal and informal communication?

In this comparison, we see that both courses have the same learning objective and outcome. However, the first course focuses on formal learning, thus not fully supporting group work. Because the second course also integrates video conferencing, the potential tool set will expand, and the resulting activities that allow students to apply and synthesize is much greater. This additional tool set better facilitates informal communication, thus supporting the overall motivation of the group to complete the project.

Taking advantage of synchronous, informal communication. It does not make a lot of sense to use the video conferencing environment to present a lecture, a task well handled in an asynchronous environment with a slideshow. How does a teacher capitalize on the synchronous abilities to promote interactivity, as well as formal and informal communication? Teachers new to video conferencing tend to create slideshows that they upload in the whiteboard space, and then use those slideshows to guide discussion. This strategy can either work or fail, depending on how the teacher structures the slideshow and the subsequent dialogue opportunities. Consider these two examples below:

Example A: *Teacher puts main points on slideshow, and begins lecture, rotating through slides.*

Teacher: Thank you for joining us today. Our topic is on how to use active listening in the online classroom. Active listening is defined as . . . To prepare yourself for active listening, you should . . . When the speaker is done talking, you should . . . Final steps include . . . Are there any questions?

Table 7.2. A comparison of an asynchronous only vs. asynchronous plus video conferencing lesson

Type of Online Course	Learning Outcome Objective and Verb	Online Tools	Activities
Asynchronous	Groups will **apply** and **synthesize** research findings to create their own multimedia presentation on best practices in online teaching.	<ul><li>Discussion boards</li><li>E-mail</li></ul>	Analyze research findings and report on discussion board. Communicate through e-mail with group to establish work schedule and duties. Post work in progress to discussion board.
Asynchronous + Video Conferencing	Groups will **apply** and **synthesize** research findings to create their own multimedia presentation on best practices in online teaching.	<ul><li>Discussion boards</li><li>E-mail</li><li>Audio/video chat</li><li>Whiteboard</li><li>Application sharing</li><li>Breakout rooms</li></ul>	Analyze research and discuss in video conferencing. Use application sharing to show potential examples of multimedia that could be included in the discussion. Teacher has groups meet in breakout rooms to discuss timelines and duties. Post work in-progress to the discussion board, and notify group members through e-mail. Schedule chat sessions as needed by the group to bring project to completion.

Example B: *Teacher puts a few main points in the slideshow, but also includes activities on some of the slides, and opportunities for interaction and microphone sharing.*

Teacher: Thank you for joining us today. How is everyone?

Students: (each take a turn saying hello)

Teacher: Our topic today is how to effectively use active listening. We'll go over a few key points, and then you'll have an opportunity to practice active listening with each other today. If you have prior training in active listening, can you show me a smiley face?

Students: (click or type a smiley face, as appropriate).

Teacher: OK, I can see this is new to some of you, and a refresher activity for others. Active listening is defined as….To prepare yourself for active listening, you should…..When the speaker is done talking, you should….. Now, let's try it out. I'm going to show you a script of an upset parent. I'd like someone to raise their hand to volunteer to read the script.

Student A: (raises their hand using electronic "hand")

Teacher: Great, thank you! Who will volunteer to be the active listener?

Student B: (volunteers)

Teacher: Ok, student A will read the script. When she is done, student B will respond using the active listening techniques you see on the slide. Just go for it, don't think too much about it.

Student A & B: (take turns reading script and with active listening)

Teacher: Great! Thank you for going first. I'd like each of you to share your reaction to the activity, and then the rest of the class will give feedback on the experience.

Students: (take turns processing the experience of active listening)

Teacher: Now, I'm going to pair you up and send you into breakout rooms to practice further. Each person should take a turn reading the script, while the other is the active listener. When both parties have had a chance to read and respond, signal me that you're ready to return to the main classroom.

And so on...

Another way to take advantage of video conferencing to promote informal communication is to allow students to type in the text window while you are speaking, or to send private messages to one another during a session. In this way, the discussion has the potential to become multi-layered, and the instructor can choose to address particular comments or not. Overtly address these skills after one or two introductory video conferencing sessions. Make students aware that the instructor has the ability to view all messages, including private messages, and your expectation is that rules of netiquette apply during private messaging, as well.

Finally, as you gain comfort with your software, try using breakout sessions. In a live classroom, a teacher might typically conduct a lesson, and then break students into pairs or small groups for discussion or projects. Breakout rooms serve the same purpose in an online environment. Use the breakout room to provide students the opportunity for increased discussion among themselves. We know one creative online high school teacher who used the breakout room to isolate a student who was behaving inappropriately during a live session. He had to ask for permission to return to the main session. Although it is not recommended to associate breakout rooms as a space for punishment, teachers sometimes have to think on their feet, especially when dealing with younger learners!

Learning to take full advantage of the interactive capabilities of video conferencing software takes time. After a full year of use, and over 60 video conferencing sessions this last year, the author is still learning new techniques everyday. Focus your attention on creating activities that promote interaction and allow for informal communication.

> *Power Tip: Whiteboards Integrate External Resources and Multimedia to Save Time*
>
> One approach we appreciate in materials design for conferencing or lessons is to integrate existing external resources and appropriate multimedia. Just as a regular teacher plans a class lesson where that teacher might assign readings from a text, bring handouts to class, show videos on certain topics, and so forth, the online teacher can use the same approach. Again, a successful online teacher focuses on designing and facilitating interactive and engaging learning experiences to achieve completion of course objectives. You can do that effectively by integrating an existing multitude of resources already on the Web into your lessons. This is not cheating. This is an example of what it means to be a life-long learner who searches for relevant information on a topic to achieve goals. Spend your limited time on developing connections with your students, instead of reinventing content that possibly already exists on the Web. Focus your energies on the experience of facilitating a great video conference ... create an experience where the student has an emotional response to the interaction.

Structuring Video Conferencing and Whiteboards for Success

Desktop video conferencing to groups of students at multiple locations is still in its infancy (Beuschel, Gaiser, & Draheim, 2003; Moore & Kearsley, 2005). However, as more schools, both in K-12 and higher education, adopt video conferencing software, this approach will become more of the norm. For example, K-12 Virtual Academies has virtual high schools around the country that have teachers interacting synchronously with all their students through Elluminate.

Getting started. If you are new to video conferencing, there are a couple of easy ways to get started.

1. Purchase a webcam.

2. If your school has not purchased video conferencing software, use one of the free IM software (such as Yahoo or MSN IM) that has video conferencing capabilities.

3. If you do have video conferencing software, spend time learning to use it before you schedule a live conference. Use the software's recording feature to create a tutorial, or an introduction to a weekly lesson, that you can then post online. Whenever you record in video conferencing, a URL is generated for the recording—no need to upload any files to a server! You can literally create a tutorial or introduction to a weekly assignment in the time it takes you to speak into the camera!

Getting your students started. Allocate time to train participants in video conferencing prior to sessions, in order to avoid using session time to deal with technical or new user issues (Johnson & Gardner, 2004). Once your familiarity and comfort level with the tool has increased, schedule an open discussion session with your students, perhaps virtual office hours, or a question/answer session—something that does not require a lot of preparation or coordination on your part. See Figure 7.3.

Figure 7.3. Example video conference assignment

2. Build Community in a Facilitated Chat
This week's chat is worth 40 points.
We will meet in Breeze to participate in a live video chat. You should have your webcams set up and available for use at this session. Review our guidelines for participating in Breeze. Login at http://breeze.boisestate.edu:8080/virtualoffice

1. Choose one session for participation:

- Thursday, Feb. 9, 5:30 PM MT
- Saturday, Feb. 11, 11:00 AM MT
- Monday, Feb. 13, 6:00 PM MT

2. Expect a minimum of 60 minutes for chat. Groups may choose to go longer, if they desire.

3. Prepare for a small group chat. **Each group member** is responsible to bring **at least one** pertinent question/issue/point from the week's assigned reading to the chat discussion. **Each group member** has equal time for discussion on their question. During this session, we will also explore the Breeze environment to prepare you for your experience teaching in Breeze with your partner.

The main goal of the first session is to introduce your students to video conferencing and to help them understand the functionality of the tool itself.

Prepare your students for conference by providing them the following information at least a week in advance, if possible:

1. A URL and time to log on. Be sure to address various time zones if that is relevant for your students. If you have students around the globe, provide a time zone converter URL.

2. A prerecorded tutorial that explains the tools inside the conferencing software (camera, whiteboard, text chat features, for example).

3. Directions on how to set up their camera, audio, and speaker settings.

4. Rules for netiquette during video conferencing (see Chapter VI for examples).

Figure 7.4. Example guidelines to set up a video conferencing session

---

EDTECH 582: Online Teaching

Guidelines for Using Breeze Video Conferencing

Time Zone Converter: http://www.timeanddate.com/worldclock/converter.html

Before the Meeting:
Here is some online documentation that you might wish to browse before the meeting:
http://livedocs.macromedia.com/breeze/5b/participants/wwhelp/wwhimpl/js.html/wwhelp.htm

To Join the Meeting:
To join the meeting click the following link:
http://breeze.boisestate.edu:8080/virtualoffice

Please login prior to our scheduled session to set-up audio and test for connection issues!

Troubleshooting & Login Issues
Breeze compatibility test:
http://www.macromedia.com/software/breeze/productinfo/meeting/meeting_intro.html
Unable to login to meeting: http://www.macromedia.com/cfusion/knowledgebase/index.cfm?id=tn_19546
Additional troubleshooting FAQs:
http://www.macromedia.com/cfusion/knowledgebase/index.cfm?id=tn_18815

Login and Audio Setup Information: We have upgraded to Breeze 5 so the login involves a two step process. First, Click the button to enter as a guest. Then, when the new screen appears type your name into the box and click enter.

Once students login to their first session, take the time to go through the main navigation bar, point out the functionality of some basic tools, and then begin a basic question/answer session. Give your students plenty of opportunities to talk to help overcome shyness they will initially feel. Ask open-ended questions that give them time to elaborate. Record this session, and e-mail the URL to your students after it is completed. Although they may or may not need this recording for any purpose, having the recording helps students understand what level of information will be made available to them after subsequent video conferencing sessions.

Practical tips on using video conferencing and whiteboards. Here we share lessons learned when it comes to working with video conferencing and whiteboards:

• E-mail participants the day before your scheduled session, even if you have already included this information in an agenda or lesson plan. Include the URL for the meeting, the time, and the topic.

• Problems will occur during conferencing. Participants will get dropped and have to reenter the room, you may forget to turn on the microphone

Figure 7.5. An introductory session to Breeze

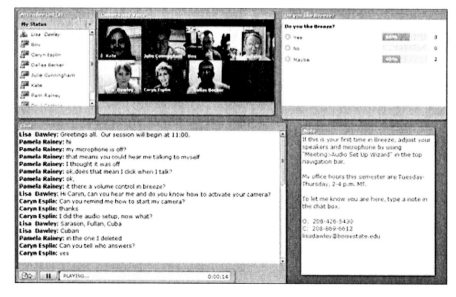

and find yourself talking to thin air, multimedia in the whiteboard area may not function as you had anticipated (check it beforehand, if possible). Just accept these problems, trouble shoot as quickly as possible if required, and move on.

- Become aware of your physical presence on camera. Bright clothing helps you stand out visually, avoid light colors. Women may find they look better on camera with heavier makeup than normal. Look straight at the camera as much as possible while you participate. This appears to users as if you are looking directly at them. Play with lighting, a light directly in front of you helps improve visibility. Be aware of what is in the background behind you for the best professional presentation.

- Check your microphone level at the beginning of each session. Ask participants if your volume is ok.

- Avoid distractions. Close doors, turn off cell phones, and attend to children, if necessary.

- Learn to control your speech and pacing. Watch recordings of yourself to learn if you pause a lot, or say "umm" or "ok" throughout your dialogue. Know what you want to say ahead of time. Practice, but keep the pacing quick when presenting information. What seems quick to the speaker often appears slow and boring to the recipients. Go through your key points quickly and efficiently. Keep slides moving in slideshows to promote visual interest.

- Incorporate graphics and other multimedia that visually support main ideas when developing materials for presentation in the whiteboard area. Keep graphics audience appropriate; use cartoons for the kids, but consider using photos with adults. Play with font style and color, use sans serif font like Arial for large chunks of text becaue this improves readability online. Use serif fonts, like Times New Roman, for titles.

- If students live in various time zones, allow them to schedule their own meeting times when working on group projects.

- Consider offering options for video conferencing, especially with adult learners who may have other time commitments. For example, offer students three sessions and require attendance at one. Also, offer optional sessions for those who want or need extra support. Send recorded sessions to students who were unable to attend.

- When using the polling feature, be sure to broadcast results to participants so they understand where they stand compared to others in the class.

- If a student violates rules of netiquette during a video conference, remove them from the session and deal with it appropriately at another time. Apologize to the class for the inappropriate interruption and move on. This indicates to all students that you have a zero tolerance policy for rude behavior online.

- If your software offers file sharing, use it the same way you would in a live session to offer handouts to the participants. If you are using a slideshow as part of your presentation, you might also want to provide that through file sharing so they can download it to their own computer.

Example Uses for Success

Learning Objective Outcome	Video Conferencing Activities
Interactivity and connection	<ul><li>Invite a special guest to participate on webcam with your class. Have the class prepare interview questions for the guest.</li><li>Start a social club that supports learning, such as a Spanish Club or Reading Club. These sessions can be hosted weekly or monthly, with an assigned topic or book for open discussion.</li><li>Host your first live session as an "Icebreaker." After covering some of the basics of how your video conferencing program operates, ask students to introduce themselves one-by-one. Follow-up with open ended questions, such as, "What are you hoping to get out of the course?" "Why did you enroll in the class?" "What do you think of synchronous learning?"</li><li>During a busy week, when student projects and papers are due, and tension is high, offer an optional support session one evening.</li></ul>

continued

Knowledge: defines; describes; enumerates; identifies; labels; lists; matches; names; reads; records; reproduces; selects; states; views	• Conduct a new student orientation at the beginning of a program or school year. Use the time to introduce students to program requirements. • Use the polling feature to have students identify main points from a required reading. • Create a tutorial: record yourself providing basic information in a content area, or modeling the use of a piece of software or a Web site, and share that recording with students. • Foreign language teachers can pull up vocabulary lists in the whiteboard area. One student can read a word aloud while another has to define it.
Comprehension: classifies; cites; converts; describes; discusses; estimates; explains; generalizes; gives examples; makes sense out of; paraphrases; summarizes; traces; understands	• Offer virtual office hours where students can login to meet with you to discuss assignment or projects in-progress. • Have students come to the session with one topic from the main reading that they would like to discuss further. Have them lead the discussion. • If a student requires feedback on a project/problem, record a session of yourself offering feedback and additional resources, if necessary.
Application: acts; administers; articulates; assesses; charts; collects; computes; constructs; contributes; controls; determines; develops; discovers; establishes; extends; implements; includes; informs; instructs; operationalizes; participates; predicts; prepares; preserves; produces; projects; provides; relates; reports; shows; solves; teaches; transfers; uses; utilizes.	• Some video conferencing software, such as Elluminate, provides users with both a private and shared graphing calculator. The graphing calculator can be used to perform and illustrate such mathematical functions add, subtract, multiply, divide, logarithm, sine, cosine, and so forth. • Have users participate in cybermentoring. For example, preservice teachers can tutor students in K-12 classrooms while under the supervision of the university supervisor. Each participant can be in a separate location, thus making it possible for the supervisor to assist pre-service teachers. • Invite students to serve as a teaching assistant for a designated period of time. They can be responsible for developing the topics or questions for a discussion session, can write up a summary of the session, and can facilitate the actual discussion itself.

continued

Analysis: breaks down; correlates; diagrams; differentiates; discriminates; distinguishes; focuses; illustrates; infers; limits; outlines; points out; prioritizes; recognizes; separates; subdivides	• Share Excel charts and diagrams in the whiteboard area. Have students break into pairs to interpret data. Pairs return to the main room and share their finding with others. • Share a newspaper clipping in the whiteboard area. Have students analyze the clipping to determine whose needs are being served by the news item, as well as whose needs might not be served. • Use application sharing to model how to write a research paper. Outline a paper in Word, and then begin writing the paper with your students' input.
Synthesis: adapts; anticipates; categorizes; collaborates; combines; communicates; compares; compiles; composes; contrasts; creates; designs; devises; expresses; facilitates; formulates; generates; incorporates; individualizes; initiates; integrates; intervenes; models; modifies; negotiates; plans; progresses; rearranges; reconstructs; reinforces; reorganizes; revises; structures; substitutes; validates.	• Create breakout rooms for students to do collaborative writing projects. For example, assign a topic of study with four questions. Each pair of students can have two questions to research. The pair can meet in the breakout room, put their questions into one document, and begin editing their combined work. • Have students create their own recorded tutorials in the video conferencing environment. For example, in my online teaching course, students created tutorials on how to use wikis and blogs. These tutorials can be shared with other professionals in their field, with the community, or with peers. This approach empowers the learner to teach others what they have learned. • If teaching a foreign language, use the breakout rooms to give students opportunities to practice speaking to each other.

continued

Evaluation: appraises; compares & contrasts; concludes; criticizes; critiques; decides; defends; interprets; judges; justifies; reframes	• Have students use application sharing to conduct portfolio presentations to the instructor and peers at the end of a class. At the end of the whole class presentation, meet with the student individually and let them evaluate their overall performance on the portfolio and presentation using a rubric.
	• Ask math students to explain the way each one of them solved a math problem in their heads. Write each procedure on the whiteboard, then compare and contrast the different approaches.
	• At the end of any discussion, bring closure to the session by "processing" the session. Give each student the opportunity to reflect on something they take away from the session—a new learning, a new question, or thought. Say, "Let's bring closure to our class by reflecting on something new you learned tonight. We will start at the top of the list (participant list) and go down one by one. Linda, would you like to start?" You can also offer the option to pass if the student chooses not to speak.

Example Lesson Plan

Figure 7.6. Example lesson plan using video conferencing

Weeks 4 & 5 Agenda: Effective Use of Online Teaching Tools

Greetings and welcome to Weeks 4 & 5 of class. Last week you began to identify criteria for what counts as quality in an online course – quality instruction, design, assessment, and interaction. This module we move our focus from the big picture of comparing online courses and learning management systems to specifically examine the effective use of online learning tools such as chat, e-mail, discussion forums, blogs, and video conferencing in particular. *Just exactly what technology tools are online teachers using, and what are those tools' strengths and weaknesses?*

You will participate in a class chat inside Breeze to discuss features of specific online teaching tools. Additionally, you will begin work with your assigned partner to begin design on a tutorial or chat inside Breeze that will be made available to assist other educators to further their knowledge about online teaching. This activity provides you the ability to provide professional development to your peers, one of the ISTE Standards for Technology Leaders.

Objectives

1. Identify learning objectives best achieved using various online teaching tools.
2. Analyze strengths and weaknesses of online teaching tools.
3. Continue community building by participating in a facilitated, small group chat.
4. Plan for a Breeze professional development project with your assigned partner.

Readings

1. **Chapter 5 & 12:** Ko & Rossen
2. **Chapter 1:** Palloff & Pratt
3. **One additional peer-reviewed research article of your choice** (see Activity #1)

---

continued

Resources

OTTER: Online Teaching Tools and Tips http://www.otter-project.com/ – great list of online teaching tools reviewed with comparison charts, links, and referenced readings

Educational Technology Journals

       National Education Technology Plan
       Technological Horizons in Education Journal
       Journal of Education Online
       American Journal of Distance Education
       Learning & Leading with Technology
       Contemporary Issues in Technology & Teacher Education
       European Journal of Open & Distance Learning
       Journal of Asynchronous Learning Networks
       Journal of Distance Learning Administration
       Journal of Online Teaching and Learning
       Distance-Educator.com

Chat

How to Use Blackboard Communication Tools http://www.cwru.edu/net/csg/CI/virchat.html
Using Chat in the Classroom http://safety.ngfl.gov.uk/schools/document.php3?D=d38
Educational Chat Rooms http://www.siec.k12.in.us/~west/edu/chat.htm
Teachers.net: Special Education chat board http://teachers.net/mentors/special_education/
NASA chat http://education.jpl.nasa.gov/students/chat.html
ePals.com Classroom Exchange http://www.epals.com/chat/

Breeze

1. Guidelines for Participating in Breeze http://edtech.boisestate.edu/ldawley/582/breeze_sessions.htm

2. How to use the Breeze admin panel http://breeze.boisestate.edu:8080/p46235047/

3. Breeze Resource Center, including tutorials on Breeze http://www.macromedia.com/resources/breeze/

continued

ACTIVITIES FOR WEEKS 4 & 5	DUE DATE

1. Build Community in a Facilitated Chat
This week's chat is worth 40 points.
We will meet in Breeze to participate in a live video chat. You should have your webcams set up and available for use at this session. Review our <u>guidelines</u> for participating in Breeze. Login at <u>http://breeze.boisestate.edu:8080/virtualoffice</u>
 	
  1. Choose *one* session for participation:
 	
   • Thursday, Feb. 9, 5:30 PM MT
 	
   • Saturday, Feb. 11, 11:00 AM MT
 	
   • Monday, Feb. 13, 6:00 PM MT
 	
  2. Expect a minimum of 60 minutes for chat. Groups may choose to go longer, if they desire.
 	
  3. Prepare for a small group chat. **Each group member** is responsible to bring **at least one** pertinent question/issue/point from the week's assigned reading to the chat discussion. **Each group member** has equal time for discussion on their question. During this session, we will also explore the Breeze environment to prepare you for your experience teaching in Breeze with your partner.
	Participate by Monday, Feb. 13; see available dates

2. Plan for a Breeze Professional Development Training with Your Partner **This activity is worth 100 points.** This activity is a first for our program at BSU. Congratulations for having the tenacity to work on the cutting-edge of online teaching. In this assignment, you will work with a partner over the period of the next six weeks to plan, coordinate, and host a video chat in Breeze as a way to provide professional development to other online teachers. <u>ISTE Standards for Technology Leaders</u> (the standards on which our program is accredited) require our students to not only learn about topics relevant for educational technologists, but to also provide professional development to other educators on those topics. This activity is one means to achieve that standard. These training sessions will be made publicly available here at the <u>Center for Online Educators</u>, and announcements will be sent out through our mailing list. Please see the <u>guidelines</u> for this activity. Enjoy!	Deadline: host partner Breeze chat by Tuesday, March 26 at the latest.

continued

> **Grading**
> Participation in chat this week is credit/noncredit. See guidelines for rubric on Partner Professional Development activity.

Wow! This is really powerful learning we are entering into over the next 6 week period. You will definitely emerge from this period more highly informed and experienced as an online educator. The work will take some coordination of times and activities, but I anticipate the outcome of the learning experience to be more than worth it. Enjoy this time getting to know another colleague in your own pursuit of professional development.

Resources

Teaching through Technology: Video Conferencing http://www.ag.ndsu.nodak.edu/ag-comm/videoconf/videoconferencing.html

Examples of Recorded Video Chats:

Expert Chat: http://breeze.boisestate.edu:8080/p27012193/

Tutorial: http://breeze.boisestate.edu:8080/p46248383/; http://breeze.boisestate.edu:8080/p46235047/

Video Intro to Online Lesson: http://breeze.boisestate.edu:8080 p22592683/

Student Portfolio Presentation of ID project: http://breeze.boisestate.edu:8080/p71552846/

Informational Session (lecture format): http://breeze.boisestate.edu:8080/p91889612/

References

Beuschel, W., Gaiser, B., & Draheim, S. (2003). Communication needs of online students. In A. Aggarwal (Ed.), *Web-based education: Learning from experience* (pp. 203-222). Hershey, PA: Idea Group Publishing.

Cavanaugh, C. S. (2001). The effectiveness of interactive distance education technologies in K-12 learning: A meta-analysis. *International Journal of Educational Telecommunications, 7*(1), 73-88.

Conrad, R., & Donaldson, J. A. (2004). *Engaging the online learner: Activities and resources for creative instruction.* San Francisco: Jossey-Bass.

Digital Bridges. (2006). Welcome to K-12 video conferencing. Retrieved July 5, 2006, from http://www.netc.org/digitalbridges/vc/

Johnson, T., & Gardner, S. (2004, April). *Learning technology implementation: Cyber-mentoring.* Poster Session at the Annual Meeting of the American Educational Research Association, San Diego, California.

Johnson, T. E., Maring, G. H., Doty, J. H., & Fickle, M. (2006). Cybermentoring: Evolving high-end video conferencing practices to support preservice teacher training. *Journal of Interactive Online Learning, 5*(1), 59-74.

McFerrin, K., & Furr, P. (2006). *Learning in online and desktop video conferencing courses: Are some students plugged in and tuned out?* Paper Presented at the Annual Meeting of the Society for Information Technology & Teacher Education. Retrieved July 5, 2006, from http://www.aace.org/conf/site/pt3/paper_3008_148.pdf

Moore, M., & Kearsley, G. (2005). *Distance education: A systems view.* Belmont, CA: Thomson Wadsworth.

Rainey, L. (2005). Use of webcams. Retrieved July 5, 2006, from http://www.pewinternet.org/pdfs/PIP_webcam_use.pdf

Rainey, L. (2006). How the internet is changing consumer behavior and expectations. Retrieved July 5, 2006 from http://www.pewinternet.org/ppt/2006%20-%205.9.06%20SOCAP.pdf

Suler, J. (2004). The online disinhibition effect. *CyberPsychology and Behavior, 7*, 321-326.

Yermish, I. (2000). A case for case studies via video conferencing. In L. Lau (Ed.), *Distance learning technologies: Issues, trends and opportunities* (pp. 208-217). Hershey, PA: Idea Group Publishing.

Chapter VIII

Assessment and Survey Tools

As all educators know, assessment is a critical component of the teaching and learning cycle. In general, assessments for online classes are established immediately after desired learning goals are defined, and they offer opportunities to evaluate learners the same way they are evaluated in a live classroom (Conrad & Donaldson, 2004). What varies between an online classroom and live classroom are the types of *assessment tools* and *techniques* available to the online teacher. What tools are available to the online teacher to accomplish assessment goals? Can those tools serve more than one purpose, and be used for a variety of assessment strategies?

Some assessment tools commonly used by online teachers include a course survey, exam and testing tools that come in the LMS, Internet assessment tools such as HotPotatoes, Quia, ExamBuilder, rubric tools like RubiStar, and quiz creation tools such as QuizStar. Other online tools, such as e-mail and discussion forums, are also used throughout the assessment process.

Figure 8.1. Example of an online test. Used with permission

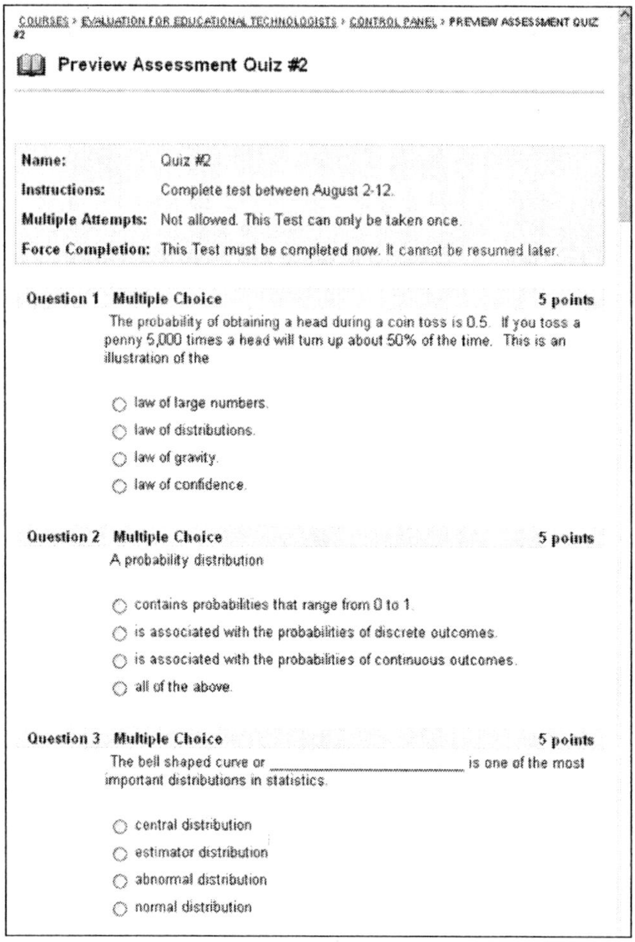

At the time of this writing, assessment tools available within many LMSs are limited to survey and exam tools that utilize multiple choice, essay, true/false, matching, fill-in-the-blank, and ordering types of questions. These exams have the option to be programmed, therefore, creating random questions, or the options to display one question at a time or all at once, for the test to be taken in a limited time period, and also the option to display or not display correct answers to students after completion of the test. Figure 8.1 shows an example of an online test. After submission of the online test, grades are then automatically recorded in both the instructor and student grade books. This automatic grading feature is a boon for many instructors. In addition to survey tools inside an LMS, a quick search on the Internet revealed the following survey tools: Survey Monkey, Zoomerang, SurveyPro, SurveyGold, Survey Solutions, Key Survey, Survey System, Surveylogix, Infopoll, Statpac, SurveyView, and SurveyCrafter, to name a few.

While many teachers use this form of testing as an integral aspect of their instruction for both formative and summative assessment, other instructors who might typically utilize more authentic forms of assessment are struggling. How does a teacher who might typically use a portfolio or project-based learning, for example, conduct assessment in an online environment? Does tool availability inside the LMS have to determine the instructor's pedagogical approach? The answer is whole-heartedly no! In fact, it is suggested that such narrow use of evaluation strategies can encourage minimal reproduction of knowledge, focusing students on lower level cognitive skills (Centre for Study of Higher Education, 2002). How can the online teachers use a variety of technology tools to provide authentic and traditional forms of assessment that encourage rich and meaningful learning experiences?

In this chapter, we examine the strengths and weaknesses of various online assessment and survey tools, explore the need for assessment as part of the teaching cycle in online learning, and provide examples of assessment strategies aligned with learning objective outcomes.

Strengths and Weaknesses

Table 8.1 illustrates the varied strengths of weaknesses of online assessment tools.

Strengths of assessment tools. Some of the benefits of assessment tools include their ability to be set up on a demand basis and can be reused for multiple classes; this is a time saver for the instructor. Another potential benefit in some learning platforms is the ability to modify the exam questions to the student's level of knowledge as the student progresses through the exam, or to give the students multiple attempts to correctly answer a question once they have reviewed material prompted during the exam. Web-based surveys

Table 8.1. Strengths and weaknesses of online assessment tools

Strengths	Weaknesses
• Online exams are time savers for the instructor. Exams can be reused from semester to semester, and grading happens automatically within the LMS. • Online exams provide instant feedback to the student, thus relieving some of the anxiety inherent in online learners due to the lack of face-to-face contact with the instructor. Students can know immediately how they did on a test, and thus modify their schema on a given topic currently under study. • Tests can be programmed to become progressively harder based on correct answers, thus testing to the level of the student's knowledge base. • Cheating can be overcome by programming the exam to pull randomized questions from a larger pool of questions or by having tests proctored. • Surveys are helpful tools for the instructor to gather information on the student, the student's experience of the curriculum, or a particular assignment. • Research shows that many students perform better with online tests vs. paper-based tests. • Some assessments, such as games and simulations, can be fun for the learner and increase motivation. • Authentic assessments such as projects and portfolios help students develop real world skills and empower them to take responsibility for their own learning.	• Exams and surveys are a very limited approach to educational assessment. • The inclusion of exams and surveys as the only assessment tool in an LMS can lead new online teachers to believe that traditional testing is a necessary component of online teaching. • Incorporating assessment tools outside the LMS, such as simulations, can add an extra time burden to the instructor's workload. • Students may need training in how to create or use authentic assessments such as online portfolios. • When using assessments external to the LMS, the instructor will have to record grades manually.

offer a fast, easy, inexpensive, and flexible way to collect data. These tests can offer immediate feedback, in the form of grades and/or comments (De-Paolo & Sherwood, 2006). Survey and exam tools can be useful for gathering survey and background information from students, or for performing statistical analysis in a statistics course, for example. A Web-based survey can be used by students to collect and analyze data in any type of class where the students engage in inquiry (DePaolo & Sherwood, 2006). There is some evidence that many students perform better with online tests vs. paper-based tests (MacCann, 2006).

Assessments can effect motivation and emotional experience in an online course. For example, games and simulations that are not graded, but are required, can be a fun way to learn and to provide opportunities for self-assessment of learning. Authentic assessments tap into deep intrinsic motivation because they are representations of the individual's overall learning experience. A timed online quiz might produce great anxiety, especially if it is tied to a final course grade. There is evidence from brain research that shows affect and motivation actually impact the learning process, thus influencing the way new synapses grow in the brain. This point is critical because new synapses equates learning.

Weaknesses of assessment tools. All assessment approaches, whether online or not, have their weaknesses. Those weaknesses particular to online assessment tools include sole use of exams and surveys, and only assessment tools (designated as such) currently provided in many LMSs offer a severely limited approach to educational assessment. Teachers new to online environments might not realize they have the ability to use multiple tools and approaches to assess their students, and thus revert to using only online testing due to lack of experience or misunderstanding.

However, the reverse side of the above issue is that learning to use and apply online assessment tools and techniques takes time and experience. The extra time involved in creating assessments can be a burden on the instructor's workload. In addition to the instructor needing additional training and experience, online students might also need training or directions in how to use online assessments, such as how to set up a Web-based portfolio, or how to access assessments not included in the LMS. Finally, some weaknesses of using external assessments might include: (1) instructors have to record grades manually from one platform to the LMS gradebook, and (2) inability of instructor to get feedback reports on students' progress or experience in external tools. This would require students to notify the instructor through e-mail when they have completed an externally located assessment.

Understanding Assessment Tools: Part of the Teaching Cycle!

Assessment is a critical component of the teaching and learning cycle. In its most simplistic form, assessment can take the form presented in Figure 8.2.

While most educators would agree that planning, teaching, and assessing are basic processes in the teaching and learning cycle, many are unclear about exactly which forms of assessment to use to gather the information they need for effective teaching and learning. Teachers or instructional designers must consider the purpose of the assessment. Who is being served by the assess-

Figure 8.2. The teaching and learning cycle

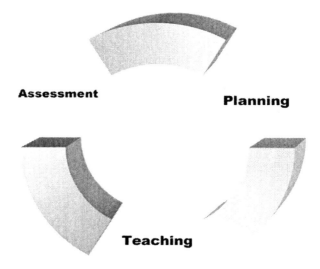

ment? Kellough and Kellough (1999) report seven *purposes* of assessment that help frame our understanding:

1. To assist student learning.
2. To identify students' strengths and weaknesses.
3. To assess the effectiveness of a particular instructional strategy.
4. To assess and improve the effectiveness of curriculum programs.
5. To assess and improve teaching effectiveness.
6. To provide data that assists in decision making.
7. To communicate with and involve parents (if appropriate). (p. 418)

Using authentic assessment. Make learning authentic and based in real-life, as much as possible. Give your students opportunities to engage in activities that are authentic and meaningful in purpose. Studying for a quiz and taking a test is not meaningful (unless your objective is to prepare for a state exam, for example). Studying vocabulary words and creating a crossword puzzle using those words is not meaningful (although it might be fun). Help your students make connections between the topic at hand and how it relates to their lives. The more you can make learning authentic, the more engaged students will be (Conrad & Donaldson, 2004). For example, if you are teaching preservice teachers, creating a portfolio of their work as a class project is meaningful. This portfolio can be used in their interviewing process for a job once they graduate from the program. If you are teaching a course on Web design to high school students, can they create Web sites that have meaning to them personally? Perhaps they are interested in online gaming and want to establish a site for online gaming fans. You get the idea—assign work that is meaningful and empowers learners.

Formative and summative assessments. There are two forms of assessment data teachers collect: formative and summative. *Formative assessments* collect information for the purposes of providing in-progress feedback to the student and teacher to support the learning process. There is often a self-reflective component to formative assessment. For example, a student might be keeping a reflective journal summarizing daily class events. The teacher can then read the journal and respond with any comments to further assist the student's learning. ISTE (2000) supports the use of online testing as part of a continual formative assessment cycle for the learner, and states it "is less intrusive that summative evaluations given at the end of a unit of study" (¶ 23).

Summative assessments serve the purpose of collecting data at the conclusion of a teaching and learning cycle, and are often used for reporting purposes. They answer the question, "To what extent was the learning goal met?" For example, many teachers will assess students at the completion of a unit of study. Those assessment data are then collected and eventually reported in the form of a grade on the report card. In our current era of school accountability, summative assessments are viewed as critical forms of data, however, it should be acknowledged that for the individual student, formative assessments are to be understood as the most important assessment practice (National Center for Fair & Open Testing, 1999). A pre- and post-test process is a commonly used summative assessment strategy.

So how can we, as online teachers, use an LMS or other Web-based assessment tools to collect both formative and assessment data? To understand some assessment techniques we can use online, we first have to understand there are different types of formative and summative assessments, each serving different purposes. These include self-assessment, peer assessment, instructor assessment of the student, student assessment of the curriculum, and student assessment of the instructor.

Self-assessment. Self-assessment is used to promote the students' reflections on their own learning. This assesment gives the power to internalize long-term, higher order learning, and provides student ownership in the learning process. Students who self-assess learn more about themselves as writers, readers, thinkers, and learners. Conrad and Donaldson (2004) state, "Evaluation of critical thinking and reflection requires assessment methods that encourage individual expression. ... the instructor may intersperse self assessment activities through the course ... that allows learners to explore ideas in a non-threatening environment" (p. 25). Because self-asssessment creates ownership and promotes accountability of the self in the learning process, it can be used as a technique to promote the concept of life-long learning. Self-assessment can be used both as a formative and summative assessment technique. An important aspect of self-assessment is goal setting based on outcomes of the self-assessment. Once students have reflected on their learning, they are able to note achievement toward their goals and

Figure 8.3. Example of a student blog used to reflect on course readings

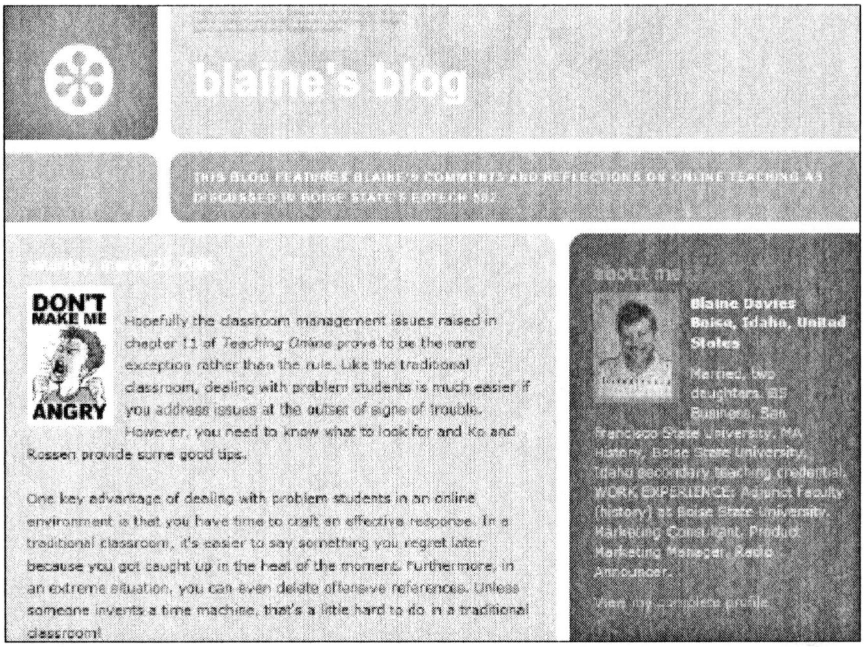

modify the goals if needed. The effective teacher can step in to assist the learner toward that end.

Examples of online self-assessment include keeping reflective journals on class readings, activities, or group work (use blogs or word processing; see Figure 8.3).

Additional approaches to self-assessment include the use of personal portfolios, which can be hosted on Web pages or assigned to a discussion board, self-evaluation of work using rubrics, and interactive online quizzes that provide immediate feedback to the learner without grading.

Peer assessment. Peer assessment is a valuable assessment strategy that creates engagement, community building, and critical reflection on the learning process. Often done informally, peer assessment usually takes the form of feedback to peers, either with or without a rubric. It is not recommended to use peer assessment to assign students' grades, as this can destroy the trust and collaborative environment in the class.

One online technique for peer assessment includes exchanging journals through e-mail or a discussion board, and writing feedback in a journal or posting comments to a blog. Peers can also provide feedback to work posted in discussion forums using guidelines (a rubric, certain number of words, specific questions to be addressed, "state one strength and one area for improvement," etc.). Groups can reflect on their progress in chat or video conferencing breakout rooms. At the completion of group work, survey students on group process and post the results. Have the groups reflect on their findings and offer suggestions for improving group effectiveness.

Teacher assessment of student learning. The most traditional form of assessment is completed for the purpose of accountability such as assigning grades, demonstrating required competencies, to determine a student's thought process, or what the student has learned in relation to lesson objectives.

Some strategies for assessing student learning might include use of course survey tools to create exams, quizzes, tests, or feedback forms. Teachers without access to LMS testing tools can use online testing tools such as Hot-Potatoes, Quia, ExamBuilder, SurveyMonkey, or Zoomerang to incorporate external testing sources into their class. Teachers can also provide rubrics with assignments. One technique I like to use is to create student portfolios in the discussion forum. Each student is assigned a discussion forum for the student's portfolio. This allows students and the teacher to see progress of work throughout the semester and feedback on assignments. It is a great opportunity to incorporate self and peer reflection, as well. Finally, many educators are also using performance management software, such as Inform™, to assess learning in relation to achievement of standards.

Curriculum assessment. The fourth potential area to assess is curriculum. Curriculum assessment is done to improve the design of the course, content, and materials, and can be done by students, instructors, peer teachers, or subject matter experts. Ultimately, assessment of curriculum results in an improved learning experience for the student. Formative curriculum assessment is conducted at the end of a lesson, unit, or project. More traditionally, students participate in summative curriculum assessment by completing online evaluations at the end of a course.

Teachers can ask for additional curriculum feedback using survey tools, anonymous discussion forums, e-mail, or chat. A favorite technique includes the use of "exit slips," an anonymous survey or discussion forum that asks for student feedback on the course, and is usually completed at the end of a lesson.

Student assessment of the instructor. Finally, the last area of potential assessment is instructional assessment. The main goal of instructional assessment is to improve the teaching process. For instructional assessment to be effective the teacher must be open to feedback and the feedback must come in the positive form of "areas for future growth." Instructional assessment is usually conducted at the completion of all courses by a student survey. Good instruction can also be established at the beginning of the semester by surveying students on their preferred learning styles, preferred forms of communication, and so forth. Instruction can also be assessed at the completion of a lesson or unit, also. A simple question, "What could I have done to better facilitate your learning experience?" is often very revealing. Another simple technique I have used are phone calls to students midway through the course asking if I can do anything to better facilitate their learning experience.

Assessment Tools in LMSs

Although any tool in an LMS can be used for assessment purposes (for example, feedback can be sent by e-mail, video conferencing can be used to demonstrate learning, etc.), there are several tools inside most LMSs designed specifically for assessment purposes. These include quiz and survey tools, student tracking or progress reports, the gradebook, and course statistics. Some platforms have also included portfolios and wikis to assist students in demonstrating learning.

Quiz and survey tools. Quizzes and surveys can be graded or nongraded, timed or untimed, allow single or multiple attempts, and offer a variety of question formats such as multiple choice, drag and drop, essay, fill in the blank, and so forth. A question pool can be created, and questions can be pulled at random from the pool. Teachers can also write feedback responses for correct or incorrect answers. This feature is particularly helpful when giving ungraded quizzes to test comprehension of basic course concepts. The prompt then refers the student to reread a particular section of the text or course materials, and reanswer the question. Images can also be uploaded to online quizzes, and work well with drag and drop questions, or to increase visual comprehension of the question being asked.

Figure 8.4. Open-ended peer feedback survey

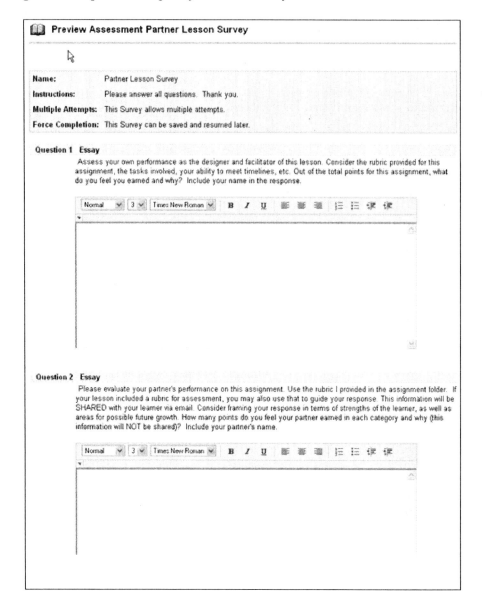

These various levels of features creates some interesting combination of testing and surveying options. Compare these two tests for example:

Test 1: Multiple choice→one hour→one attempt→randomized questions→ proctored

Test 2: Essay→untimed→multiple attempts→open book

Notice that the structure of the first test requires memorization of facts recalled quickly under a stressful testing environment. The second test emphasizes comprehension and analysis of course readings in a less time-intensive environment. Which test would you rather take? Why?

Online testing offers the teacher a means to provide students with ongoing, real-time assessment of learning when used as a formative assessment strategy (Wellman, 2006). Online tests can also be proctored in some educational settings, which beneficial to those tests that require memorization and where cheating might be a concern. Figure 8.4 shows an example of an open-ended survey used to gain peer feedback on a collaborative assignment.

Student progress reports & tracking. Depending on your LMS, you may have student tracking and progress report features. Student progress features track students progress through various assignments, usually in the form of a checklist or a bar showing the percentage of assignments completed.

In Figure 8.5, we see that the student's "learning path" shows three of the weekly assignments completed at 100%, while the fourth week has 0% completed. This tracking feature can be useful to the student who is enrolled in multiple courses or is working through the course nonsequentially, and it also serves as reminder where they are in the course (Ko & Rossen, 2004). It is also useful to the instructor who can look at her class and view all the students' progress.

Other student tracking features include forms of course statistics that the instructor can query to see how often the students log on, where students spend their time when they log on, number of postings, and other quantitative data that might help inform the teaching process.

Beginning teachers can sometimes overemphasize these statistics, and we would encourage teachers to stay focused on final course outcomes and

Figure 8.5. Example of student tracking in an LMS

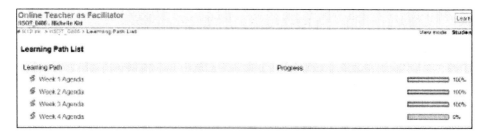

Figure 8.6. Course statistics showing access by day of week

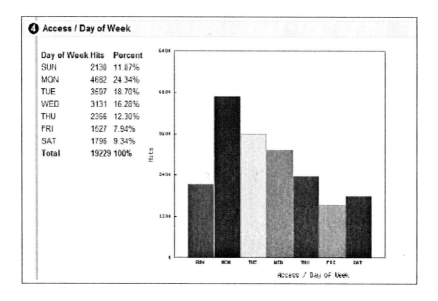

requirements, not the number of hits, views, or posts that a student makes. You can, however, use these statistics to get some useful information: the time of day the majority of students log on (useful for planning synchronous sessions), students who are not accessing the course at all (good in the initial week of class to see who needs help or may have dropped the course), students who are obsessive in their interaction (sometimes indicating anxiety or perfectionist tendencies that can be coached). Be wary of the statistical data that shows how long a student is logged into a course; these data are inaccurate because students will often open a site and leave their computers for extended periods of times.

Data tracking is typically available in other areas of online courses, as well, such as statistics that show how many times a post has been viewed, whether or not the instructor has viewed a post, the date and time of the most recent post, and so forth. Adapt your instructional strategies to the level of tracking available to yourself and students. You may find yourself needing to include confirmation postings or e-mails if you have limited tracking capabilities, for example.

Gradebooks. Most LMSs include a gradebook where instructors can record grades and students can access their individual grades at any time. Students really appreciate the ability to see their overall progress in a course at any given time.

Gradebooks are a very handy tool for the online teacher because their functionality continues to expand over time. For example, if you have your students take an online exam, the grade is automatically recorded in the gradebook. This gives the student immediate feedback, and you do not have to manually grade the exam. The gradebook will also calculate and display averages so you have an understanding of where student grades are falling for a particular assignment—useful for insight into your curriculum design. If you notice that students are making lower grades than normal on one particular assignment, this is a clue that you need to revisit your instructional strategy or materials for that assignment.

Figure 8.7. Example of an online gradebook

Week 1: Introductions	Week 2: Blog	Week 2 Best Practice	Week 3 Online Course Comparisons	Week 3: LMS Comparisons	Week 4: Chat
Assignment	Assignment	Assignment	Assignment	Extra Credit	Assignment
Pts Possible 40	Pts Possible 10	Pts Possible 40	Pts Possible 40	Pts Possible 40	Pts Possible 40
Weight 0%	Weight 0%	Weight 0%	Weight 0%	Weight 0%	Weight 0%
40	10	40	40	40	40
40	10	40	40	10	40
40	10	40	40	0	40
40	10	40	40	40	40
40	10	40	40	0	40
40	10	40	40	40	40
40	10	40	40	40	40
40	10	40	40	0	40

Items in a gradebook can be weighted, modified, managed into different orders, and sorted. Final class grades can be automatically calculated. And in some LMS software, such as eCollege™, comments can be attached to individual grades. So as an instructor is grading an assignment, the instructor can write comments that are automatically inserted into the gradebook along with the grade, and an e-mail is generated to the student. This level of cross-functionality is quite a timesaver for the online teacher.

For those teachers without online gradebooks, an Excel™ spreadsheet can be created to track and calculate student grades. However, teachers have to take the next step and manually notify their students of their grading progress.

Other Online Assessment Tools

Web-based survey tools. Although most LMSs contain the ability to create quizzes or surveys, it is still helpful to become familiar with other online survey tools. These tools are used by students in many types of courses to collect and analyze data relevant to the course topic. As an instructor, you might also need to collect data from parents, colleagues, or the community, something you are unable to do with LMS survey tools. Commonly used survey tools include QuizStar™, Quia™, SurveyMonkey™, and Zoomerang™.

These types of products also allow you more customization of the look and feel of the survey, where the user can create a variety of assessment sections, upload graphics and logos, change colors, and so forth (DePaolo & Sherwood, 2006). The surveys can be accessed by anyone with a password and do not require a special login to the LMS. Lastly, users may still need to employ other software such as Access and Excel to created customized reports and summarize data. Even with this potential shortcoming, Web-based survey software offers many advantages that make it a valuable resource for instructors (DePaolo & Sherwood, 2006).

Games and simulations. One of the latest educational trends is the use of online games and simulations in learning. Many online games have evolved into complex learning environments, serving purposes beyond assessment.

For example, in this simulation, preservice teachers can practice their classroom management techniques while working with simulated students in a classroom. Based on the actions they take, they receive various responses from

Figure 8.8. SimSchool: A simulation for preservice teachers to practice classroom management skills

students. This is self-assessment at its best, but the simulation also strives to teach the learner appropriate classroom management techniques.

Online games can be rich in experience for the user; they strengthen their ability to solve problems (quests), select avatars to represent the self, and interact with other players as a team and find solutions. There are many forms of educational games and simulations. One of the latest trends is a game that learners can design themselves. Examples of educational games and simulations include Quest Atlantis™, AquaMoose 3D™, World Hunger™, Racing Academy™, and Elemental™. Additional resources are located at the end of this chapter.

Portfolios. Web-based portfolios offer an exciting opportunity for students to showcase their learning and work to the public. Students can be required to upload key "artifacts" that are representative of their learning over the span of a unit or course. A few LMSs now include portfolio storage. For those that do not have this feature, there are several alternatives. First, if your students are proficient in html, can ftp, and have hosting space, they can create a Web-based portfolio that they maintain themselves as a Web site. This is empowering for adults as it allows them to share their work with the larger community. Younger students might have access to Hyperstudio software.

Figure 8.9. Example of discussion boards used for portfolios

You can also consider using a blog or wiki as a portfolio environment. As a last resource, consider turning your discussion forums into portfolio space.

Assign each student a discussion board, and title it with the student's name, for example, "Lisa Johnson's Portfolio." They can then use threads to attach and upload artifacts to their portfolio. Peers and the teacher can also provide comments to artifacts by using the "reply" feature. I have found this to be an easy and effective way to integrate portfolios in the online classroom.

Rubric generators. Once you move away from using online testing as your only assessment strategy, you will find yourself creating a lot of rubrics to guide assessment! You may provide rubrics to students for discussion board postings, role plays, assessing group work, projects, and more. The rubric formats offered to teachers by RubiStar™ and MyT4L™ are easy to use, powerful tools. They offer the teacher sample rubrics, example critieria, and categories.

Encourage your students to use these tools to develop their own rubrics, and then let them assess themselves and report this information to you. This turns responsibility for learning over to the learner, and increases engagement and empowerment. Of course, the instructor will always have to oversee and facilitate this process, but I have found this technique valuable, especially when students have worked on long papers or projects. It gives the instructor insight into how students view their work.

Blogs and wikis (see Chapter IX). Because blogs and wikis are "owned" by the student, they are an excellent source for assessing student learning. Provide guidelines with a rubric for posting work in a blog or wiki, and then assess accordingly. Try using Blogger.com™ and pbwiki™ with your students. By doing a quick search on Google™, you will find that many educators at all grade levels are now integrating these tools into their instructional set.

If you are not comfortable using blogs or wikis, you can still have your students engaged in reflective journaling. Using a two column journal in word processing (see Figure 8.10), have them make note of important pages and concepts from their readings. In the right column, they can then discuss applications of these potential concepts to their own practice. The journals can be posted to the discussion form two or three times during the course, and peers and instructors can comment on the entries.

Structuring Assessment for Success

If you are designing the online course or materials, it will be your role to plan assessments. Consider these strategies during your planning process:

- Design learner-centered assessments that include self-reflection.

- Design and include grading rubrics to assess contributions to the discussion.

- Include collaborative assessments through publicly posting papers along with comments from students (and yourself).

- Encourage students to develop skills in providing feedback by providing guidelines to good feedback and modeling what is expected.

Figure 8.10. Example of a two-column reflective journal
Reflective Journal
Week 5

K&R Chapter 3: Course Conversion	Thoughts, Comments, Questions
• Distinction between using the Web to "complement" what you do in class or to "recast" your entire class. (p. 36)	This, to me, is an important distinction. Doing a few things to complement work done in an on-ground class really is fundamentally different than recasting an entire class. It seems the thinking process for the two types of activities needs to be very different.
Two examples	I was very impressed with what these instructors did. Partly because they seemed to venture out on their own to create something that worked for them. I get very concerned about schools that want an online component, buy a CMS, but do not really help faculty maximize its potential. As teachers, we know motivation is important. Well, it seems to me that motivation is important for instructors as well and I do not always see the incentives for instructors to do the kinds of things these folks did. I think schools need to create a culture where this kind of work is rewarded. There are many of types of incentives that could be used to help instructors do these things. A few that come quickly to mind: • Release time to either "complement" or "recast" • Financial incentives • Include these kinds of activities more prominently in the criteria for promotion and tenure • Provide high quality faculty development to help instructors see how these kinds of things can make them better instructors (and helping us recast our perceptions of what a teachers does)

continued

"It turned out that putting all his lectures online was much more difficult and time-consuming that he thought it would be." (p. 41 and p. 49)	I would love to see the development of high quality lecture materials available for online use. For example, for a statistics course, perhaps a big textbook company (or someone willing to make a big investment) could produce a large number of very high quality little lecture chunks on a large number of mini-content areas. The instructor could then pick and choose which "chunks" to use and when to use them.

Rather than replacing the teacher, use of these chunks would free up the instructor to do other things with students.

I mention this because I remember spending huge numbers of hours in the Multimedia class creating animations and narrated PowerPoint presentations. I was very proud of work I did and I think the material was pretty good, but the "production values" looked a little cheap because I was using a cheap microphone, Microsoft Producer, and QuickTimePro, all of which are pretty low-end tools.

It seems to me that while there are so many extraordinary things that are happening in online education, this is an area that may be lagging behind. |
| "The missing element here is instruction design." (p. 45) | About a million years ago, I had a methods class where the teacher said, "Always begin by asking 3 simple questions: (1) What do you want your students to learn?, (2) How are you going to teach it?, and (3) How will you know if your students have learned it?" I have had to adapt to this a bit to accommodate a constructivist predisposition, but I must say that I have kept his words in mind in the ensuing years, and their simple wisdom has never failed me.

I sometimes think instructional design folks get a little full of themselves and make the process more complicated then it needs to be. |
| Tips for Writing Online Text (p. 49) | Very helpful. There is danger is going overboard on the graphics, but reading a lot of screen text for me is hard, and I appreciate when the page gives the reader a little chance to breathe. (This journal is a pretty good example of what not to do ☺.) |

- Use assessment techniques that fit the context and align with learning objectives.

- Design assessments that are clear, easy to understand, and likely to work in the online environment.

- Ask for and incorporate student input into how assessment should be considered. (Palloff & Pratt, 2003, pp. 101-102)

As you consider formative and summative assessments in order to evaluate achievement of learning objectives, also consider needed assessments to evaluate critical thinking, group work, assessment of the curriculum, as well as your own teaching. Here is a simple planning tool you can use to begin considering the assessments you will integrate online.

One important principle of assessment is the concept of triangulation, that is, using multiple sources of data to inform our evaluation. So, anticipate your online course will incorporate multiple assessments through its duration. Assessments should also be varied so students have multiple ways to demonstrate their learning (Ko & Rossen, 2004).

Table 8.2. Assessment planning tool

Assessment Need	Technique/Strategy	Online Tool
Achievement of learning objectives: formative		
Achievement of learning objectives: summative		
Critical thinking		
Group work		
Assessment of the curriculum		
Assessment of instruction		

Staying learner centered with assessments. If the emphasis of your course is on learner-centeredness, then it illustrates that you want your assessments to be learner centered, as well. Opportunities for reflection are the foundation of a learner-centered classroom. What mechanisms, assessments, and tools can be used to support reflection on self, peers, and the curriculum? Many instructors use authentic assessments that run throughout an extended period, or the entire course, to achieve this purpose. For example, consider having students keep reflective blogs where they reflect on the readings, activities, and their learning in the course. Students can also keep a Web site where they upload examples of their work throughout the semester, thus creating an electronic portfolio. These sites can be shared with the instructor or peers midway and at the end of the course.

Other approaches to supporting reflection would include self and peer assessment of a given activity or assignment using a rubric or a simple survey that asks several prompt questions. In video conferencing, students can reflect on the class discussion by using the last five minutes to "bring closure" to the session—a time when each student speaks one at a time to share something new they learned in the session. Students can also have the opportunity to "pass," if they have nothing to share. Offering the "pass" option is a form of student empowerment, and makes the student responsible for learning.

At the beginning of a course, use the survey tool or e-mail to gather basic information about your students: name, contact information, special needs, and concerns they might have about the course. This nongraded activity introduces your students to online testing tools in a nonthreatening way.

Giving feedback. Online students want and thrive on instructor feedback and students can experience isolation online; therefore, feedback is one mechanism to overcome this isolation and get a sense of "how am I doing in this class?" Timeliness in feedback is an important key. Students are motivated when they understand their work is taken seriously and is not sitting on a teacher's desk, virtual or otherwise. During the first week of class, explain to your students how often and what types of feedback will be available.

The type of feedback you provide may vary from assignment to assignment. It is not reasonable, for example, to expect that you would respond to every discussion post. It is reasonable to expect that you would provide written comments in addition to a graded rubric when assessing a project portfolio. Here are some guidelines to consider when writing feedback:

- Always start by noting at least one area of strength, an intriguing comment, an interesting idea. Then, instead of pointing out "weaknesses" or "problems," instead, discuss "areas for improvement" or "areas for additional consideration." This type of distinction in language may seem nit picky, but it serves a very important purpose. The first set of words implies a right and wrong way to learn, and the student got it wrong. How motivating is it to be wrong? The second set of words implies a *strengths-based* approach to learning, something we want to model if we truly support the idea of life-long learning. That is, we all have strengths than can be identified and built off of to achieve the next goal in our learning process.

- With discussion board posts, operate as a facilitator, not evaluator. Use your posts to paraphrase, ask questions, extend the dialogue, point out new information, and summarize a topic up to that point. Do not overly praise one individual or put down another.

- Consider using public feedback on individual or group assignments. Post the feedback to the discussion board, include the rubric and your comments. However, never post any students' grades in a public space. These should be sent separately in an e-mail, or the student should be prompted to visit the gradebook to see grades.

- If a student has done extremely poor work, consider sending an e-mail instead of posting public feedback. In your public feedback, you can write, "See my e-mail, and let us talk." This type of feedback remains respectful to the individual, and at the same time, makes students aware that you have standards that are being maintained in the course. In the e-mail to the student, explain your concerns with the work and suggest a phone or chat conference to clear up misunderstandings or concerns.

- When using peer feedback, provide guidelines or direction on how that should be accomplished. Give question prompts or have them use rubrics. Peer feedback is particularly helpful to instructors running large sections of online classes, as it provides additional opportunities for feedback, and requires students to view criteria from a fresh perspective (Ko & Rossen, 2004).

- Always read your feedback before posting or e-mailing. Typos and grammatical errors are common, or something you said could be misinterpreted if it is not clear.

- Be concise in your feedback. Get to the point.

- Consider copying individual lines written by the student into your message, and then use a different color text to respond. This promotes visual clarity, and helps the student understand the pieces of the work that stood out to you.

- Individual feedback is not always possible or appropriate. Instead, consider awarding a grade for weekly participation and then offer group feedback. Group feedback is feedback written to the entire class. The instructor can sum up or summarize the overall postings or assignments that week and offer additional thoughts. Group feedback can also promote coherency in the class because the instructor is speaking to everyone at once, yet taking the time to point out individual student contributions (see Figure 8.11).

Figure 8.11. Example of instructor feedback to entire class

Reflections on Week 1

As I read over your detailed responses to this assignment, I was left with a general impression that we have a talented and quite intelligent group of folks in our class. I also had these questions: "Do principles of andragogy apply to all ages?" and "Do adult online learners need to be taught in different ways than adult on ground learners." I'd like to respond to these questions in several ways.

First, for many years, I specialized in elementary education, and teaching elementary school teachers. My specialty was in classroom pedagogy and technology integration. I understood the term "pedagogy" to mean the study of teaching in general and did not apply it to any particular audience. And after all, the students I taught were adults, not kids. And my expertise was in teacher professional development – I definitely understood how teachers learn. As I began to specialize more and more in educational technology, the audience broadened. I was now working with teachers at all levels, school district technology coordinators, trainers in the corporate and government sectors, and software designers. And still, I emphasized best practice in teaching, or what I described as *pedagogy*. My understanding of pedagogy differs from Gibbons and Wentworth, as I never considered good pedagogy to be teacher-directed instruction in the first place.

I was introduced to the term "andragogy" several years ago. In my mind, andragogy does not always necessarily reflect a particular age group (adults over 25, for example), but represents an *ideal teaching practice* based on supporting self-motivated, mature, life-long learners. As Dallas described in his post, his ideal is becoming harder and harder to achieve in K-12 schools, as we are in a time of accountability and heavily influenced by federal legislation such as the No Child Left Behind (NCLB) Act. Since education beyond K-12 doe snot have these heavy influences for accountability and high-stakes testing, there is flexibility for education. In higher education, we are governed by principles of academic freedom. In the corporate section, learners are governed by return on investment. There is room to address principles of best practice.

---

continued

So these days, I still use the term "pedagogy" in a generic sense to discuss best practice in teaching, and possibly how to accommodate for factors a teacher might encounter in the schools, such as testing, parents, and pre-prescribed curriculum in K-12 schools. When I use the term "andragogy," however, I am specifically referring to Knowles' conception of best teaching practice, and tend to apply it toward a mature or adult audience, most often after high school. Can the principles of andragogy be applied in elementary, junior or senior high? And the answer is: most definitely. However, the focus of this course will be on working with adult learners, in general, and with adult learners in online learning environments, in particular.

And I also need to express that we are seeing new trends in distance learners. Kelly mentioned this idea in her post, as well. In the past, typically distance education was preferred by those who lacked access to traditional learning. Now, we are moving to the point where distance learning components are being integrated across our entire campus in a majority of our courses. We have an emergent population of young adults who grew up as gamers and Internet users, and feel quite at home in Internet based environments. Our Director of Academic Technologies informed me last semester they are not even going to distinguish hybrid classes in our course catalog anymore as it is assumed there is some online component to all classes. We are seeing a huge paradigm shift in education happening before our eyes. More on this to come throughout our course.

So who is right? Caryn and Paul gave us their own interpretations of andragogy. Julie offered an insightful critique of "collaborative" online learning. Do Gibbon and Wentworth have the answer? Knowles? Fidishuan? Or Dr. Dawley? ☺ From my perspective of andragogy, there is no true "right," as much as there are multiple perspectives. And a strong learner and educator will value those multiple opinions as they continue to seek and develop their own personal constructs on issues as part of their learning process.

Making assessment fun. What? Assessment can be fun? With formative assessments, in particular, a lot of enjoyment is experienced by students who are involved in checking their own understanding as they go through the course. Integrate online simulations appropriate to your content area. They help students develop the ability to self-diagnose and give guided practice using prompts. Inject humor where appropriate, and ask evaluative questions in unique and humorous ways, such as "If George Washington was alive today, how would you explain to him what you learned this week?" With younger students, integrate some quick online assessments such as word searches or crossword puzzles. Use a popular slideshow template to create a game of Jeopardy™ in your subject area. Try to incorporate games where appropriate to meet your assessment needs—games are fun!

Example Uses for Success

Learning Objective Outcome	Assessment Activities
Interactivity and connection	• Mid-way through a group project, have groups assess their progress and work style. Share results with group and discuss strategies to move toward completion. • After completing a project in pairs, have students meet in chat or email to share what they each learned. • Have students lead an online study session in chat where they can prepare for an upcoming exam. Each participant should prepare several questions and answers prior to the chat.
Knowledge: defines; describes; enumerates; identifies; labels; lists; matches; names; reads; records; reproduces; selects; states; views	• Labeling of online graphs or diagrams. • Use an online multiple-choice test, open-book. • To test vocabulary in a foreign language class, create a matching test (if your software includes that option) where students drag and drop the vocabulary word on top of the associated picture.
Comprehension: classifies; cites; converts; describes; discusses; estimates; explains; generalizes; gives examples; makes sense out of; paraphrases; restates (in own words); summarizes; traces; understands.	• Have students explain data presented in graphs and charts on the whiteboard. • Offer an online quiz with formative feedback built in the answers. • Automated interactive modules where students work through activities receiving automated feedback. Non-graded. • Using breakout rooms in video conferencing, have students work in pairs to practice active listening on a given topic for the week. One student shares her understanding of an assigned reading, and the other student has to paraphrase and repeat back what he heard. Take turns.

continued

Application: acts; administers; articulates; assesses; charts; collects; computes; constructs; contributes; controls; determines; develops; discovers; establishes; extends; implements; includes; informs; instructs; operationalizes; participates; predicts; prepares; preserves; produces; projects; provides; relates; reports; shows; solves; teaches; transfers; uses; utilizes	<ul><li>Publication of documents on the Web.</li><li>Students can create tutorials/materials for others on topics they are learning. For example, students in a music education course might create a Web site, "Resources for the Online Music Educator."</li><li>Create a slideshow demonstrating application of course concepts to the student's own work. For example, in an instructional theory course, a special education teacher can develop a slideshow illustrating how those principles apply to her work in special education.</li></ul>
Analysis: breaks down; correlates; diagrams; differentiates; discriminates; distinguishes; focuses; illustrates; infers; limits; outlines; points out; prioritizes; recognizes; separates; subdivides	<ul><li>Peer editing of papers using a rubric.</li><li>Have students reach a paper or research article, and summarize the article by providing an outline of the paper.</li><li>Encourage students to participate in setting goals and objectives for the course, if possible. Let them prioritize the objectives, and suggest possible learning activities.</li></ul>

continued

Synthesis: adapts; anticipates; categorizes; collaborates; combines; communicates; compares; compiles; composes; contrasts; creates; designs; devises; expresses; facilitates; formulates; generates; incorporates; individualizes; initiates; integrates; intervenes; models; modifies; negotiates; plans; progresses; rearranges; reconstructs; reinforces; reorganizes; revises; structures; substitutes; validates	• Online role-play where a scenario is read, and students adopt a role in the scenario. The role-play occurs over a set time period (a week, for example) inside a discussion forum. Include a minimum participation requirement. • Encourage students to keep individual blogs where they can reflect on, and integrate their thinking, about course readings or assignments. Promote peer collaboration by requiring a minimum number of responses each week. • Students create class demonstration portfolios by either uploading artifacts of their work to either (1) a discussion board that has been set up with their name, or (2) to a Web page they maintain. • Allow a choice of student-created projects at the end of a course to demonstrate synthesis of course topics. If students are old enough, have them create their own rubrics for assessment. Incorporate peer assessment and instructor feedback throughout their design process. • Set up a class wiki where each student has a page for specific contribution on a given topic. For example, in a course on networking, each student is assigned to write about a given topic such as servers, server maintenance, hubs, routers, etc.
Evaluation: appraises; compares & contrasts; concludes; criticizes; critiques; decides; defends; interprets; judges; justifies; reframes	• Rhetorical, ethical or other questions and a web forum that learners must use to share their reflections, with a minimum participation requirement. • Create an "Aha!" board where students can share Aha moments as they occur during the class. • "Bumper sticker" – at the conclusion of a unit or course, ask students to sum up their experience or knowledge as it would fit on a bumper sticker. • Have students present their portfolios to you and peers via video conferencing. • Create a likert-scale survey for students to complete at the end of the course assessing (1) instructional strategies, (2) curriculum, (3) their own learning satisfaction, and (4) effective use of the online learning environment.

Example Lesson Plan

Figure 8.12. Example lesson plan using a survey tool

Overview: Comparing Learning Management Systems & Project Planning

Greetings and welcome to Week 12 of class! You have worked hard over the last several weeks. Your online lessons are now complete – what an experience for you, as a teacher and a learner! Let us spend some time reflecting on where we have come to date, as well as where the remainder of the course is going. In my mind, this was a successful learning experience in many ways, but only you can tell me about that – thus, the survey you will find at the beginning of our tasks in this time period. :)

This week, we will also examine attributes of different Learning Management Systems (such as Blackboard, WebCT, eCollege, Desire2Learn, Moodle) by conducting LMS comparisons.

That is it, enjoy!

Objectives

1.   Evaluate yourself and your student in your online teaching experience by completing a survey.

2.   Compare and contrast features of various Learning Management Systems.

Resources

Edu-tool.com http://www.edutools.info/index.jsp

---

continued

ACTIVITIES FOR WEEKS 12	DUE DATE
1. Reflection: complete class survey Please complete the survey located in this week's assignment folder.	Deadline: midnight MST on Tuesday, April 12.
2. Course Management System Comparisons Blackboard is one type of course management system (CMS). CMSs are also sometimes referred to as learning management systems (LMS), e-learning platforms, or online course delivery platforms. However, there is a difference between a CMS and LMS (if you send me an e-mail stating the difference and showing me a link, 5 points extra credit for you this week!). In a CMS, one can make a distinction between learner tools and support tools. As an online student enrolled in this course, you are now very familiar with Blackboard's *learner* tools such as threaded discussion, chat, and email. In creating and teaching your online lesson, you began to work with and assess *support* tools such as course customizing and administration tools. Your task this week is to compare several online platforms by analyzing various tools and features. You will post and discuss your results in the general discussion forum. 1. Go to the Edu-tool.com site at: http://www.edutools.info/index.jsp 2. Click the tab, "Course Management Systems," read the page. 3. Click on "Compare Products/By Features" on the tab at the top. 4. Note you can compare features in three categories: Learner Tools, Support Tools, and Technical Specifications. 5. Conduct a comparison of a minimum of three features in learner tools, three features in support tools, and one in technical specifications.	Deadline to post: midnight MST on Tuesday, April 12.

continued

ACTIVITIES FOR WEEKS 12	DUE DATE
2. Course Management System Comparisons 6. You will be provided with a list of online course platforms that meet your query. Choose at least three platforms to compare. 7. Here you are at last! A list showing a comparison of all features. Copy this URL; you'll need it for your post this week (see below). 8. After reviewing the features of your various platforms, choose one to investigate further. Visit the Web site of that platform. See if you are able to download/enroll in a test course. Learn more about learner and support tools available on the platform. 9. In the Discussion Forum for Week 12, create a post that (1) provides the URL from step #7, and (2) discuss the various options available in your investigated platform. How did your investigated platform support/ not support the type of course(s) you might envision offering online? What are the issues that might be involved in using the platform you investigated? How might these issues be resolved?	Deadline to post: midnight MST on Tuesday, April 12.

Grading
Pass/no pass, all criteria must be addressed. 10 points.

Resources

Assessment in Online Education: http://breeze.boisestate.edu:8080/p34813439/

Authentic Assessment Toolbox: http://jonathan.mueller.faculty.noctrl.edu/toolbox/whatisit.htm

Cheating in Online Assessment: http://www.westga.edu/~distance/ojdla/summer72/rowe72.html

Electronic Portfolio Resources: http://www.uvm.edu/~jmorris/portresources.html

Electronic Student Portfolio: http://www.iport.iupui.edu/teach/teach_studenteport.htm

ExamBuilder: http://exambuilder.com/

Hot Potatoes: http://www.halfbakedsoftware.com/

How to Write a Good Survey: http://www.accesscable.net/~infopoll/tips.htm#Balance%20rating%20scales

Jeopardy Template: http://www.graves.k12.ky.us/tech/jeopardy_instructions.htm

Kathy Schrock's assessment site: http://school.discovery.com/schrockguide/assess.html

My T4L Rubric Maker: http://myt4l.com

Online Assessment Strategies: http://www.flinders.edu.au/flexed/resources/assess.htm

Puzzle Maker: http://puzzlemaker.school.discovery.com/

Quia: http://www.quia.com

Quiz Center: http://school.discovery.com/quizcenter/quizcenter.html

Sample Student Multimedia Evaluation Rubric: http://www.ncsu.edu/midlink/rub.mm.st.htm

Self-Assessment in Portfolios: http://www.ncrel.org/sdrs/areas/issues/students/learning/lr2port.htm

Social Impact Games: http://www.socialimpactgames.com/Survey Monkey http://www.surveymonkey.com/

Twenty Top Tips for Writing Effective Surveys: http://ezinearticles.com/?20-Top-Tips-To-Writing-Effective-Surveys&id=2622

WWW4Teachers (RubiStar & QuizStar): http://4teachers.org/

Zoomerang: http://info.zoomerang.com/

References

Bransford, J. D. (1999). *How people learn: Mind, brain, experience, and school.* Washington, DC: National Academies Press.

Centre for the Study of Higher Education. (2002). Online assessment. Retrieved December July 6, 2006, from http://www.cshe.unimelb.edu.au/assessinglearning/03/online.html

Conrad, R., & Donaldson, J. (2004). *Engaging the online learner: Activities and resources for creative instruction.* Jossey-Bass.

DePaulo, C. A., & Sherwood, A. L. (2006). Instructional uses of Web-based survey software. *The Journal of Educators Online, 3*(1), 1-19.

ISTE. (2000). Accelerating and tracking student achievement. Retrieved July 6, 2006, from http://www.iste.org/Content/NavigationMenu/Research/Reports/Research_on_Technology_in_Education_2000_/Achievement/Accelerating_and_Tracking_Student_Achievement.htm

Kellough, R. D., & Kellough, N. G. (1999). *Secondary school teaching: A guide to methods and resources: Planning for competence.* Upper Saddle River, NJ: Prentice Hall.

Ko, S., & Rossen, S. (2004). *Teaching online: A practical guide.* Houghton Mifflin.

MacCann, R. (2006). The equivalence of online and traditional testing for different subpopulations and item types. *British Journal of Educational Technology, 37*(1), 79-91.

National Center for Fair & Open Testing. (1999). *The value of formative assessment.* Retrieved July 6, 2006, from http://www.fairtest.org/examarts/winter99/k-forma3.html

Nguyen, D. D., & Kara, D. S. (2000). *Summative and formative evaluations of internet based teaching.* In L. Lau (Ed.), Distance learning technologies: Issues, trends and opportunities (pp. 22-38). Hershey, PA: Idea Group Publishing.

Palloff, R. M., & Pratt, K. (2003). *The virtual student: A profile and guide to working with online learners.* San Francisco: Jossey-Bass.

Wellman, G. S. (2006). Comparing learning style to performance in on-line teaching: Impact of proctored vs. un-proctored testing. *Journal of Interactive Online Learning, 4*(1), 20-39.

Chapter IX

Blogs and Wikis

Blogs and wikis are two recent Web-based tools gaining popularity with online educators. Currently, over 32 million Americans are reading 8 million blogs (Njuguna, 2005). Situated in the context of student empowerment, open knowledge, and democratic freedom, blogs and wikis provide the individual learner a worldwide forum for publishing or contributing their thoughts, writing, and expanding knowledge base. They are documented tools for promoting reflective writing (Hernández-Ramos, 2004).

A blog, or Weblog, is a Web page that serves as personal journal for an individual (see Figure 9.1).

Blog entries are dated, and are usually open to comments from the outside world. Blogs can also include audio or video clips, known as a vblog. One of the highly touted benefits of blogs includes the empowerrment of the author through the writing process. The individual student owns and directs the content of the blog. Unlike discussion forums which might constrain think-

Figure 9.1. Example of a blog site

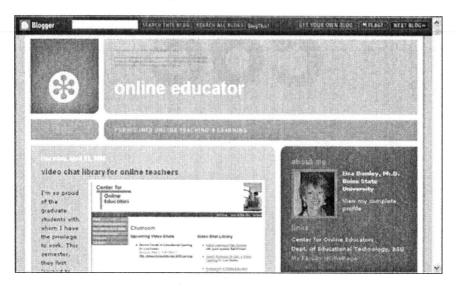

ing into a hierarchical format, the student decides the direction the blog will take. In effect, the student becomes expert on a given topic. This results in increase in higher-order thinking skills as the student constructs knowledge over time. An additional benefit of the blog is its lack of boundaries for student publication. Discussion forums constrain the ability to view the student's writing to a single set of classmates. Blogs open up a student's writing to the world, thus enabling the student as a global citizen.

Wikis, as defined by their founder, Ward Cunningham (2005), are "a collection of Web pages which can be edited by anyone, at any time, from anywhere" (¶ 11). The WikiWikiWeb™, established in 1995, was the first wiki site and provides extensive historical and FAQ information for those wishing to learn more about using wikis (see Figure 9.2).

Users of wikis appreciate their ability to support democratic freedom, simplicity, and power.

One of the most common examples of wikis used today in education in Wikipedia™, a free online encyclopedia that anyone can edit worldwide. Started in 2001, Wikipedia™ is part of a larger parent foundation, Wikimedia™. Wikimedia's™ goals include the development and maintenance of multicultural open content, and to provide that content free-of-charge to the

Figure 9.2 The WikiWikiWeb™. Used with copyright permission

public. In addition to offering Wikipedia, the foundation also offers Wiktion-
ary™, Wikiquote™, Wikisource™, Wikibooks™, and Wikijunio™, a youth
oriented project. When using wikis in the learning process, students become
authors of content that is shared and built upon by others around the world.
Wiki projects can be incorporated into a lesson, unit, or course of study.
For example, students taking a course in European history might choose to
participate in or create a wiki project on the Middle Ages wherein articles
are created or linked to provide a chronology of historical information from
that time period.

Wikis have two writing modes, a *document mode* where contributors write
collaborative documents using a third person voice, and a *thread mode* used
by contributors carry out threaded, signed discussions. When users enter a
wiki, its default state is in *read*, and looks like a normal Web page. When
the user wants to edit a wiki page, they must access the *edit* state (Augar,
Raitman, & Zhou, 2004). Most wiki editors use *wikistyle,* a simple coding
syntax similar to html.

In this chapter, we examine the strengths and weaknesses of blog and wiki
tools, explore the need for learner expression in online learning, and provide
sample activities aligned with learning objective outcomes.

Strengths and Weaknesses

Table 9.1 illustrates the varied strengths of weaknesses of using blogs and wikis.

Strengths of blogs and wikis. The main strength of a blog or wiki appear obvious—the ability to self-express in a public forum. Blogs and wikis are being used by many instructors to support the writing process, reflection in learning, provide student empowerment, and to promote the idea of students as experts in their own learning process. Each tool promotes social and peer interaction and collaboration, increases positive student/teacher relationships, develops critical thinking ability, and improves flexibility in teaching and learning. Working with blogs and wikis gives students an authentic learning experience.

Using blogs and wikis can serve a variety of purposes in the educational context, depending on the needs of the instructor and students. Emphasis is placed on the writing experience itself, not the technology, and students often report great enjoyment in the writing process when blogging. Blogs also make it easy for the teacher to provide written feedback to the student in the form of comments to blog entries the student has posted. These formats also offer parents of younger learners an opportunity to see and participate in the student's learning experience (Ferdig & Trammel, 2004).

Because blogs and wikis operate in a Web-based interface, learning to use the tools is achievable by most students who are computer savvy. Tools and tutorials are often free and readily available to the user. It is easy to create and type in a blog, as users do not need any special knowledge of html (Hernández-Ramos, 2004). Once a student understands how to use a blog or wiki in the classroom environment, the student is then able to take that skill and use it for work or personal interests. Blogs are also able to incorporate many advanced features such as video, graphics, audio, add-ins, mash-ups, and hyperlinks (Hernández-Ramos, 2004). Add-ins and mash-ups refer to live RSS feeds that provide interactive data to the user. These might take the form of a live opinion poll, or an interactive map showing live snow conditions. Overall, there are many strengths and benefits to incorporating wikis and blogs in the educational experience.

Table 9.1. Strengths and weaknesses of blogs and wikis

Strengths	Weaknesses
• Provides a forum for learner expression • Supports democratic principles • Learner controls content • Learner becomes the expert • Work is published to a worldwide audience • Work is open to feedback from others • Can be made private, public, or password protected • Blogs and wikis can be cross-linked to other blogs and wikis • Ease of use: bloggers do not need to know html or any other coding language • Tools are free and easy to maintain • Lots of support and tutorials available • Can serve multiple purposes • Students enjoy the writing experience • Emphasis placed on the writing, not the technology • Available anytime, anywhere • Automatic archiving • Blogs make it easy for the teacher to provide written feedback • Authentic learning experience • Promotes peer learning and cooperation • Parents can participate online with younger students. • Learning to use blogs and wikis is a skill that be used outside the classroom • Blogs can integrate graphics, audio, video, hypertext links, add-ins, and mash-ups.	• Blogs and wikis are not currently part of most LMS packages; teacher and student must use blog and wiki tools independently • A student's work is open for public criticism, and has the potential to create a negative learning experience for student unless guidelines are provided for moderation • Accuracy and verifiable sources are one of the touted weaknesses of blogs for reporting purposes. • Blogs are less editable than wikis • Wiki pages are basic in text layout and design; interfaces are not visually engaging at this time • Most wikis require knowledge of "wiki-style," an editing code similar to html • Requires typing skills • Confidentiality issues with younger students requiring parental permission • Wikis have the potential to be accidentally edited or deleted.

Weaknesses of blogs and wikis. For those online teachers currently using an LMS, learning another tool set outside the LMS costs time. Although most blog and wiki interfaces are fairly easy to learn, there is still an investment in learning to use, and teaching your students to use the new tool. The required technology skills include the ability to type and use a Web browser. Typing extensive amounts of writing might be overwhelming for younger students. Care should also be taken to ensure that younger students' confidentiality and privacy are protected, especially when using blogs. Check with your district's Acceptable Use Policy, and make sure you have parental permission before beginning.

Once published, blogs have less ability for editing than wikis, because they are single-authored. There is also the possibility for negative, critical, or inappropriate feedback to blog entries. A student's age should guide the teacher's decision on whether the blog or wiki project should be made accessible to outsiders, and if so, to how large a group. Both wikis and blogs have the ability to add password protection, and this might be an important feature for some age groups.

Because the very nature of wikis is to allow cross collaboration and editing among shared Web pages, wiki entries can be accidentally edited or deleted. To overcome this problem, instructors (or the wiki host) can incorporate usage guidelines. Wiki software often implements tracking and authentication mechanisms, thus deterring inappropriate posts or editing. A student is required to login to edit the wiki and each edit is attributable to a specific individual.

In addition to the usage guidelines, tracking and authentication mechanisms were implemented to deter students from making inappropriate posts and deletions from the wiki. Because students had to log in to edit the wiki, every post or edit could be attributed to an individual student (Augar, Raitman, & Zhou, 2004).

Understanding Blogs and Wikis:
Learner Empowerment through Expression!

Social interaction as an important aspect of the teaching and learning process has been discussed in research for decades. Social learning theorists and constructivists understand learning as a process of "meaning making" on the individual part of the student, with much of learning occurring through transactional relationships, conversations, and social interaction. Through the student's writing, discussions, projects and activities, the educator is able to better understand the student's individual meaning making process and thus better facilitate their learning over a course of study (Ferdig & Trammel, 2004).

The nature of blog and wiki content provide the perfect forum for student expression of learning, thinking, and meaning making. In addition to the benefits of students publishing their own writing, students have the opportunity for additional cognitive scaffolding when receiving feedback or revisiting their own work (Olson, 1994).

Some theorists (Williams & Bartlett-Bragg, 2005) suggest that tools such as blogs and wikis can provide new ways of offering pedagogies that put students at the center of learning process, instead of the teacher or content. As students own their blog, their thoughts, comments, and links are information constructed by them. This information is shared, and commented on by others in the class, including the teacher. The course can center on student's ongoing construction of knowledge. Compare this pedagogical approach to a traditional LMS where content is provided by the teacher, the teacher designs the lessons and discussion activities, and the teacher usually facilitates the types of discussion to be held in forums or in chat.

Because blogs and wikis also incorporate hyperlinks to other Web sites, students are able to demonstrate their understanding that knowledge is relational, contextual, and that they are producers in the knowledge-making process (Ferdig & Trammel, 2004).

The use of links in blogs and wikis takes on more importance than in discussion threads. Links are often used in blogs and wikis to establish credibility of the author's statements. Blogs and wikis give full control to the author, empowering the learner to take charge and assume responsibility for their own learning process. Over time, students participating in these formats often view themselves as part of a larger or global society, and understand that exploration with their voice and opinions is an important part of shaping not only a knowledge base, but society itself.

Purposes of blogging. Blogs are used for many purposes, both in and out of education. Lamb (2005) offers us a framework for consider eight purposes in the educational realm:

1. **Blogger as diarist:** The most common type of blog is used as a personal diary. Good for all ages, especially helpful in courses where autobiographies are being studied or where personal reflection is used as an authentic assessment tool.

2. **Blogger as enthusiast:** These blogs focus on a particular content area or area of interest for the author. For example, a student in a music class might create a blog on the Rolling Stones or a student studying abroad might chronicle their travels through various cities.

3. **Bloggers as institutional outreach:** Used by institutions and corporations, these blogs are used to support the mission of the institution, and are often located on the institution's Web site.

4. **Bloggers as journalists and news reporters:** Many newspapers, and individuals, are moving toward a blog format for publishing factual information. Some of these blogs are receiving a lot of attention for reporting stories more quickly than news services. Up for controversy is the objectivity involved in the reporting on this form of blog. Thus, we have a fifth category.

5. **Bloggers as news pundits, advocates, and columnists:** The majority of news blogs, especially those created by individuals or students in the learning process, focus on commentary and personal opinion in news and world events. For educators supporting news blogs in the classroom, it is recommended that students be aware of the differences in subjective and objective reporting, and that their mission is clearly stated in the blog itself.

6. **Bloggers as stars:** Created by celebrities, sport stars or other famous individuals, these blogs can be used in the classroom to introduce and generate excitement about the concept of blogging.

7. **Bloggers as promoters:** Basically, these blogs promote the act of blogging.

8. **Bloggers as specialists:** These blogs are written by content area "experts," although this concept could easily apply to any student studying a specific topic area in a course. These blogs can be limited to a selected audience (a class or school) or made available publically. Examples of

these blogs in education might include students publishing blogs on an area under study such as 18th century France or Marketing Trends in the Fashion Industry.

While many bloggers write with the intention of informing a dedicated reader base, Williams and Jacobs (2005) inform us that bloggers goals are often larger in scale:

It is also a means of reaching a wider audience; an unknown mass of "netizens", ready and willing to respond to the opinions and commentaries of bloggers in a manner not dissimilar to that afforded a talkback radio host. With a "soapbox" all to themselves, blogs provide their maintainers with the rare opportunity (for the vast majority, at least) to act as an oracle of information. (p. 233)

Structuring Blogs and Wikis for Success

Before introducing your students to blogs or wikis, we should start at the end. That is, as the instructor you first need to establish the purpose of the blog or wiki and what criteria will be used to assess work. In the following section, we first look at successful implementation of blogs and then wikis.

Assessing blogs. Prior to your students beginning to use blogs, you have to determine what criteria you will require as part of your grading process. A well-designed rubric can help students get focused on the purpose of the blog in your classroom—which may be different from purposes for which they have used blogs in the past. What outcomes are you seeking? Will you evaluate peer participation, amount of postings, content of postings? Here is a sample blog rubric to consider:

Getting started with blogs. The best way to begin using any new tool with students in education is to first use it yourself. Begin by becoming familiar with blogs. Spend time visiting a variety of blog sites, especially those used in education. Consider blogging yourself by either responding to another

Figure 9.3. Rubric for assessing reflecting thinking in blogs

Blogs, Weeks 3-9	Did Not Meet Requirements	Met Some Requirements	Met Most or All Requirements	Total Points
Reflective thinking, application, and synthesis of readings	Little reflection, no evidence of ability to discuss "theory into practice." The blog does not contain links to other sites.	Some reflective thinking, ability to relate readings to personal experience, does not take it to next level by making multiple connections and exploring potential solutions and use of concepts. The blog may or may not include links to other sites.	Entries makes connections between readings and practice, proposes solutions and potential use of concepts. The blog includes links to other sites.	30
Quoting of reading material	Less than 1 quote/ concept *per chapter* is provided and discussed.		At least 1 quotes/ concept *per chapter* is listed and discussed.	30
Responds to peers: Offer your insights, suggestions, further questions, praise when deserved. Your goal is to assist your peers in furthering their own learning via thoughtful reflection.	Responds to less than one peer per week.	Responds to at least one peer's blog entry per week.	Responds to at least two peer's blog entries per week.	20
Weekly Participation	More than 1 entry is late.	Most blog entries are up-to-date, with 1 entry or less being late.	Blog entries are kept up to date each week	10

person's blog, or by setting up your own. To locate blogs of interest, try Google's *Blog Search* as a blog search engine.

Once you have some exposure and experience with blogs, begin by modeling blogging for your students. Consider setting up your own blog for the class where students can see the progression of a blog over a few weeks. Discuss the purposes of blogging, how and when it is done, and rules of etiquette. Have your students first post responses to your blog entries. When there is a comfort level on the part of the teacher and students, begin to require assignments where they participate in other's blogs, locating blogs of interest and posting responses.

Finally, introduce your student to creating their own blog (see "Resources" for more information how and where to host blogs). Blood (2002) describes a three-step process in the blogging process: scouring, filtering and posting. The student visits multiple Web sites relevant to the topic to find information to which they will respond, critique, or hyperlink. Encourage them to include links to the outside, to invite others, especially experts, to comment on their blog entries. Assist your students in understanding the public nature of blogs and that anyone can see and keep copies of their work, even if it is edited at a later time.

Power Tip: Blogs, Kids, and Safety

I am so intrigued with my blog that I introduced my step-daughter, 14, to blogging last night. Just for fun we sat down and started creating her personal blog together. As we worked our way through the template together, I started getting those alarm signals that go off when we engage kids with Internet technologies that expose them to the world, literally.

I began to worry about who would see her blog, whether she should post a picture of herself, how much personal information she should share, and whether others could e-mail her. I talked with her about the need to not disclose her identity—she was already very aware and savvy. After creating her site, we worked through each of the settings, deciding together how much access she wanted others to have.

I was pleased to see that Blogger.com™ does offer some security for younger users. For example, the ability to comment to her posts is restricted to her members only—those she has invited to her blog. All her family has access to the

---

continued

blog—great for monitoring blog activity. She chose not to make her e-mail address available, and has not included a picture of herself or mentioned her last name.

While all her choices were right, I am still left with that slightly uneasy feeling about introducing her to blogs in general. Annette Lamb has a great reference site for blogs used for a variety of purposes with kids and others: http://escrap-booking.com/blogging/bloggers.htm.

Tracking New Posts and Responses. When you have an entire class of students hosting their own blogs, it becomes apparent very quickly that students and the teacher need an easy way to keep up to date with new entries, as well as new comments posted to existing entries (Gibson, 2004). RSS and Atom feeds are forms of syndicated news feeds that are being added to many blogs. This allows readers to "subscribe" to a blog, and receive new entries in blogs via a *feed reader.* Some examples of popular feed readers include Google Reader, Sage (for Firefox), Pluck, and Planet. However, feed readers do not pick up new comments that subscribers might make to a blog entry. Blog owners can overcome this problem by choosing notification through e-mail when a new entry is made to their blog.

Adding Video to Blogs. It is easy to insert audio and video clips into blogs. All you need is a built-in camera, Webcam, or digital video camera. An inexpensive webcam can be purchased for around $30. Sightspeed™ is a free, cross-platform video blog recording tool that can be used to record video clips up to 60 seconds and then post them to your blog.

Power Tip: Using Add-In and Mash-Ups

If you are involved in presenting any kind of information on the Web (Web sites, blogs, etc.), then you want to know about add-ins and mash-ups. Add-ins and mash-ups allow us to integrate live feeds from other sites into our own.

For example, create a live map showing all the ski conditions around Tahoe at Skibonk.com™. Try clicking on any of the links or information in the map—you will immediately see the power of add-ins.

continued

Some other examples: integrate a daily news feed to display on your site, insert a live map into your site, or insert a live poll.

What we are doing in reality in using a javascript script tag to call that dynamic feed into our own site. Not familiar with javascripting? No problem! Use the converter at http://www.rss-to-javascript.com/ to create the code for you! Then all you have to do is paste that code into your Web site or blog. What could be easier?

Getting started with wikis. Teachers should first begin to learn about wikis using the same process previously described for blogging. Gain exposure to wikis as a user. Participate in the creation of wiki before getting your students involved. For educational purposes, wikis offer the advantage of being more comprehensive in their involvement of all class participants on one project, thus promoting more peer interaction and collaboration. They can easily become the focus of an entire course or unit of study. For example, consider a course with the topic of "Politics and Trends in Education." This type of conceptual course easily lends itself to students researching and publishing historical information in a wiki format. The teacher serves as facilitator of the project, and can lead students to resources, contacts with experts, and coordinate outside contact with other participants on the project.

To get started, consider participating in a wiki project that has been started by others. Wikipedia offers a list of open projects. For those interested in starting their own wiki, SeedWiki or PBWiki offer free accounts with a easy-to-use WYSIWYG interface.

Example Uses for Success

Learning Objective Outcome	Activities
Interactivity and connection	• Encourage students to contact experts in their topic area of participate in their blog or wiki. • Coordinate two or more classes to participate in the same wiki simultaneously. • Have younger students invite parents or relatives to respond or participate.
Knowledge: defines; describes; enumerates; identifies; labels; lists; matches; names; reads; records; reproduces; selects; states; views	• Students watch a video clip online and restate the main points of the clip in their blog. • Students read online documentation on the civil war and are then asked to list five causes of the war in their blog. • Students create a list of all the Greek gods and post that information to a wiki along with supporting Web sites.
Comprehension: classifies; cites; converts; describes; discusses; estimates; explains; generalizes; gives examples; makes sense out of; paraphrases; restates (in own words); summarizes; traces; understands	• Have students read examples of postings from hate groups on Yahoo and then discuss these types of groups in their blog. • Play an online game related to course content and then have students describe their experience of the game in their blog. • Have students read information on a given theory, locate five examples of that theory in practice on various Web sites, and post the information on a wiki.

continued

Application: acts; administers; articulates; assesses; charts; collects; computes; constructs; contributes; controls; determines; develops; discovers; establishes; extends; implements; includes; informs; instructs; operationalizes; participates; predicts; prepares; preserves; produces; projects; provides; relates; reports; shows; solves; teaches; transfers; uses; utilizes	• Students can collect historical information on stocks related to a specific industry, chart and post that information on a wiki. • Students can design their own project on a wiki and submit a call for participants. • Encourage students to become "experts" in an area of interest, and set up and administer their own blog.
Analysis: breaks down; correlates; diagrams; differentiates; discriminates; distinguishes; focuses; illustrates; infers; limits; outlines; points out; prioritizes; recognizes; separates; subdivides	• Encourage students to collect data such as how many students eat lunch in the cafeteria, and the type of lunches eaten, then diagram this data and share it on a school blog. • In an auto repair course, students can create a wiki that outlines the chronological development of engines from 1900-today. • Students in world events courses can read newsclippings from famous world leaders, analyze leaders priorities as stated in their speeches, then post their analysis and comparisons of world leaders in their blogs.

continued

Synthesis: adapts; anticipates; categorizes; collaborates; combines; communicates; compares; compiles; composes; contrasts; creates; designs; devises; expresses; facilitates; formulates; generates; incorporates; individualizes; initiates; integrates; intervenes; models; modifies; negotiates; plans; progresses; rearranges; reconstructs; reinforces; reorganizes; revises; structures; substitutes; validates	• Two instructors can set up a collaborative wiki project wherein students can outline and divide responsibilities for collecting and posting information. Communication can occur via e-mail or webcam. • Advanced students can create and facilitate their own wiki on a given topic. • Students can create a personal opinion blog that reviews latest events, trends or news on a given topic. • Advanced students can teach other students how to set up a blog.
Evaluation: appraises; compares & contrasts; concludes; criticizes; critiques; decides; defends; interprets; judges; justifies; reframes	• Students visit an assigned Web site. In their blog, they describe the purpose and goals of the organization. Describe the intent behind the website, and whether the site could be modified to better meet the organization's goals. • Have students set up a blog that examines multiple views of any topic. For example, a blog entitled "The Whole Picture" might explore and interpret multiple viewpoints of any given event. • Provide students with a rubric for evaluating blog or wikis. Have them compare and contrast three blogs or wikis using the rubric, and then report their findings.

Example Lesson Plan

Figure 9.3. Example lesson plan introducing use of blogs

Overview: Online Teaching Best Practice

What exactly is best practice in online teaching? And who is it that is setting the standards for what counts as quality online teaching and learning? The answers (and there are multiple answers) to these questions, as well as others relevant to online teachers, are evolving on a daily basis right now. Our field is still emerging, with new research coming out monthly. To help you develop a foundation in online teaching best practice, this week you will choose three questions from the sets of questions provided below, and then begin some research using the resources provided. Choose questions that are meaningful for you. Do not worry about finding the "right" answer or extensive information. Often, there is limited information available.

The medium you will be using to communicate your findings this week is a blog. We will be maintaining reflective blogs throughout most of the semester. A blog, or Weblog, is a great way to journal online. Blogs can serve a variety of purposes, but for our class, your blog will be a mechanism for sharing your reflections, thoughts, suggestions, and comments on readings and course content. They are also a mechanism for communicating with peers in a way that offers the author control over the blog itself. Here is a blog I maintain called OnlineEducator. Over half of you surveyed in the course have not used a blog. If this is your first exposure, relax and enjoy. :) As you use the blog this semester, consider whether blogging is a tool that can be integrated into your own online teaching.

Objectives

1.   Explore and begin to identify best practice in online teaching.

2.   Further synthesize online educational concepts and trends through peer writing critique.

3.   Reflect on course readings and your own learning by starting a reflective blog.

Readings & Resources

1.Chapter 1, Ko & Rossen

Information Resources
        Distance-Educator.com
        TLC Teaching Tips
        Center for Online Educators
        CNN: Students Prefer Online Courses
        Growing by Degrees: Online Education in the US, 2005
        2005 Horizon Report: 5 Year Trends
        Rubric for Online Instruction
        MERLOT
        OTTER
        Online Pedagogy: Best Practice Resources

continued

Educational Technology Journals
National Education Technology Plan
Technological Horizons in Education Journal
Journal of Education Online
American Journal of Distance Education
Learning & Leading with Technology
Contemporary Issues in Technology & Teacher Education
European Journal of Open & Distance Learning
Journal of Asynchronous Learning Networks
Journal of Distance Learning Administration
Journal of Online Teaching and Learning

ACTIVITIES FOR WEEK 2	DUE DATE
QUESTIONS FOR WEEK 2 ASSIGNMENT **(choose three questions to answer)** **Group 1: Defining Online Teaching & Learning** Define online teaching and learning. Describe various models used in online teaching and learning (hybrid, fully online, Web-based, LMS, etc.). Describe qualities of a successful online environment. What percentage of faculty are now teaching online in some capacity, and/or what percentage of classes are now online? **Group 2: Politics & Trends in Online Education** Discuss the rationale and causes behind the recent boom in online learning. Whom does it benefit and how? What are the current national and state level politics behind online teaching & learning? Where does NCLB fit in the picture? Are there trends around the country that support online learning in general? Describe these trends. Where are we headed in online education? What are future trends, predictions, pilot projects are being tested? What are the latest tools and technologies being used by online teachers? **Group 3: Online Teachers & Learners** What are personality traits of those learners who are successful in online courses? What percentage of students drop-out of online courses? When do most adult learners access online courses? What is the typical pattern for accessing online material? Describe qualities of a successful online teacher. What issues must a teacher consider that are specific to teaching in an online environment? Who is teaching online—where did they receive their training, if any? What teaching standards exist for online teachers? Where can online teachers access materials to integrate into their online courses?	

continued

1. Create your blog OK, this is exciting stuff! Let's create your blog. We'll be using a free blog tool called <u>Blogger</u>. Go to Blogger's home page. Follow the steps on the right to create your blog. You are free to use another blogging tool, if you so choose. After you create your account in Step 1, see this tutorial for setting up your blog. <u>http://breeze.boisestate.edu:8080/p46248383/</u>. While you are viewing the tutorial, note there are scroll bars at the bottom and right side to adjust the display. (And please ignore the last 10 seconds of the tutorial—it was my first time recording in Breeze last semester :) ***When finished, post the title and URL of your blog in the Week 2 discussion forum.***	Deadline: midnight MST on Sunday, January 29.
2. Answer THREE questions Post your answers for each question in your blog. *Create a separate blog entry for each question.* I would strongly recommend that you do all your writing in Word, and then copy and paste into the blog window. *Include at least one reference and URL in your answer. Answers should be approximately 100 words each.* It's also ok to write in the first person or include personal experience as a part of your response.	Deadline: midnight MST on Tuesday, January 31.
3. Respond to three classmates Write a critical response to at least three classmates in their blog. In your response, offer your insights, suggestions, further questions, praise when deserved. Your goal is to assist your peers in furthering their own learning through thoughtful reflection. Each response must also include one URL to promote further thinking/discussion on the topic.	Deadline: midnight MST on Thursday, Feb. 2

Grading

Grading is pass/no pass this week, 10 points for setting up the blog and 40 points for the remaining activities. You receive full credit when all criteria have been completed.

continued

Criteria for Assignment
• Set up blog
• Answers at least three questions
• Includes appropriate references/URLs in response
• Answers are approximately 100 words each
• Responded to at least 3 classmates, one in each area. Include a URL.

Good luck! It is my hope and intention that this introductory assignment will answer some initial questions you have about online teaching best practice, and provide you a basis for beginning a more in-depth inquiry throughout the rest of the semester.

© 2006 Lisa Dawley, Ph.D.

Resources

Blogger.com: http://www.blogger.com

Bloggers as…: http://escrapbooking.com/blogging/bloggers.htm

Blog Glossary: http://www.marketingterms.com/dictionary/blog/

Bloglines: http://www.bloglines.com/

Blogs and Blogging: A Homerun for Teaching, Learning, and Technology: http://escrap-booking.com/blogging/index.htm

EdBlogger Praxis: http://educational.blogs.com/edbloggerpraxis/2004/02/bloggg.html

Google Blog Search: http://blogsearch.google.com/

Google Reader: http://reader.google.com

Kelly's Music & Computer Blogs: http://kellysmusic.biz/blog/

Livejournal.com: http://www.livejournal.com

Netcraft: Of Blogs and Wikis: http://news.netcraft.com/archives/2004/03/26/of_blogs_and_wikis.html

PB Wiki: http://pbwiki.com/

RSSTop55 - Best Blog Directory And RSS Submission Sites: http://www.masternew-media.org/rss/top55/

Sage: http://sage.mozdev.org/

Seedwiki: http://www.seedwiki.com/

Sightspeed Video Blogging: *http://www.sightspeed.com/*

Smart Writers: How to Blog: http://smart-writers.com/how-to-blog.html?source=google&campaign=486219

Teachers' Blogs: http://www.teachersblogs.com/

WikiWikiWeb: http://c2.com/cgi/wiki?WikiWikiWeb Wikipedia http://www.wikipedia.org/

Wiktionary: http://www.wiktionary.org/

Wikiquote: http://www.wikiquote.org/

Wikisource: http://www.wikisource.org/

Wikibooks: http://www.wikibooks.org/

Wikijunior: http://www.wikijunior.org

References

Augar, N., Raitman, R., & Zhou, W. (2004, December). *Teaching and learning online with wikis.* Paper presented at the Annual Meeting of the Australian Society for Computers in Learning in Tertiary Education. Retrieved July 6, 2006, from http://www.ascilite.org.au/conferences/perth04/procs/augar.html

Blood, R. (2002). *The weblog handbook.* Philadelphia: Perseus Books Group.

Cunningham, W. (2005). *Wiki getting started FAQ.* Retrieved July 7, 2006, from http://c2.com/cgi/wiki?WikiGettingStartedFaq

Farmer, J., & Bartlett-Bragg, A. (2005, December). *Blogs @ anywhere: High fidelity on-line communication.* Paper presented at the Annual Meeting of the Australian Society for Computers in Learning in Tertiary Education.

Ferdig, R., & Trammel, K. (2004, February). Content delivery in the "blogsphere." *T.H.E. Journal Online.* Retrieved July 6, 2006, from http://www.thejournal.com/magazine/vault/articleprintversion.cfm?aid=4677

Gibson, B. (2004). A learning blogosphere. The Community Engine. Retrieved July 6, 2006, from http://thecommunityengine.com/home/archives/2005/03/a_learning_blog.html

Hernández-Ramos, P. (2004). Web logs and online discussions as tools to promote reflective practice. *The Journal of Interactive Online Learning, 3*(1). Retrieved July 6, 2006, from http://www.ncolr.org/jiol/issues/PDF/3.1.4.pdf

Lamb, A. (2005). *Bloggers as* ... Retrieved July 6, 2006, from http://escrapbooking.com/blogging/bloggers.htm

Njuguna, W. (2005, April). *Blogs, with strengths and weaknesses, gain.* 2005 ASNE Reporter. Retrieved July 6, 2006, from http://www.asne.org/index.cfm?id=5692

Olson, D. (1994). *The world on paper: The conceptual and cognitive implications of writing and reading.* New York: Cambridge University Press.

Williams, J. B., & Jacobs, J. (2005). Exploring the use of blogs as learning spaces in the higher education sector. *Australasian Journal of Educational Technology, 20*(2), 232-247. Retrieved July 6, 2006, from http://www.jeremybwilliams.net/AJETpaper.pdf

Chapter X

Learning to Use
Multiple Tools

A successful online teacher has many tools available. The focus of this book has been to help you determine which technology tools to integrate into instruction to help your students achieve their various learning objectives. Often it requires the use of multiple tools to get the job done—this is true for students, as well as teachers. In any given hour, for example, I might use Rubistar™ to design a rubric for a discussion board, paste that rubric into a lesson that I am designing in Dreamweaver™, and paste that lesson inside an html editor window inside Claroline™. I will then e-mail my students to let them know the current week's lesson is available, and create and attach a Word™ version of that lesson plan so they do not have to log into the online class to see what is coming up. Whew!

Every year, there are more ways to connect with others with the use of technology and interaction with media. The average American home now has 26 different electronic devices for communication, and the Consumer Electronics

Association of America now tracks sales and consumer preferences for 53 separate technologies (Rainey, 2006). Parikh (2003) encourages us to leverage multiple Internet technologies, combined with appropriate instructional activities and materials, to achieve our learning goals.

There is no one way to plan or decide which set of integrated technologies will best meet all your students' needs. These decisions are dependent on the technologies available to you and your students, special needs that might need addressing, objectives of the course, availability of broadband, what is allowed in Acceptable Use Policies, as well as your own comfort level in using the technology itself, and planning to integrate the technology for learning.

In the next section, we explore several situations that definitely require a teacher to use multiple online teaching tools. These cases highlight the complexity involved in these decisions, and provide you some initial "food for thought" and potential solutions. At the conclusion of this section, is a list of commonly used software and online teaching tools. It takes time and practice to learn which tools will get you to the point where you want to be. Even if you have been a "brick and mortar" teacher for many years, moving into online teaching will be a new world. Be patient with yourself and your learning process. And realize there will always be more to learn.

Dealing with Inappropriate Online Behavior

New online teachers are concerned often about class management—how do I deal with "problem" students? Problems can take many forms, but the worst problem that needs immediate attention is students who engage in inappropriate online behavior such as flaming, spamming, sexual harassment, or any type of activity that seeks to destroy the collaborative community you are working to create or impinges on another student's ability to learn.

Flaming or harassment can occur in chat, video conferencing, in discussion boards, through e-mail, or phone. Here are steps you can take using your online tools to deal with this situation:

First, get familiar with your institution's policy for these issues. All universities have Student Codes of Conduct, for example. Most K-12 school districts have Acceptable Use Policies. If your school does not have a policy, then write your own. This document should be made available to students the first day of class in a document folder, and it should be referenced for review in the assignment for the first week. At the first sign of inappropriate behavior, take action! If an inappropriate behavior is occurring that impacts another student's ability to learn, immediately suspend the disruptive student's ability to post or use communication tools until the matter is cleared up. Continue to allow that student access to course content and have the student e-mail assignments directly to you. Consult with your principal or department head and notify Affirmative Action, if required. Then, e-mail or call the student to discuss the situation. Explain how the student's actions were a violation of policy, and what the resulting consequences will be for this violation and future violations (usually suspension upon the second violation). After making copies of the offending posts, delete the posts, and make a class announcement (if the flaming occurred in a public area) that the discussion thread has been closed.

Typically, the violator and the harassed student are asked not to have direct communication any longer in the course, and should not be grouped for any future assignments. The harassed student should be encouraged to know the student's best interests are protected, and that the student should notify you immediately if they are contacted or harassed in the future.

Complications like these are few, but they do arise. Be prepared. Your job is to ensure the safety of the learning environment for those who choose to learn. The school, school policy, and the law are there to back you up.

Finally, less threatening, but still cause problems, are the students who are "whiners" or "know-it-alls." Often their goal is gain attention through antagonizing, usually the instructor. We often find these students are the least knowledgeable about the content under study. They make statements in threaded discussion for instance, "None of this week's readings were anything new to me. We studied this in my last class. I did not learn anything." The best strategy to use with these students is to give them the attention they desire, but in a positive, not negative form. For example, a positive response to the above statement might be, *"Hi Todd (always include the first name), I am so glad to hear you have former experience with this week's course readings. We can all learn from your experience. How have you been able to apply these concepts in your own work? Has it made a difference? How so? Thanks in advance for sharing!"* This type of response lets that student know they were heard, encourages a positive dialogue from here on out, and reframes a negative into a positive. You also model positive problem solving to the remainder of the class by using this approach. This can be a win/win situation.

Create a Teaching Style that Works for You and Your Students

What is your online teaching style? This style may or may not vary from the way you might teach in a regular classroom or computer lab. Spend your time with initial online teaching experiences getting acquainted with your own habits and preferences. Also, explore the use of new Internet technologies as they emerge. You may find a whole new adventure waiting for you and your students. As technology tools become more interactive, many instructors find themselves reinvigorated to explore new terrain with their students.

Do you prefer to log in daily or twice a week? Do not require more of your students than you are willing to do. Are you a morning or evening worker? If you are a morning person, late evening chats will most likely be unsuccessful. Do you enjoy providing lengthy feedback or does a quick response in a discussion forum fill the bill? Are most of your students adults and frequently log in late at night or on the weekends? Do you teach elementary students whose parents need to reach you during the day? Getting to know yourself and your students is critical when planning the types of assignments and tools that will be most successful in your online class.

Learn the Capability of Your Particular LMS

If you use a LMS to teach online, you may find that you have to supplement your teaching experience with additional technology tools. All learning management systems are not created equal. Features and capabilities can vary from platform to platform. And updates are frequently issued that provide new capabilities. Check the manuals or tutorials that came with your LMS. See if the company has established an online discussion forum or materials database that has more information. Try searching in Google using search terms such as "Blackboard chat tutorials" or "WebCT discussion forum ideas." Many schools or universities offer on-site trainings for their LMSs, particularly if the platform is new or recently updated. Again, the idea is collaborative life-long learning that reaches out to others to keep yourself educated on the capabilities of your online platform. It can be a great inspiration to learn new ideas and share your own work with others. You will begin to identify what tools you need to add in addition to what is offered inside your LMS.

Keeping Current in Online Teaching

Our field is constantly changing and new online teaching tools and practice emerge daily. Growth of online courses, tools, grants, professional development opportunities, and conferences makes it difficult to know how to keep up and where to focus our attention. An easy to way to cover daily highlights

Figure 10.1. The Center for Online Educators chat library. Used with permission

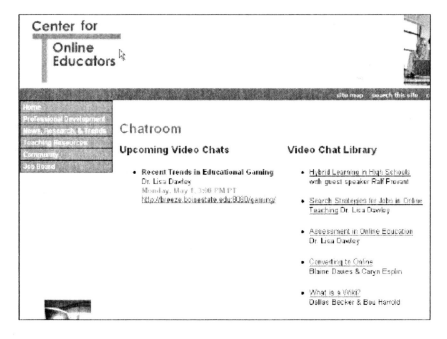

is to subscribe to DistanceEducator.com. This daily newsletter recaps news in distance learning from around the country. You will receive a convenient daily e-mail showing top headlines. We often come across news stories that we are able to pass on to our students and colleagues.

Participate in at least one conference per year, either live or online. Sign up as a presenter. Again, the idea is to share your knowledge as you also learn from others. Also, consider joining an online community related to your subject area. The Center for Online Educators hosts monthly chats on topics of interest to online teachers, for example.

Finally, let the power of e-mail serve you in your quest. There are many resources where you can get free newsletters and research reports to keep in touch with the latest news. Consider subscribing to newsletters from eSchoolNews.com, educatoronline.org, or to the Pew Internet Reports that provide fascinating research trends on Internet usage by teens, adults, in education and otherwise. If you are a blog fan, subscribe to several blogs using Google Reader, a free RSS/Atom aggregator that will forward daily blog entries to you, so you do not have to check multiple blogs to see if they have been updated.

Power Tip: Subscribe to the Pew Internet Reports

You absolutely must get acquainted with the Pew Internet Reports! They are a fascinating look into how the Internet is changing our lives. The reports go quite deep into teen and adult usage and trends. They will help you understand what tools and technologies are commonly used by your students, and how you can tap into that knowledge to promote better learning.

- Go to http://www.pewinternet.org/, type the word "teens" or "adults" in the search box. Choose one report to skim and report findings on how teens are using Internet technologies in today's world. What ideas do you have for capitalizing on that information to more effectively facilitate learning?

---

continued

- Sign up for e-mail notification of new Pew Reports ... keep in touch with emergent trends, stay knowledgeable! http://www.pewinternet.org/signup.asp

Finding Resources for Online Teachers

So where do you find all those great resources you need to embed into your online lessons? You will come across a lot of resources by subscribing to some of the resources listed above. Another approach is to consider which people are the major players in your subject area. Teaching science? Consider checking out NASA, Discovery Channel, or NOVA for interesting video clips. Teaching history? Check out the History Channel's Web site for awesome audio recording of famous speeches throughout the 20th century. Investigate databases such as MERLOT that were created for teachers to share lesson ideas about integrating technology.

A second search strategy would be to Google using relevant search terms such as "history lessons online," "virtual field trips," or "algebra online tutorials." These types of searches will often lead you to directories containing multiple references to your required materials.

Also, many companies are now catering to the needs of online educators. The Center for Online Educators offers free resources to online teachers including links to curricular resources, multimedia, design needs such as graphics and typography, a discussion forum for sharing ideas and information, and an online teacher job board.

Enjoy the Benefits of Online Teaching

Many people have described the process of learning to teach online as being both exciting and frustrating. On the one hand, we are always learning new things—new techniques, new strategies, new technology tools to improve our teaching. On the other hand, lots of things are always changing. If you are a person who dislikes change, you will not enjoy being an online teacher! Online teaching has both benefits and drawbacks. Instead of focusing on the drawbacks, recognize the positive attributes of teaching online that cannot be achieved with regular classroom teaching. First, online teachers have the ability to customize their work schedule around other aspects of their lives. This level of freedom is invaluable to many educators.

Second, many online courses contain students from around the world in one course. I have been privileged to have students from Japan, the Ukraine, the Philippines, and all around the United States in a single course. This phenomenon does not happen in regular classrooms. We benefit from the global perspectives our students bring to class, and learn that geographical boundaries do not negate our commonality as human beings.

Power Tip: Taking Off on Weekends

Good morning. It is Saturday, and there is coffee brewing on the stove. This morning I was contemplating the lifestyle of online teachers, and how the phrase "24/7, anywhere, anytime, anyplace" has affected the way I teach. I am left with the question, "Can I take off on weekends?" The logical part of my brain says, Of course. Everyone deserves a weekend off. Another part of me, however, gets a little anxious if I do not log in over the time when many students are completing their work.

If you read books on online teaching, you will get some fairly common advice that teachers should visit their online classrooms several times a week. If you talk with online teachers, you will find a wider range of approaches—teachers who log in everyday, those who login 2-3 times per week, and those who login once a week or less.

I suppose what interests me most are my students' perspectives on how often their teacher should log in, how immediate they should receive feedback on their work, and how quickly their posts should be responded to. The newer a student is to online education, the more quickly they will want and expect feedback on their posted writing/work. Now, mind you, I cannot cite this claim from any research; this is based on my own personal experience. I have questioned what causes that expecta-

---

continued

tion. Why? Well, let us say I am teaching on campus, a three hour class that meets once per week. A student hands in a paper. When do they get that paper back? A week later, at the earliest, sometimes two weeks if the writing is intensive or I am overloaded that week. However, to wait a week or two to give feedback in an online class gives me butterflies—not to mention my students. What is it about online learning environments that creates the need for instant educational gratification?

I have explored a variety of informal approaches to assist my students with the expectation of my availability. In my syllabus, I discuss my availability (that I login 2-3 times per week), that they can e-mail or call if they need more immediate assistance, and I provide an instant messenger address that I try to keep open whenever I am online. If I am going to be off-line for more than two days, or out of town, I will post an announcement letting folks know about it in advance. Part of my professional responsibility, I believe, is educating online learners about the nature of online learning, and setting the tone for how my online classroom operates.

Now, I am going to finish up my cup of coffee, post this blog entry, and head off for some fly fishing this weekend. Hope yours is a good one, too.

Finally, online teachers are pioneers in developing educational frontiers. By teaching online, we are given the opportunity to continually grow as learners and teachers, and embody the very essence of what it means to be a life-long learner. We can stay invigorated by keeping up to date with emerging tools, trends, and practice. We gain a perspective of the world that goes beyond our home, neighborhood, or hometown, and we influence an emergent trend in education that is shaping the nature of how we think about ourselves as members of society. The implications are huge. The opportunities are endless. I invite you to join the adventure. Remember to bring your tool kit.

Example Lesson Plan

Figure 10.2. Example lesson plan integration use of multiple tools

---

Week 6 Agenda: Hybrid Teaching and Learning

Last week's readings in Chapter 12 of Ko and Rossen introduced you to the concept of a hybrid, or blended, learning environment. As Caryn pointed out in her Breeze discussion last week, p. 240 outlines several approaches to hybrid learning. As access to broadband Internet continues to grow, and more and more universities adopt learning management systems, hybrid courses will become the norm, not the exception. We have almost reached this point at Boise State University.

This week, we will explore hybrid learning more in-depth by giving you a hands-on opportunity to begin basic design of hybrid environment. You will create a sample hybrid class in Blackboard CourseSites, a 30-day free trial of Blackboard. This activity will achieve two goals: (1) you will be able to demonstrate application of learning on hybrid course design, and (2) gain hands-on experience using the administrative control panel in Blackboard. So let us get started!

Objectives

1. Reflect on course readings and your own learning by posting in your blog.
2. Continue to plan for a Breeze professional development project with your assigned partner.
3. Demonstrate application of hybrid learning design by creating your own Blackboard CourseSite.
4. Gain experience using the administrative control panel in Blackboard.

Readings

1. **Chapter 12:** Ko & Rossen (review)
2. **One additional article on hybrid learning**

Resources

Hybrid Course Website: U of Wisconsin http://www.uwm.edu/Dept/LTC/hybrid/

---

continued

Grading

This assignment is worth 40 points. Any missing requirements (see above) will be deducted at 4 points each.

The ability to work in the administrative control panel will be useful to you in the coming weeks as you begin your TA assignments in a live Blackboard course. If you are interested in learning more about options for online course design, consider enrolling in our new course offered this summer—EDTECH 597: Online Course Design.

Resources: Other Cool Tools

Center for Online Educators: http://www.educatoronline.org

Learning Management Systems (LMS)

Blackboard- Used by many schools and universities around the country**WebCT**- Another popular LMS

ECollege- Another popular LMS

Claroline.net - Free LMS to educators, based on principles of constructivism

Nicenet.org- free e-learning platform for your classroom

Moodle- Another free LMS available to you; constructivist orientation, open source, available in 40 languages!

Web Courseware Comparisons- links to comparisons of online platforms

Edu-Tool.com- online platform comparison tool, great resource

HTML/CSS Editors

FrontPage: Microsoft's official site for FrontPage. It has interactive tours and FAQs

FrontPage World: Tools, tips and secrets of FrontPage

Dreamweaver MX: The professional designer's dream to Web design

TopStyle Pro: Edit HTML, CSS (cascading style sheets), and XHTML in one program!

Image Editors

Photoshop 7.0: Adobe's premiere software for photos and images.

Photoshop Elements 2.0: A simplified version of Photoshop, easy to. use and inexpensive

PhotoImpact
Paint Shop Pro

Microsoft's Picture It!

The Gimp: free open source software
Corel Draw 12

Adobe Illustrator: industry-standard vector graphics software
Macromedia Fireworks: import files from all major graphics formats and manipulate both vector and bitmap images to quickly create graphics and interactivity. Images can be easily exported to Dreamweaver, Flash and third-party applications

Groundlayerz.com: Links to free trial downloads of many image editors, animation, screen capture, image compression programs
Blue Armadillo: free image batch conversion utility; convert an entire folder of images from one format to another

Animation Editors

Adobe AfterEffects: powerful tools you need to produce visually innovative motion graphics and effects for film, video, DVD, and the Web

Macromedia Flash: interactive content and video
GIF Construction Set: instant gif animation using a wizard, inexpensive
Animagic: powerful gif animation tool

Sound Recording

GoldWave: Free download of an easy-to-use audio recording software

Audacity: Free sound recording software, easy to use

Chat

BoldChat: Free live chat tool you can integrate into your course, good for 1-on-1
ParaChat: Another freebie, nice for group chats up to 100
QuickChat: Similar to ParaChat, easy-to-use, just cut & paste java applet code!
RogerWilco: Real-time live voice chatting technology, download & go!
Yahoo Messenger Voice Chat: Free voice chat download

Video Conferencing Software

Window NetMeeting 3: audio/video conferencing, file exchange, chat
Breeze: audio/video communication, training, collaboration online

Elluminate: audio/video conferencing, whiteboard, application sharing

Video Editing & Compression

iMovie: The product of choice for video editing on Macs Sorenson Squeeze
Quicktime Pro: Movie and animation software Simulations

RoboDemo: record screen activity to create interactive flash tutorials, free trial!
SnagIt: ability to capture anything on your screen is simply unmatched

Camtasia Studio: tools to record, enhance and publish professional demos, training and tutorials

Firefly: rapidly develop robust software simulations, free trial

Discussion Boards

Snitz: free bulletin board software

Yahoo Groups: free discussion board and calendar tools

Presentation Software

PowerPoint: Microsoft's official Web site with tips, tutorials

ezedia: Multimedia authoring software, kids can use it!

AntiVirus

Norton AntiVirus: total security protection for PC or Mac

McAfee: virus protection

References

Parikh, M. A. (2003). Beyond the Web: Leveraging multiple internet technologies. In A. Aggarwal (Ed.), *Web-based education: Learning from experience* (pp.120-130). Hershey, PA: Idea Group Publishing.

Rainey, L. (2006). *How the internet is changing consumer behavior and expectation*s. Retrieved on July 6, 2006, from http://www.pewinternet.org/ppt/2006%20-%205.9.06%20SO-CAP.pdf

About the Author

Dr. Lisa Dawley is an associate professor and chair at Boise State University, Department of Educational Technology. She also the founder and director of the *Center for Online Educators*. Dr. Dawley received her PhD in education from the University of California at Santa Barbara. Her areas of interest include the pedagogy of emergent internet-based technologies, online teaching and learning, and teacher professional development. She co-authored one of the first texts on integrating the internet into the classroom, and has published articles in the *American Educational Research Journal, Teacher Education Quarterly, Teaching Education*, and *Research in the Schools*. Dr. Dawley is also the recipient of the Distinguished Research Award from the Association of Teacher Educators, and was an invited participant at Stanford's Summer Institute at the Center for Advanced Study in the Behavioral Sciences.

Index

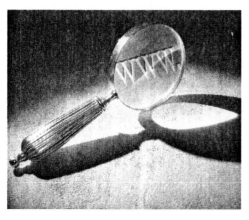